HTML5 for Flash Developers

Leverage your Flash skill set and learn to create content
using a wide range of HTML5 web development features

Matt Fisher

PUBLISHING

BIRMINGHAM - MUMBAI

HTML5 for Flash Developers

Copyright © 2013 Packt Publishing

First published: July 2013

Production Reference: 1220713

Published by Packt Publishing Ltd.
Livery Place
35 Livery Street
Birmingham B3 2PB, UK.

ISBN 978-1-84969-332-5

www.packtpub.com

Cover Image by Siddharth Ravishankar (sidd.ravishankar@gmail.com)

Credits

Author
Matt Fisher

Reviewers
Brad Manderscheid
Anirudh Prabhu
Mike Robinson

Acquisition Editors
Antony Lowe
Rukhsana Khambatta

Lead Technical Editor
Neeshma Ramakrishnan

Technical Editors
Vrinda Nitesh Bhosale
Aniruddha Vanage
Zafeer Rais

Copy Editors
Alfida Paiva
Gladson Monteiro

Project Coordinator
Amey Sawant

Proofreader
Stephen Swaney

Indexer
Rekha Nair

Production Coordinator
Melwyn D'sa

Cover Work
Melwyn D'sa

About the Author

Matt Fisher, Senior Developer at *Jam3* (www`jam3.com`), is passionate about technology. Whether it is building large-scale multi-user online applications or programming a model plane to fly itself, he brings that passion with him to every project. An interactive web and systems developer by day and an electronics-obsessed person by night, Matt's diverse and highly-valued skill set makes him stand out from the crowd. Matt's fascination with technology and programming began at a young age and today, most of his technical and programming skills are self-taught. In the recent past, Matt has also been a part-time professor at both colleges and universities in Toronto, as well as an advisory board member. His website, `www.fisherinnovation.com,` gives a detailed description of his work.

I would like to thank all of my colleagues at *Jam3* (www.`jam3.com`), my close friends, family, and of course my beautiful better half, Lindsay Munro, for all of their inspiration and support during the time spent writing this book. It would have been impossible without all of you.

About the Reviewers

Brad Manderscheid is currently a Senior Developer for *Bader Rutter and Associates* and lives in Milwaukee, WI. He specializes in mobile and games and has a strong passion for creating rich, interactive experiences for both desktop and mobile devices. He previously spent the better part of a decade making documentary films, working as a freelance developer and consultant for large companies and agencies across the country, and has built everything from mobile applications to large CMS applications and multi-player games for the Web.

He is currently working on his own publication, *Beginning HTML5 Game Development Using CreateJS*.

Anirudh Prabhu is a software engineer at Xoriant Solutions with four years experience in web designing and development. He is responsible for JavaScript development and maintenance in his project. His areas of expertise are HTML, CSS, JavaScript, jQuery, and SASS. He has completed an MSc in Information Technology from Mumbai University.

He has also been a technical reviewer for *Apress's Pro JavaScript Performance*.

When not working, Anirudh loves to read, listen to music, and do photography.

Mike Robinson is a Senior Web Developer at *Globacore*. Solving problems with code is something he loves to do and has been fortunate enough to have made a great career of it for over 10 years. He's passionate about crafting beautiful experiences and intuitive interactions using clean, concise, and manageable code.

I would like to thank my lovely wife Jessica and my son Will for their ongoing love and support while I spent my free nights and weekends reviewing this book.

www.packtpub.com

Support files, eBooks, discount offers and more

You might want to visit www.packtpub.com for support files and downloads related to your book.

Did you know that Packt offers eBook versions of every book published, with PDF and ePub files available? You can upgrade to the eBook version at www.packtpub.com and as a print book customer, you are entitled to a discount on the eBook copy. Get in touch with us at service@packtpub.com for more details.

At www.packtpub.com, you can also read a collection of free technical articles, sign up for a range of free newsletters and receive exclusive discounts and offers on Packt books and eBooks.

http://PacktLib.packtpub.com

Do you need instant solutions to your IT questions? PacktLib is Packt's online digital book library. Here, you can access, read and search across Packt's entire library of books.

Why Subscribe?

- Fully searchable across every book published by Packt
- Copy and paste, print and bookmark content
- On demand and accessible via web browser

Free Access for Packt account holders

If you have an account with Packt at www.packtpub.com, you can use this to access PacktLib today and view nine entirely free books. Simply use your login credentials for immediate access.

Table of Contents

Preface

HTML5 for Flash Developers has been specifically written for Flash developers ready to dive right into HTML5 development. Starting off by analyzing each of the elements that make up HTML5, we will then begin learning how to utilize them by comparing their features to typical Flash development.

What this book covers

Chapter 1, *Why HTML5?*, begins by answering why learning how to develop in HTML5 can be an incredibly important skillset to acquire. We will continue with a complete overview of all of the different technologies that make up HTML5 and how they are utilized.

Chapter 2, *Preparing for the Battle*, covers the important process of preparing assets such images, audio, and video for the web. This chapter also covers many of the important aspects of JavaScript development and how they differ from ActionScript 3.

Chapter 3, *Scalability, Limitations, and Effects*, aims to inform you about many of the limitations that HTML5 developers regularly encounter while developing for the web today. We will also take our first detailed look into the newest addition of Cascading Style Sheets, CSS3. Finally we will overview some of the most interesting new additions to HTML development by looking at HTML5 Web Workers, Web Sockets, the Canvas element, and finally WebGL.

Chapter 4, *Building Robust Applications with HTML5*, continues to look deeper into JavaScript development by aiming to structure code in an object-oriented manner. Comparisons to ActionScript 3 class structure, usage, and syntax are made as well as an overview of some libraries and frameworks to aid in building robust HTML5 applications.

Chapter 5, Code Once, Release Everywhere, looks at applications and code libraries that enabled developers to easily target multiple platforms with a single application build, minimizing development time and maximizing public usage. We will spend a good portion of our time diving into the CreateJS framework and all of its packages. Finally we will cover how CSS3 media queries can allow for targeted element styling on a wide variety of screens.

Chapter 6, HTML5 Frameworks and Libraries, continues to dig into the wide variety of amazing framework and libraries available to you when developing your next HTML5 application. We begin by checking out one of the most popular libraries online today, that is jQuery. Along with the jQuery JavaScript library, we will look at how the jQuery Mobile project can transform a simple HTML document into a mobile-friendly user interface. Finally we will check out other open source projects such as Google V8, Node.js, and Three.js.

Chapter 7, Choosing How You Develop, looks at many of the popular code editing platforms that are available to HTML5 developers. We will overview many of the absolute necessities most developers require from coding environments when developing for the web. We will also take some time to check out the Adobe Edge Animate platform which brings a Flash-like user interface for creating HTML5 animations.

Chapter 8, Exporting to HTML5, continues to look at more software that allows you to write your HTML5 applications in platforms like Adobe Flash and compile them directly into HTML5. We will overview many popular platforms that export to HTML5 such as Jangaroo, Haxe, and Google's Dart.

Chapter 9, Avoiding the Roadblocks, attempts to display and discuss many of the typical issues developers face when working with many of the new additions to HTML5. In this chapter, we will develop a simple 2D side scrolling game and examine where common issues occur.

Chapter 10, Preparing for Release, concludes this book by discussing many of the common tasks usually performed on HTML5 applications prior to publishing them on the Internet. We will discuss proper browser testing methods and the utilization of "nightly" web browser releases. We will discuss many ways to benchmark your HTML5 content with external applications and browser plugins to enable you to inspect for runtime issues. Finally we will discuss methods to automate processes that web developers find themselves doing repeatedly by using applications like Grunt.

What you need for this book

For a complete understanding of the book, the following software are required:

- HTML5-compliant web browser (Google Chrome, Firefox, Opera, and so on.)
- An HTML5-friendly text editor (Sublime, Dreamweaver, Aptana, and Adobe Brackets)
- Access to the Adobe Creative Cloud https://creative.adobe.com/
- Adobe Flash
- CreateJS toolkit http://www.adobe.com/ca/products/flash/flash-to-html5.html

Access to the Internet to download up to date versions of open source libraries and frameworks.

Who this book is for

This book has been specifically targeted at developers with experience with developing web application and games in Adobe Flash who are ready to add HTML5 development to their skillset.

Conventions

In this book, you will find a number of styles of text that distinguish between different kinds of information. Here are some examples of these styles, and an explanation of their meaning.

Code words in text are shown as follows: "We can include other contexts through the use of the include directive."

A block of code is set as follows:

```
this.setX = function(x) { _xVal = x; }
this.setY = function(y) { _yVal = y; }
this.currentX = function() { return _xVal; }
this.currentY = function() { return _yVal; }
this.currentWidth = function() { return _widthVal; }
this.currentHeight = function() { return _heightVal; }
```

When we wish to draw your attention to a particular part of a code block, the relevant lines or items are set in bold:

```
this.setX = function(x) { _xVal = x; }
this.setY = function(y) { _yVal = y; }
this.currentX = function() { return _xVal; }
this.currentY = function() { return _yVal; }
this.currentWidth = function() { return _widthVal; }
this.currentHeight = function() { return _heightVal; }
```

New terms and **important words** are shown in bold. Words that you see on the screen, in menus or dialog boxes for example, appear in the text like this: "clicking the **Next** button moves you to the next screen".

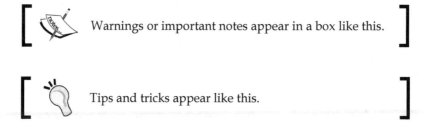

Warnings or important notes appear in a box like this.

Tips and tricks appear like this.

Reader feedback

Feedback from our readers is always welcome. Let us know what you think about this book—what you liked or may have disliked. Reader feedback is important for us to develop titles that you really get the most out of.

To send us general feedback, simply send an e-mail to feedback@packtpub.com, and mention the book title via the subject of your message.

If there is a topic that you have expertise in and you are interested in either writing or contributing to a book, see our author guide on www.packtpub.com/authors.

Customer support

Now that you are the proud owner of a Packt book, we have a number of things to help you to get the most from your purchase.

Downloading the example code

You can download the example code files for all Packt books you have purchased from your account at `http://www.packtpub.com`. If you purchased this book elsewhere, you can visit `http://www.packtpub.com/support` and register to have the files e-mailed directly to you.

Downloading the color images of this book

We also provide you a PDF file that has color images of the screenshots/diagrams used in this book. The color images will help you better understand the changes in the output. You can download this file from `http://www.packtpub.com/sites/default/files/downloads/3325OT_ColoredImages.pdf`.

Errata

Although we have taken every care to ensure the accuracy of our content, mistakes do happen. If you find a mistake in one of our books—maybe a mistake in the text or the code—we would be grateful if you would report this to us. By doing so, you can save other readers from frustration and help us improve subsequent versions of this book. If you find any errata, please report them by visiting `http://www.packtpub.com/submit-errata`, selecting your book, clicking on the **errata submission form** link, and entering the details of your errata. Once your errata are verified, your submission will be accepted and the errata will be uploaded on our website, or added to any list of existing errata, under the Errata section of that title. Any existing errata can be viewed by selecting your title from `http://www.packtpub.com/support`.

Piracy

Piracy of copyright material on the Internet is an ongoing problem across all media. At Packt, we take the protection of our copyright and licenses very seriously. If you come across any illegal copies of our works, in any form, on the Internet, please provide us with the location address or website name immediately so that we can pursue a remedy.

Please contact us at `copyright@packtpub.com` with a link to the suspected pirated material.

We appreciate your help in protecting our authors, and our ability to bring you valuable content.

Questions

You can contact us at questions@packtpub.com if you are having a problem with any aspect of the book, and we will do our best to address it.

1
Why HTML5?

Before getting started, it is important that you understand what **HTML5** is, how it works, and how it relates to what you already know as a Flash developer. This book uses **Adobe Flash** (CS6) as a reference when comparing functionalities of HTML5 with what Flash developers are commonly used to while creating applications in Flash. Therefore, a solid understanding of both the Adobe Flash IDE as well as ActionScript 3 will be required to properly follow the examples within this book.

In this chapter you will learn:

- What HTML5 actually is and what technologies are included within it
- Reasons for adding HTML5 development to your skillset
- Avoiding the initial issues involved in transitioning from Flash development
- Modern browser compatibility with HTML5 functionality

Understanding HTML5

As a Flash developer, you have probably worked with **HTML** on a frequent, if not daily, basis as a platform for publishing your compiled Adobe Flash **SWF** files on the Web. Although web browsers with **Flash Player** installed can view standalone SWF files, it is normal practice to embed Flash content within an HTML document. Thanks to the simplistic syntax and availability of HTML, many people who are not even developers have learned traditional HTML development techniques. Unfortunately, early HTML specifications fell short in many areas of displaying content online. Common tasks such as creating rich interactive experiences, sharing multimedia assets, or creating web-based user interfaces to act in a more typical software-like manner became a massive chore, if not impossible. In the recent past, Flash has been the obvious choice when developing and integrating assets such as video and audio playbacks, web-based games, 3D interactive graphics, and inline advertisements. Lately, many of these features on the Web have been remade using HTML5 allowing users to access the content in the same manner, but without the use of technology such as Adobe Flash Player.

The ability to build quality web-based content that can be globally accessible from any device is the key to a successful product or service. Facebook, Google, and Twitter are all using HTML5 to better the user experience of their applications and deliver content to users without the need for third-party plugins. More businesses are saving time, resources, and money during their application development process by utilizing the HTML5 development stack to target not only web browsers on desktop and mobile, but also installable applications on both platforms as well.

Transitioning your Flash development skills to HTML5 is a fun process that will not only open you to more opportunity professionally, but enable you to better analyze what tool is right for the job at hand. Adobe Flash isn't going anywhere anytime soon, but the same can easily be said for HTML5.

Since many developers flock to Flash development from previous web and application development technologies that may have had nothing to do with HTML, let's start by covering the essentials of the HTML5 stack.

What is HTML5?

HTML5 is the fifth and latest version of the HTML standard developed by the World Wide Web Consortium (`http://www.w3.org/`). Being a new version, it brought some new features to the existing HTML specification as well as removed some of the old outdated features. Many of these new and existing features are starting to closely resemble the feature set within Adobe Flash, thus opening many new facets of web development, which are not reliant on paid applications or browser plugins such as the Adobe Flash Player.

The development of the HTML5 specification is still a work in progress and is scheduled to be finalized and released sometime in 2014, but most of the modern web browsers today support many features of the specification already.

Generally, references to HTML5 refer to a suite of features and technologies surrounding the usage of not just HTML but **Cascading Style Sheets** (**CSS**) as well as **JavaScript**. Without the use of CSS and JavaScript, plain HTML documents, even HTML5 documents, will remain extremely simplistic in their functionality and look and feel. Therefore, learning HTML5 is effectively learning three technologies simultaneously. As tedious as that sounds, Adobe Flash is setup in a very similar way. The Flash IDE allows easy creation, editing, and referencing of assets to be used within your application. To integrate these assets into a dynamic interactive application requires the use of **ActionScript**. HTML5 is very similar to this such that HTML and CSS will be your Flash IDE and JavaScript will be the replacement for ActionScript. With all this in mind, let's continue by reviewing the standards on which HTML is built.

HTML standards

The **World Wide Web Consortium** (http://www.w3.org/) or **W3C**, is responsible for creating the standards on which HTML is developed today. These web development standards have been created as an attempt to unify the syntax and functionality developers create web pages with, as well as the feature set integrated in web browsers to enable these features in HTML. By writing web applications in a compliant markup that follows the HTML specification standards, developers can better ensure that their content will be displayed properly no matter how a user chooses to view it.

HTML syntax

Though it may look trivial, HTML syntax is the core of all web pages. Regardless of whether it is hardcoded within an HTML file, compiled from another programming language source, or injected into a document during application runtime, HTML syntax is the blueprint for the assets used within an HTML page. The better a developer understands HTML syntax and its limitations, the easier it will be for them to build their applications.

HTML syntax is written with the use of tag elements which are wrapped in angle brackets. HTML tags come in two different varieties: paired or empty elements. Paired HTML tags are the most common and the first tag style that one usually uses when creating an HTML document. The html tag is used to declare what is within an HTML document and usually sits on the first and last lines of an HTML file:

```
<html>
   Add your HTML content here.
</html>
```

As you can see in the previous example, paired tags open and close a container for more HTML elements to sit inside. Tags are always formatted the same, the only difference between each tag in the pair is that a forward slash is used to declare that a tag is closing an element. Therefore, <html> will not pair with any tag that does not contain the same internal value. HTML tags are case insensitive, and in the early days it was common for developers to always use capitals when writing tags. That tradition has now disappeared and you will almost always see tags written in lower case.

Empty HTML tags are written without the use of a closure tag. For example, when placing an image reference within an HTML document, there is no further HTML element content that can be placed within that image. Therefore, image references in HTML are formatted such as <imgsrc="my_image.jpg">. The image is referenced within the img tag by appending the src parameter with its value set to the image location.

If you have managed to use **Adobe Flex** to build any of your Flash content and utilized the **MXML** user interface markup language, you may have got the hang of closing empty tag elements with syntax such as `<imgsrc="my_image.jpg" />`. In HTML5, this trailing forward slash is not required but will still render your content properly if you happen to append it. For best use case, try to get in the habit of not using it in your HTML5 projects.

HTML is a tricky beast when it comes to debugging; a document with HTML errors in the syntax will not display errors on loading like a traditional Flash application. Writing clean and concise HTML is the key to maintaining an error-free, standard, compliant web page. There are many applications and tools available to aid in developing clean HTML code, some of which will be covered later in the book. The W3C has created a robust HTML syntax validation service, which will check a publicly available website for HTML errors (`http://validator.w3.org/`).

HTML elements

Every version of the HTML specification has a specific list of tags available to developers while creating HTML documents. The current list of elements within the HTML5 specification as defined by the W3C can be found within their language reference documentation (`http://www.w3.org/TR/html-markup/elements.html`).

Within the HTML5 specification are some very interesting new elements available to developers with regards to media integration into web pages. For example, Flash requirements for media playback can now be avoided when embedding audio or video into a web page with the addition of the `audio` and `video` tags. These exciting new media tags are covered in more depth in *Chapter 3, Scalability, Limitations, and Effects.*

Bringing in the style

Cascading Style Sheets or CSS is the primary method used for styling HTML elements. Like HTML, there is a set list of styles in CSS that you can apply to elements in an HTML documents. To get an idea of what CSS attributes are available to you, head over to `http://www.w3schools.com/cssref/` for the entire list. CSS can be applied to HTML elements in a number of different ways. Traditionally, CSS syntax is stored within an external `.css` file and referenced from within the `head` element in an HTML document. However, CSS can be appended to elements within the HTML document directly by adding a `style` parameter to almost any element within the `body` tag:

```
<imgsrc="my_image.jpg" style="border:5px solid #000000;">
```

The previous example uses the `style` parameter within an image element to apply a 5-pixel thick black border around the image referenced in the `src` parameter.

Downloading the example code

You can download the example code files for all Packt books you have purchased from your account at `http://www.packtpub.com`. If you purchased this book elsewhere, you can visit `http://www.packtpub.com/support` and register to have the files e-mailed directly to you.

What if you had five images or even 100 images in your page that needed the same styles applied to each element? Applying the exact same `style` parameter to each image tag is not only time consuming but will result in code that is oversized and possibly extremely hard to maintain or update. CSS can target a single element or a group of elements by using a `class` or `id` HTML parameter:

```
<div id="photo-gallery">
  <imgsrc="photo1.jpg" class="photo">
  <imgsrc="photo2.jpg" class="photo">
  <imgsrc="photo3.jpg" class="photo">
  <imgsrc="photo4.jpg" class="photo">
  <imgsrc="photo5.jpg" class="photo">
</div>
```

In the previous example, we attempted to display a group of different images within an HTML document. Each image, referenced with an `img` element tag, also has a `class` parameter appended to it with the `photo` value. The `class` HTML parameter can be used and re-used on almost any element available and allow you to reference a group of elements rather than modifying each element directly. All of the images are also encased in a `div` element. `div` elements are used as containers to display content in. In this case, the `div` element has an `id` parameter set to `photo-gallery`. The `id` HTML parameter is very similar to `class` with the exemption of being able to re-use the same value of `id` within the same HTML document.

Editing HTML, CSS, and JavaScript can be simplified by using a code editing application setup to aid with HTML5 syntax. Applications like **Aptana** (`http://aptana.com/`), **Dreamweaver** (`http://adobe.com/products/dreamweaver.html`), and **Sublime Text** (`http://sublimetext.com/`) are all recommended. However, if simplicity is your thing, feel free to use something else.

With all this in mind, writing CSS to style this photo gallery could be done
as follows:

```html
<!DOCTYPE html>
<html>
  <head>
    <title>My Photo Gallery</title>

    <!-- Our Photo Gallery CSS Styles -->
    <style type="text/css">
      body {
        background-color:#000000;
      }

      #photo-gallery {
        width:100%;
      }

      #photo-gallery .photo {
        width:200px;
        border:4px solid #ffffff;
      }
    </style>
  </head>
  <body>
    <div id="photo-gallery">
      <imgsrc="photo1.jpg" class="photo">
      <imgsrc="photo2.jpg" class="photo">
      <imgsrc="photo3.jpg" class="photo">
      <imgsrc="photo4.jpg" class="photo">
      <imgsrc="photo5.jpg" class="photo">
    </div>
  </body>
</html>
```

Instead of applying style parameter to each and every element in the document,
we can now use the style tag within the head element to place our raw CSS code.
In the previous example, HTML elements are selected in three different ways. To
start, the body of the document had the background color set to black by using its
hexadecimal value. We select the body tag element by simply using the tag reference.
This method of selecting raw elements can be used on a wide variety of elements
within your document but will affect all elements with that reference. The next
method of selection is by looking for elements with a specific ID. To designate the
use of an ID, # is placed in front of the ID value. Therefore, #photo-gallery will

be selecting the div element with the id parameter set to photo-gallery. We set the width parameter of the gallery container to 100%, which is calculated from the browser width when viewing the HTML document. Finally, to style each one of the images in the gallery, we style the class which was applied to each one of the image tags in the body of the HTML document. Since the class HTML parameter can be applied to an unlimited number of elements in an HTML document, we can specifically target the classes within another element by chaining the CSS element selection together. Classes are selected in CSS by appending . to the start of the class name. Therefore, #photo-gallery .photo will select only the elements with the photo class name inside the element with id of photo-gallery:

Passing it over to JavaScript

Styling HTML elements with CSS only gets you so far. HTML and CSS are effectively the Flash IDE from the perspective of a Flash developer. What is missing is the code that drives the interaction and functionality within your application. While using Flash, ActionScript is the weapon of choice when creating robust applications. While developing HTML5 content, JavaScript will be doing the grinding, allowing you to bring life to your HTML elements.

What is JavaScript?

JavaScript has been around since the mid 1990s and has grown up to be one of the most popular scripting languages available. JavaScript brings life to HTML documents by adding features such as content modifications, animations, 3D graphics, form submission, and data retrieval all without having to reload the active HTML document. Features such as these allow web content to act more like traditional software applications rather than static web pages.

Unlike ActionScript 3, JavaScript is a true scripting language as it requires no preprocessing or compiling to be run. Just like HTML and CSS, a JavaScript document's source is sent to user upon request and executed on client side. Therefore, unlike technologies such as ActionScript, JavaScript source code is open for public viewing.

JavaScript in action

Looking back at our My Photo Gallery example, an important missing feature is the ability to view a selected photo in larger format. JavaScript is a perfect platform to add this functionality as its main usage is to bring interaction to HTML documents. Using the existing code example, we can extend its functionality by adding a new div element at the bottom of the page body to contain the larger image view. This element can be empty as we do not want a photo to be displayed by default on page load. Finally, we set an identifier on the div tag of id="photo-display", which will allow us to target the content in that element from CSS and JavaScript:

```
<div id="photo-display"></div>
```

Before integrating the JavaScript functionality, we need to append some CSS styles to div using #photo-display to allow selected photos to fill the browser window at a higher resolution, typical of most photo gallery displays. Within the CSS styles, we have already set for this example, we will append some more style properties to the #photo-display element:

```
#photo-display {
  display:none;
  position:absolute;
  top:0;
  width:100%;
  height:100%;
  background-color:#000000;
  text-align:center;
}

#photo-display img {
```

```
    margin:auto;
    margin-top:50px;
    max-height:800px;
    border:4px solid #ffffff;
}
```

This CSS will target only one specific `div` as we have used the `#photo-display` syntax to target it. To start the styles off, we begin with the most important parameter, `display:none`, which hides the element on page load. This is perfect in our case as we do not want the full-screen display visible on page load. By adding `position:absolute` and `top:0` to the style definition for our `#photo-display` element, we will display the element on top of the previous elements declared within the HTML body. The rest of the styles set on `#photo-display` are pretty self-explanatory. The next lines of CSS specifically target the `img` elements within `div` with the `photo-display` class. We can do this in CSS by chaining identifiers together. In this case, we specify these styles for image tag elements within a custom named element ID.

With the HTML and CSS to display the larger version of a selected photo in place, the next step is adding the JavaScript code for displaying the selected photo within the `#photo-display` container upon user interaction. To consolidate this example into a single file, we will add the JavaScript within an HTML `script` element:

```html
<!-- Our Photo Gallery JavaScript Source -->
<script>
  var largeImage = new Image();

  // Display a specific photo in the large
  // photo display element.
  var displayPhoto = function(source) {
    // If there is already an image inside the display
    // remove it.
    if(largeImage.src != '') {
      document.getElementById(
        "photo-display").removeChild(largeImage);
    }

    // Update the source location of the image
    largeImage.src = source;
    document.getElementById(
      "photo-display").appendChild(largeImage);

    // Display the large photo element.
    document.getElementById("photo-display").
      style.display = 'block';
```

```
   }

   // Closes the large photo display element.
   var closePhotoDisplay = function() {
     document.getElementById("photo-display").
       style.display = 'none';
   }
</script>
```

As a Flash developer, the previous function syntax should look pretty familiar. A major change within the function scope is the variable syntax. Unlike AS3, the HTML as well as the source variables are not strictly typed. This goes for all variables within JavaScript syntax and is probably one of the biggest issues Flash developers have with JavaScript.

Aside from some string manipulations to generate img HTML elements from the source variable, the method also references the document object. Every HTML document that is loaded into a browser then becomes the document object accessible from within JavaScript. The document object within JavaScript has a number of built-in properties and methods that are available to access information and elements within the view HTML document. In our example, we make use of the easily defined document object method getElementById(). As the method name implies, when an HTML element's ID is supplied, the reference to the element within the HTML document is returned for use within the script. Since JavaScript supports the chaining of properties, we can apply the innerHTML property to manipulate the inner content of an HTML element as well as the style property to change an element's CSS properties.

To enable an image to close once a user has finished viewing it, we will add a second JavaScript function to our example to revert all the changes made when displaying the photo. Since the photo-display image will be updated when the user clicks on a new image, all our closePhotoDisplay method needs to do is hide the visible element to show the full photo gallery again:

```
functionclosePhotoDisplay() {
   document.getElementById("photo-display").style.display = 'none';
}
```

Setting the #photo-display element's style.display back to none hides the entire element and reverts the user interface back to its initial state.

Adding events to each of the photos can easily be accomplished by appending an onclick parameter to the targeted element. The addition would look as follows:

```
<imgsrc="photo1.jpg" class="photo"
   onclick="displayPhoto('photo1.jpg')">
```

Now, when the image is clicked on, the onclick event gets fired and runs the JavaScript code declared within the parameter. In this case, we use this opportunity to call our displayPhoto method within our previously written JavaScript block. Within the call, we supply the required source variable, which will be the image file name as a String datatype. This will allow the proper image reference to be used within the #photo-display element. All put together, our updated div tag with id="#photo-gallery" will now look like the following:

```
<div id="photo-gallery">
  <imgsrc="photo1.jpg" class="photo"
    onclick="displayPhoto('photo1.jpg')">
  <imgsrc="photo2.jpg" class="photo"
    onclick="displayPhoto('photo2.jpg')">
  <imgsrc="photo3.jpg" class="photo"
    onclick="displayPhoto('photo3.jpg')">
  <imgsrc="photo4.jpg" class="photo"
    onclick="displayPhoto('photo4.jpg')">
  <imgsrc="photo5.jpg" class="photo"
    onclick="displayPhoto('photo5.jpg')">
</div>
```

Finally, to enable the user to close an open image within the #photo-display element, we will apply an onclick event to call our closePhotoDisplay method. Rather than applying the onclick event to the image within the #photo-display element, we will target the display itself, allowing users to click anywhere in the browser to close the display:

```
<div id="photo-display" onclick="closePhotoDisplay()"></div>
```

Putting all of these code snippets together, the gallery source now looks like the following:

```
<!DOCTYPE html>
<html>
  <head>
    <title>My Photo Gallery</title>

    <!-- Our Photo Gallery CSS Styles -->
    <style type="text/css">
      body {
        background-color:#000000;
      }

      #photo-gallery {
        width:100%;
      }
```

```css
#photo-gallery .photo {
  width:200px;
  border:4px solid #ffffff;
}

#photo-display {
  display:none;
  position:absolute;
  top:0;
  width:100%;
  height:100%;
  background-color:#000000;
  text-align:center;
}

#photo-display img {
  margin:auto;
  margin-top:50px;
  max-height:800px;
  border:4px solid #ffffff;
}
</style>
```

```html
<!-- Our Photo Gallery JavaScript Source -->
<script>
  var largeImage = new Image();

  // Displays a specific photo in the large
  // photo display element.
  var displayPhoto = function(source) {
    // If there is already a image inside the display
    // remove it.
    if(largeImage.src != '') {
      document.getElementById(
        "photo-display").removeChild(largeImage);
    }

    // Update the source location of the image
    largeImage.src = source;
```

```
            document.getElementById(
              "photo-display").appendChild(largeImage);

            // Display the large photo element.
            document.getElementById(
              "photo-display").style.display = 'block';
          }

          // Closes the large photo display element.
          var closePhotoDisplay = function() {
            document.getElementById("photo-display").
              style.display = 'none';
          }
        </script>
      </head>
      <body>
        <div id="photo-gallery">
          <!-- Place all of the images inline with a 'photo' class
            for CSS manipulation. -->
          <imgsrc="photo1.jpg" class="photo"
            onclick="displayPhoto('photo1.jpg')">
          <imgsrc="photo2.jpg" class="photo"
            onclick="displayPhoto('photo2.jpg')">
          <imgsrc="photo3.jpg" class="photo"
            onclick="displayPhoto('photo3.jpg')">
          <imgsrc="photo4.jpg" class="photo"
            onclick="displayPhoto('photo4.jpg')">
          <imgsrc="photo5.jpg" class="photo"
            onclick="displayPhoto('photo5.jpg')">
        </div>

        <!-- An empty DIV element to contain the user selected photo
          in large scale. -->
        <div id="photo-display" onclick="closePhotoDisplay()"></div>
      </body>
    </html>
```

Saving the text into an .html file and launching it in a web browser will now reveal all of our hard work. Just as before, the gallery should start by displaying the list of images by default. Once an image is clicked on, the selection will be passed to the #display-window element and displayed at 100 percent of the browser width:

Finally, clicking anywhere within the document will close the large image and return you back to the initial gallery display.

Although this example contains none of the new features of HTML5, it is a simple way of showing some of the key technologies that make up HTML and some of the methods used to reference assets in HTML.

Why bother learning HTML5?

As a Flash developer, getting yourself into the realm of HTML5 development is an extremely logical step for many reasons. Building applications with HTML5 allows you to easily reach users on desktop or mobile with rich integrated and interactive content without the need for plugins. One of the most beneficial aspects of HTML5 development is the accessibility to the development environment. Since HTML5 requires no special compiler or software for writing code, developers are free to choose their favorite setup for writing and testing their projects. Applications can be easily run and tested within any compliant web browser and tested locally without the need of a web server. This makes HTML5 one of the most accessible and easy to use technologies on the Web.

Write once, deploy everywhere

Unlike Flash applications, any device with a modern web browser can interact with HTML5 web content. So, with the help of CSS for dynamic resizing of viewable content, your HTML5 applications can be used without the need of application installation or dependencies on desktop or mobile platforms. Developers can also use technologies such as **Phone Gap** (`http://phonegap.com/`) or **Appcelerator** (`http://www.appcelerator.com/`) to easily convert their existing HTML5 web content to packaged mobile applications for market in all modern mobile operating systems. Packaged applications can be integrated and sold using common mobile application services such as Apple's **App Store** (`http://store.apple.com`) and **Google Play** (`https://play.google.com`). On top of that, **Microsoft Windows 8** desktop application development now supports a whole suite of different programming languages, one of them being HTML5 (`http://msdn.microsoft.com/en-us/library/windows/apps/br211386.aspx`). With the ability to package HTML5 content into installable applications, developers can now begin to easily monetize their work by sale on the various application distribution outlets.

Exciting new features

As just mentioned, HTML5 hosts a suite of new and exciting features, many of which will be covered in the following chapters of this book. However, to allow you to better understand why HTML5 is so exciting and important for Flash developers and the web development community, here is a more detailed list of some of those features.

canvas – 2D drawing API

Flash developers can really flex their programming abilities within the new `canvas` element and 2D drawing API. Just like the drawing API within ActionScript 3, the `canvas` HTML5 element allows developers to create dynamic graphics during runtime, all from within JavaScript. Flash game developers moving to HTML5 usually find their home within the utilization of the `canvas` element as it is the closest representation of traditional Flash development when using HTML5.

Media playback

Web developers no longer require to develop their media playback elements with platforms such as Flash or Quicktime. Audio and video can now be easily integrated into the HTML document using `audio` and `video` tags. Not only does this allow for easier and cheaper integration of playback elements into web pages but also mobile devices have no issues reading and displaying these elements from within their integrated browsers.

Offline storage

Traditionally, when web developers needed to save data locally on the user's machine, they used **cookies**. HTML5 adds a new offline storage method called **Web Storage** (`http://dev.w3.org/html5/webstorage`) that can drastically increase your applications' abilities when you have the requirement to save data for re-use. Large amounts of data like your clients user-specific application configuration can now be stored in a more secure and quicker manner.

You can now also setup your HTML5 content to be available to your users even when they go offline by utilizing the HTML5 **cache manifest**. The cache manifest is just a simple text file, which is placed on your web server. If a web browser supports the use of HTML5 cache manifests (all modern browsers currently do), the references to files and assets, which you have placed within the manifest, are all cached on the client side. Depending on whether your manifest is set to cache all the content required to run your application, the user can then go offline and continue using the application. Combined with the use of HTML Web Storage for archiving data to be resent to a web server upon Internet reconnection, you can develop applications that will allow your users to seamlessly use them despite their connection being broken. A perfect example of this feature of HTML5 in action is **Gmail** by Google (`https://mail.google.com`). By archiving message data on a user's device when accessed initially, important information such as e-mails can still be reviewed when a user goes to open a message while, say, he is underground in a subway.

Document editing

Many HTML5 elements now allow a parameter, `contenteditable="true"`, which allows users to edit all the content within the element. This feature brings a sort of WYSIWYG environment directly to HTML content. Inline document editing can be extremely handy as a developer when manipulating content within your HTML5 projects.

Drag-and-drop

HTML5 elements now have the ability to be draggable. Simple but important user experience additions such as this bring more application-like interactivity which traditionally would be built with JavaScript. Just like inline document editing, setting elements to be draggable during development can aid in finding the proper position properties.

Geolocation

The Geolocation API enables users to allow their current position to be sent to an HTML5 document for use within JavaScript. Apart from the obvious usage of a user's location in mapping applications, Geolocation values can add many new features into web documents that allow for a more interactive user experience.

File API

The File API within HTML5 allows a more interactive experience when dealing with files on a user's local machine. Local files can now be dragged into the browser and previewed within the HTML document without uploading the data to the web server.

> For a more in-depth look at the complete feature set within HTML5, visit the online W3C API documentation (http://www.w3.org/TR/html5/).

Mobile accessibility

As more devices become integrated with Internet accessibility, the need for streamlined, multiplatform applications that allow for low overhead and integrated device access is at an all-time high. Almost all modern mobile browsers already support many features of HTML5, which web developers can harness to build mobile applications that rival many natively built applications for specific mobile platforms. Features such as Geolocation, local file access and offline storage allow applications to easily integrate themselves into the device hardware that is running them.

> Any of the examples in this book can be run on any modern mobile device running an HTML5-compliant web browser. If you have an iPhone, Android, or Windows phone handy, test out the examples on your device to view how well mobile platforms run HTML5 content.

One of the biggest driving forces behind the advent of HTML5 was mobile. Mobile application development requires a slightly different approach than typical application development as the platform running the application not only has fewer resources as compared to a typical desktop configuration but also things like battery life, screen resolutions, and touch interfaces need to be taken into account. Dealing with all of these requirements while developing applications with Flash can get a little bit tricky. Flash applications traditionally tend to be a bit heavy on resource usage, though optimizations can be made to compensate for some of these issues while running applications on mobile platforms.

Flash Player on Mobile

Since the advent of iPhone, Flash developers had to deal with the fact that their web-based Flash content would never be viewable from the integrated iOS web browser. Apple made their stance on the usage of the Adobe Flash Player clear in a publicly address letter from Steve Jobs in April 2010, which stated that the Flash Player did not deliver the device or application performance that Apple required on their device.

In June 2012, Adobe released a public statement regarding the future of the Adobe Flash Player for mobile. As of August 15, 2012, Flash Player for Android will only be available to devices certified to run the Flash Player as Adobe has suspended the development of the mobile version of Flash Player. Users running Android Version 4.1+ will be unable to run Flash content within their browser and all web content will rely on the use of the technologies within HTML5.

With the Flash Player removed from the mobile market, a Flash developer's only resource, at this point in time, for creating mobile applications is developing them with **Adobe AIR** and packaging their work as standalone applications rather than on the Web.

Build on your existing skillset

Flash developers transitioning to HTML5 development have a leg up when it comes to learning tricks to create amazing applications with purely HTML, CSS, and JavaScript. Not only will all the lessons learned about handling and optimizing media elements transition over, but also their ActionScript 3 skills will allow them to understand and use JavaScript to its full potential.

ECMAScript

The time developers invest to learn a programming language such as ActionScript 3 is far from a short endeavor. Fortunately, both JavaScript and ActionScript 3 are built on the **ECMAScript** scripting language standard (http://www.ecmascript.org). In a nutshell, this means that many of the method, variable, and property syntax setups are extremely similar in look, feel, and usage. As we dig deeper and see more examples of HTML5 in action, if you have experience with ActionScript 3, you will instantly notice many similarities when utilizing JavaScript.

Avoiding the initial road blocks

All Flash developers generally have the same issues when transitioning to HTML5 development. Most of these problems arise from differences between platform syntax, as well as dealing with the interaction between each element within the HTML5 stack.

Stage versus DOM

The first and most obvious change when moving to HTML5 development is the lack of the ever important Flash Stage. Dealing with element layout, asset animations, and interactivity with HTML5 is all taken care of purely with code. Although there are many web development IDEs with drag-and-drop type interfaces, to better understand how to build cleaner web pages, this book will cover all examples with hand written code examples.

Positioning assets in the DOM

One of the biggest initial issues many Flash developers have when moving into web development is the concept of positioning content and assets within the DOM. Unless specified, HTML elements are not simply placed in DOM with X and Y position values. Since elements within an HTML document are displayed inline by default, global X and Y position values are irrelevant. When positing an element within DOM with CSS, properties such as margin, padding, top, left, right, and bottom are used instead. As mentioned, if elements are specially styled with a position of absolute or utilized within a canvas element then X and Y values can be used. On top of the issues regarding simply controlling where elements are placed within your project, there is the ordeal of making sure that all of the web browsers that may view your content display it as per your specification.

Dealing with media elements

Media optimization is the key to delivering content over the Web. When working with Flash, many of the assets used are vector-based and therefore lightweight on the compiled SWF file size. Bitmap data used within the Flash SWF is compressed during compilation, therefore automatically aiding you by minimizing file size. Since what the majority of HTML documents do is reference raw files publicly accessible on the Web, each asset used should be optimized for minimal file size while keeping the intended quality as close to original as possible. As we cover different aspects of HTML5 development throughout the chapters of this book, many optimization methods will be covered for the different types of media used in web pages.

Securing your code

Publishing content in Adobe Flash outputs a compiled binary SWF file, which is ready to be played in a compatible Flash Player. The code and assets used in the application are protected from prying eyes since the application was compiled into a single binary file. But when dealing with code and assets on the Web, the entire game changes. Pretty much everything you create and deliver in an HTML5 project, as with any website, is open for public viewing.

Code obfuscation is a practice some developers use while delivering production level client-side code. Many websites and applications are available to obfuscate your JavaScript code by rewriting the code in a hard to read, compressed format. Although this is not a foolproof way of securing code, it adds a level of deterrence when it comes to users poking around a document's source code.

Understanding client-side code usage and limitations is the key to writing secure JavaScript applications. Sensitive information should never be hardcoded into a document which can be viewed on client side. *Chapter 2, Preparing for the Battle*, covers the usage of client-side script in a more in-depth manner in comparison to ActionScript 3.

Browser and platform compatibility

One of the major changes in development paradigm when moving from Flash to HTML5 development is the need to target multiple platforms with the same code base. While developing an application using Adobe Flash, you initially set a target version of the Flash Player for your application to run within. By compiling your application into a packaged SWF, the Flash runtime will have no issues rendering your application in any compatible Flash Player. Since every browser and platform tends to display web content a little bit differently, when developing HTML5 content and applications, one must take note of the platforms and browsers that may be used to view the content to better optimize the viewing experience.

Browser functionality checks can be written into JavaScript conditions to enable users with browsers that lack the support for specific HTML5 features to still view your HTML5 content. For instance, if a user visits a page with an HTML5 video playback element within it, without the support for it within his browser, JavaScript could alternatively embed a Flash video playback application instead.

Finding a modern web browser that doesn't support HTML5 is getting harder day by day. When it comes to choosing a browser to test code in while reading this book, Firefox (http://www.getfirefox.net/), Chrome (http://www.google.com/chrome), Safari (http://www.apple.com/safari/), and Opera (http://www.opera.com/) are all great choices and available online for free.

Within the chapters of this book, many of these popular web browsers will be utilized to show how content may sometimes differ in look and usage. Due to the speed at which browser updates and changes are released, testing your site as much as possible in every browser on every platform is a very important aspect of web development. Many of these web browsers now have built-in development and debugging tools, which allow for easier optimizations of your HTML5 projects. Other applications and services are also available to ease the pain of browser testing, some of which will be used and covered in this book.

Summary

In this chapter, we have covered the key aspects of the HTML5 stack and how to use each of them in a simplistic manner. By creating a simple photo gallery web page, we not only used HTML, CSS, and JavaScript, but also the methods to reference elements in between them. Some of the new and exciting features available within HTML5 were also explained and compared with functionality traditionally created within Flash assets. The typical issues during the learning curve for Flash developers moving to web development were reviewed to allow you to be aware of these issues before finding out the hard way. Hopefully, this chapter has furthered your interest in learning more about what HTML5 can do.

The development of the HTML5 standard maintained by the W3C is an interesting but extremely in-depth topic, which will not fit within the constraints of this book. If you are interested in learning more about how HTML5 standards are created and maintained, I strongly recommend checking out and keeping up with the information on specification and syntax development W3C publishes on their site (`http://www.w3.org`).

With the platform overview out of the way, we will continue by digging further into the most important aspect of the HTML5 stack, JavaScript, and how it relates to what you already know from developing with ActionScript.

2
Preparing for the Battle

Now that you understand what technologies make up HTML5, we can start getting our hands dirty. But before we jump right into coding HTML, CSS, and JavaScript, we need to cover the fundamentals of the first step of developing a project, asset preparation. Without a design, assets, and content, your web pages won't be very appealing or, for that matter, functional. During the preparation we will also dig into the syntax specification for JavaScript and how it's related to ActionScript 3, to prepare us for full-fledged development in *Chapter 3, Scalability, Limitations, and Effects*.

In this chapter we will cover:

- The preparation of common assets such as images, audio, and video for use within an HTML5 document
- In-browser code outputs and debugging
- The basics of JavaScript and the syntax variance from ActionScript 3
- Examples of JavaScript in action and the proper methods for code execution

Preparing the asset

While developing applications in Flash, integrating assets such as images, audio, and video into a typical project can be accomplished in a couple of different ways. You may choose to integrate assets in the typical way by importing them directly in a Flash project library. The addition of an asset into a Flash project results in the asset inclusion into the compiled SWF file. Since all assets are compiled within a single file, there is no need to acquire assets from external resources such as the Internet. Assets within a compiled Flash project are inherently protected from acquisition or being referenced by public.

Unfortunately, assets internally referenced within the project library cannot be updated or changed once the project has been exported. Developing applications such as a video playback UI or photo gallery requires assets to be integrated dynamically, resulting in a single application instance that can be used infinitely. External assets may be integrated via requests for external files which are publicly accessible on the Internet. External integration allows for smaller application sizes as well as the ability to modify the external assets without the need for application updates. Unfortunately, if the file is unavailable or the user isn't connected to the Internet, the asset cannot be integrated and may result in a failure within the application.

External asset integration is the standard way of including content into web-based documents. Files that will be referenced by HTML documents are typically placed on the same web server as the HTML documents embedding them.

Assets can also be referenced from other web servers on the Internet, however the content is at the mercy of the developers or administrators with access to that content. Developer's laziness or attempts to lower bandwidth costs can result in images or other assets being embedded from external sources, moving bandwidth charges to a web server other than your own. This process is known as **hotlinking** and is frowned upon within the web development community, as you force other website owners to deal with the cost of asset distribution.

Due to lack of automatic optimization of web content as in the compiler in Flash, web developers must take it upon themselves to prepare their content and assets for web usage. Since web content is delivered on demand to users over variable Internet connection speeds, assets should be as small in file size as possible to allow playback and viewing with as little latency as possible for the end user. Let's review each of the common asset types and the proper methods for preparing each of them for embedding into our HTML documents.

 All the assets used for optimizations and conversions can be found in the downloadable examples files for book within the Chapter 02_examples directory.

Images

Adding images into your project is usually one of the first asset integration techniques used in every web-based project. All images on the Web generally come in one of three different formats: JPEG, PNG, or GIF. Each of these formats serves specific purposes and should be used according to what a design and function requires. As common as these image formats are within everyday use, it is important to understand what each format can and can't do to allow for optimized image integration into HTML documents.

> Follow this book along with the example files available for download on the Packt Publishing website (www.packtpub.com). If you don't have a copy of Photoshop CS6, a demo for the same can be downloaded and installed for free from http://www.adobe.com/cfusion/tdrc/ index.cfm?product=photoshop&loc=en_us&promoid=IICUB.

Consider this high-quality, uncompressed image in **CR2** format taken directly from a Cannon digital SLR camera. The size of this raw image is 27 megabytes and hence it isn't compatible for viewing or embedding within any modern web browser.

Even if a web browser could handle placing this image within an HTML document, the time it would take to download the image would be enormous. Despite today's common high-speed Internet connections, not many users are willing to wait more than a couple of minutes to view a single image while loading a web page. Therefore, before using this image for the Web, it must be optimized for the Web. When this CR2 image is opened in Photoshop, the Photoshop Camera RAW window will display not only the photo data and file size but also the image dimensions.

It looks like the digital camera used to take this photo saved this image at 17.9 megapixels, which makes this image 5184 pixels wide and 3456 pixels high. This image would never be used at this resolution on the Web as it wouldn't fit on a computer monitor and would need to be scaled down in order to be viewed. Scaling down an image for using it on the Web may make it smaller in size and easier to view on the Web, but the file needed to display it is still the enormous master version that will be slow to load. Let's continue by opening this file in Photoshop by selecting **Done** within the Camera RAW import window.

It is good practice to export a web-ready version of your images with the resolution your web page design requires them to be displayed at. Changing the image resolution to an appropriate size for the Web can be easily accomplished within Photoshop by selecting **Image Size** under the **Image** tab.

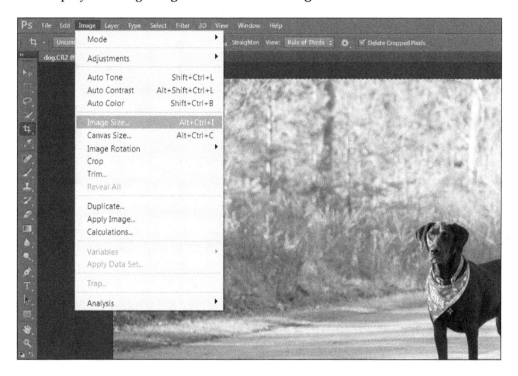

In the **Image Size** window, we can enter some more realistic values into the **Width** and **Height** parameters to see what kind of optimizations we can achieve. By using values such as 1920 x 1280, which is still a very high-resolution image for the Web, you can view what the expected output image source file size will be in the text above the **Width** and **Height** parameters.

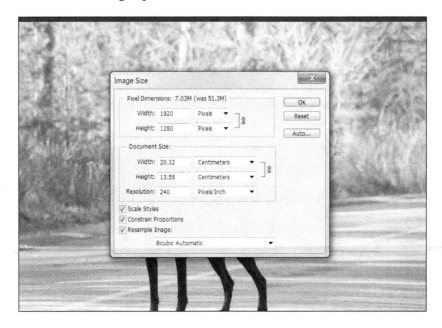

After updating the **Width** and **Height** parameters within the **Image Size** window, the resulting file size can be viewed immediately above them. Keep in mind that the file size change displayed will not be the final output size as we can still optimize this image source with techniques such as JPEG compression.

 While optimizing image sizes for usage within a specific web design, there is generally no need to export images larger in size than what is set within a design. If a thumbnail is needed within a design, exporting two images, a large and a small, is better than using a single image for both instances.

Photoshop's **Save for Web** feature located under the **File** tab can be said to be web developers' best friend. This tool allows you to easily export images from Photoshop with the specific intent of optimization for the Web in mind. Whether spicing up designs or converting assets to single instances, whenever you are going to export something from Photoshop for usage on the Web, this tool is the best way to accomplish it.

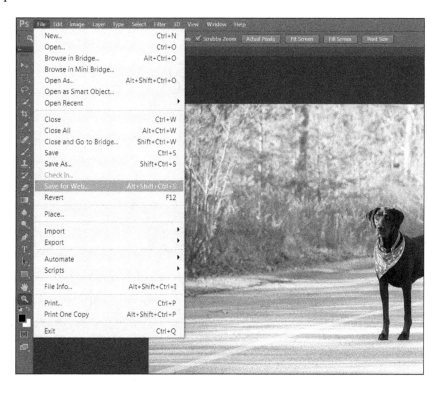

Clicking on the **Save for Web** option will open a dedicated window that will aid you in selecting the best format and compression method while exporting your data. So let's export a couple of versions of this photo to see what can be the minimum possible file size while trying to retain as much image quality as possible.

With the format type set to **JPG** to allow for better compression, select the **4-Up** tab at the top of the window to bring up side-by-side comparisons of different levels of compression on your image data. Play around with these values and see how low you can take the quality levels before you see dramatic changes to your image. While doing this, keep an eye on the expected file size to see how the level of compression is affecting the size.

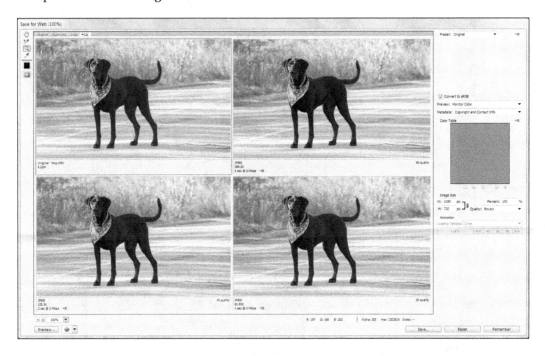

The background of this dog photo specifically takes a hit in quality as the compression level rises. This is due to the long grass creates a very dynamic and busy area where pixilation can be seen. Areas within the dog's solid color body maintain more of the original quality as the pixels in the same area are very similar in color. Another interesting feature within the **Save for Web** window is the expected time to download output each version of image has with it. You can easily change the expected bandwidth levels to see how much time it may take to deliver this image to a user over the Internet.

 Since every image is different, there is no single perfect optimization setting. Taking the time to make sure that each image looks its best at the smallest file size will reward you with a better looking website that loads quickly.

For example purposes, I have exported this image in a couple of different resolutions and compression levels using the JPEG format.

dog.CR2	27,462 KB
dog-1080x720-80compression.jpg	371 KB
dog-800x533-80compression.jpg	223 KB
dog-800x533-60compression.jpg	128 KB
dog-800x533-20compression.jpg	52 KB
dog-800x533-5compression.jpg	31 KB

As you can see from preceding the file listing, we initially started out with a 27-MB photo taken directly from a digital SLR camera. Using different exporting methods in Photoshop, we can easily get a decent version of the same image with a smaller resolution in a file that is well under 500 kilobytes. Considering that in a fully developed web page this image could be one of many, the general rule of thumb is to keep every image files size as small as possible. This will allow your content to load quickly and display properly for the design you have created.

Of course, as previously mentioned, JPG is not the only image format available for use within web pages. Let's quickly cover each of the formats and what each of them brings to the table.

JPEG

Outputting an image as `.jpeg` or more commonly `.jpg` allows for lossy image compression, which aims to decrease file size by discarding some of the data within the image. The amount of compression used when saving in JPEG format is typically user defined, allowing designers and developers to create a smaller file than the original such that is as close to its source as possible. One of the major downsides to the JPEG format is the lack of transparency support as the format contains no alpha channels.

PNG

Portable Network Graphics (PNG) is a bitmap image format that doesn't use compression when saving image data. PNG images are great for design and asset images as they retain the quality and color palette used in design and also support transparency. However, they are not typically utilized for images such as photographs, as the resulting file size will be too large due to the amount of details in the image.

GIF

The beloved GIF file, or more commonly seen nowadays as the **animated GIF** has been available for usage since CompuServe released the format in 1987. GIF images support 256 colors, transparency, as well as animations via multiple image frames. Though it is still in use all around the Web till date, due to the lack of timeline control of animated images, techniques such as sprite sheets (of which we will cover more in the following chapters) are becoming more popular for animated image integration.

Audio

Preparing audio for the Web is relatively straight forward as majority of web browsers support **MP3** audio formats within HTML5's new audio element. Aside from MP3, some browsers support the use of **OGG** audio files. Therefore, exporting audio in either of the formats will allow you to target all modern HTML5 compatible browsers and ensure that your end user hears the audio regardless of what browser they choose to view your content with.

The audio element

Creating the `audio` element, as with HTML syntax for most of the elements, is pretty straight forward. One major difference from traditional source references within HTML elements is the use of the `source` element which is encased within the `audio` element. By utilizing this new `source` element, we can reference multiple assets within the same element and load only the first file which is compatible:

```
<audio controls>
    <source src="horse.ogg" type="audio/ogg">
    <source src="horse.mp3" type="audio/mp3">
    Your browser does not support the audio tag.
</audio>
```

If a user attempts to open this element within a browser with no HTML5 audio support, the remaining internal content within the `audio` element will be displayed. In this case, we display only text, but you could easily append a reference to a Flash audio playback application or a warning styled with CSS. However, if all is well with the browser as per the given requisites, the page will display an audio playback UI that look something like the following:

The audio playback control user interface is specific to the browser displaying the data. The preceding image is what Google Chrome currently renders as its internal audio playback control user interface. Default audio controls can be removed by excluding the `controls` parameter within the `audio` tag element. Without the default control UI, you can build your own controls with images, HTML, and CSS and control them with JavaScript.

Video

As mentioned in *Chapter 1, Why HTML5?*, video integration into HTML5 documents is now easier than ever. As simple as integrating video into HTML5 documents is, it all begins with preparing the video for use on the Web. This process should not only minimize the size of the video file but also encode it with a specific codec and save it within a specific video container.

The HTML5 `video` tag supports the inclusion of multiple video container formats. While attempting to support the full range of HTML5 compliant browsers, developers must include references to the same video saved in multiple formats as not every browser supports all of the allowed video file types. Therefore, a solid understanding of video containers and codecs is necessary for web developers to properly integrate video into their documents.

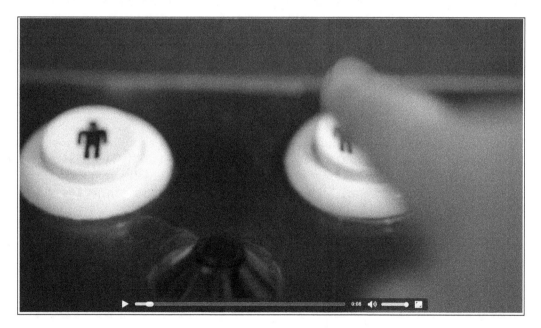

Video codecs

Codecs are used for compression and decompression of videos, to decrease file size and allow large video files to be shared using less bandwidth. Without the use of compression on video files, users would have to wait an inordinate amount of time to transfer a video over a typical Internet connection. To put this into perspective, a raw high-definition video, around 5 minutes in length, can be well over 25 GB of data. Video codecs are made up of advanced algorithms that remove similar data that blends from frame to frame. Rather than storing each individual frame as a separate image, an encoded video stores a specialized data set that is usually many times smaller than the raw source material. For viewing, the encoded data needs to be decoded from the streamlined data source back to viewable frame-based video. Codecs are the all-in-one piece of technology to get this task completed. Each of the supported video containers in HTML5 supports only one video codec, so choosing one is pretty straight forward. However, since video is usually accompanied by audio, the audio must also be run via a specific audio codec as well.

Video containers

One of the major issues while attempting to embed video into an HTML5 document is supporting all modern browsers with the same content. Unfortunately, not all the HTML5 compatible browsers available support the same video formats. Therefore, in order to support the widest range of browsers, developers must embed multiple versions of the same video file encoded in multiple formats. Since this issue is not likely to change anytime in the near future, understanding the available video containers and their corresponding codecs is an important step in preparing video for your HTML5 documents.

MP4

From the perspective of a Flash developer, the **MP4** container should be the most familiar as they are very similar to **FLV** or **F4V** files. **MPEG-4** or MP4 containers are currently supported for embedding within the video element by Internet Explorer 9+, Google Chrome, and Safari. MP4 videos must be encoded using the **H.264** codec, which was also used by FLV and F4V videos in Flash.

WebM

The WebM audio and video format is a project sponsored by Google to bring a completely open multimedia container and codec to the Web. WebM files are supported by Firefox, Google Chrome, and Opera. When encoding videos for use within a WebM container, the VP8 video codec, which is also owned by Google, is used.

GG

OGG containers are supported by Firefox, Google Chrome, and Opera. When encoding videos for use within a OGG container, the **Theora** codec is used. Since the full spectrum of browsers is covered by using just MP4 and WebM videos, encoding in OGG format is not entirely necessary. There is no harm in adding it as a failsafe anyways; only the first video file format the browser finds within the source list is utilized during display, all of the other files are ignored and not downloaded.

 Sample encoded video files as well as the high-quality master video file can be found within the `Chapter 02_examples` directory.

Video encoding software

There are many great applications available online that can encode your video content into formats compatible with HTML5. As long as the container and codec specification is met, any application or method can be used to get the job done. To aid in getting you up and running, for this chapter and the remainder of this book, here are some of the most popular encoding tools and applications web developers use to get videos on the Web in a snap.

Miro Video Converter

If you are looking for a simple way to get videos ready for the Web, look no further than Miro Video Converter, which can be found on Miro's website `http://www.mirovideoconverter.com`. This software is not only free and open source but also supports exporting videos and audios in all HTML5 compatible formats. Miro Video Converter is available for Windows and OS X and is probably the easiest way to prepare audios and videos for your HTML5 projects.

With the application installed and opened, the next step is to simply drag-and-drop your source video file into the application for queuing. If you have multiple videos, you can also add them to the queue and all of them will be encoded one after another.

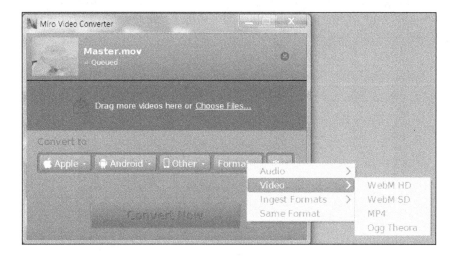

Once all the videos you require to be encoded have been added to the queue, select the **Format** option at the bottom of the window and select one of the three available formats within the convertor. Keep in mind that to enable video element playback support in every browser, you will need to encode your videos once in each format. If you require more in depth configuration in the encoding job, Miro Video Converter allows us to control basic parameters such as aspect ratio and video dimensions.

Adobe Media Encoder

Flash developers who have included videos within their projects have probably made use of the Adobe Media Encoder. This handy software comes bundled with Flash and can easily encode videos for use within Flash and HTML5 projects. Unfortunately, this application will only output videos natively in Flash video formats of HTML5-ready MP4.

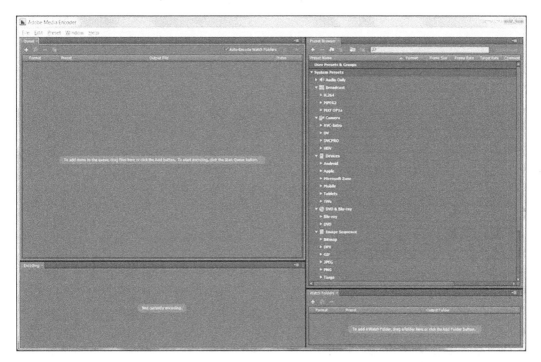

Handbrake

If you don't have access to Adobe Media Encoder, then the next easiest way to encode MP4 videos for free is by heading over to `http://handbrake.fr` and downloading Handbrake. Not only is Handbrake open source but also it is built for Windows, OS X, and Linux so it's hard to be left out in the cold.

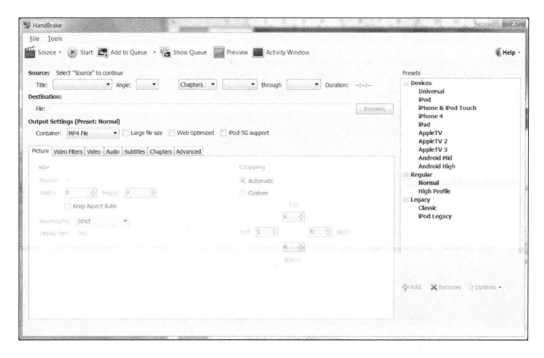

FFMPEG

Finally, my personal favorite, FFMPEG. If you are a lover of the command line as I am, this amazing piece of software is for you. When it comes to media, it's hard to say what FFMPEG can't be used to accomplish. If you're in need of high-level video transcoding, be sure to visit `http://ffmpeg.org` to learn more.

The video element

Once our video content has been encoded in the necessary formats, all that is left is to do is to reference the video from within the body of the HTML document. Just like the `audio` element, instead of the typical `src` parameter used within an tag to create a reference to the file, the `video` element supports the `source` tags within the `video` element to allow referencing multiple assets. It should be noted that if you are only embedding a single video reference, the `src` parameter within the `video` tag can be used rather than adding the `source` tags:

```
<video width="800" height="600" controls>
  <source src="my_video.mp4" type="video/mp4">
  <source src="my_video.webm" type="video/webm">
  <source src="my_video.ogg" type="video/ogg">
  Your browser does not support the video tag.
</video>
```

Again, just like the `audio` element, the `video` element allows for playback control integration by appending the `controls` parameter in the `video` tag. Videos can be played automatically on page load by appending `autoplay="true"` in the `video` tag.

Now that we have all of our assets prepped and ready for action, it's about time to start moving into the development environment. Since the web browser is our target platform, let's take some time to cover what the modern web browsers of today give us in terms of web developer tools to aid us in our development cycle.

Debugging and output methods

With the popularity of HTML5 and other heavily client-side driven web content, comes the need for a robust developer toolset to allow for easy debugging and testing of web pages. Fortunately, each of the modern browsers have adapted or integrated some very similar setups for doing just this. One of the most important features within this toolset is the JavaScript console. The JavaScript console is to web developers what the Flash Output window is to Flash developers. This is a critically important area to print data from initialized applications or websites and print statements or values specified within the code. In ActionScript, printing data to the output window is accomplished by using the `trace()` function. In JavaScript, we utilize the `console` object's built-in methods for doing the same. Consider the following example:

```
function calculateSum(a, b) {
  sum = a + b;
  console.log("The sum of " + a + " + " + b + " = " + sum);
}

calculateSum(2, 3);
```

 This example can be found within the `Console-Example` directory within the `Chapter 02_examples` directory.

This code example creates a function in JavaScript to calculate the sum of numbers and calls the method with example parameters to display the output in the browser console. Similar to traces in ActionScript, console integration in JavaScript works behind the scenes, segregated from the actual web page. The primary function of the console is to aid a developer with debugging JavaScript, CSS, or HTML properties during runtime. Not only can the developer console be used for printing data from the application but it can also be used to trigger specific functions in your code without the need for a specific event or interaction to take place.

As important as the console is, the entire user interface and interaction changes depending on what browser is being used to view the document. Therefore, understanding where to find and how to use the console in all popular browsers is an important step in helping you build robust code. Let's quickly run our simple calculate sum example in a couple of the common browsers to see how they handle the output.

Google Chrome

All versions of Google Chrome come packaged with a built-in developer toolset and it can be easily opened by right-clicking on a web page and selecting the **Inspect Element** option in the dialog box. This will reveal the developer tools window attached to the bottom of the browser window. Selecting the **Console** tab will display the JavaScript console to view the output from the web page. Opening our JavaScript `calculateSum` function example in Chrome with the console open should display something like the following image:

As you can see, the output from the `console.log()` call has been displayed along with what file and line number the call was dispatched from. Even from a simple perspective, I am sure you are starting to see how handy this tool could be if you have 100 or even 1000 lines of code in multiple files to deal with. As similar to the output window for traces in ActionScript this tool is, the cherry on top of the pie is its ability to invoke further JavaScript execution directly from the console window. Within the console, we can continue and find the sum of new numbers by calling the `calculateSum` function with the necessary values directly from the console.

Some browsers, such as Chrome, even have auto completion feature that expands the text as you type in method or property names, a feature I am sure most Flash developers wished they had within the Flash IDE.

Firebug for Firefox

Since Firefox does not come pre-packed with a robust developer toolset, a common option for web developers is to install the **Firebug** extension to enable this feature. The extension can easily be added to your Firefox installation in a couple of seconds by visiting `http://getfirebug.com`. Once installed and activated, right-click anywhere on a page and select **Inspect Element with Firebug**.

This should all feel pretty familiar to what we did within Chrome. Firebug is a great little project that almost all developers I know utilize. There are a ton of great features in all of these toolsets, many of which we will touch on in this book. Since we have a very simple HTML page open with barely anything in it, now might be a good time to see the UI and output from a more vanilla web page, so feel free to click around and check things out.

Safari

To enable the developer tools in Safari, open the **Preferences** window and select the **Advanced** tab. Select the check box at the bottom of the window labeled **Show Develop menu in menu bar** and then you can close the window.

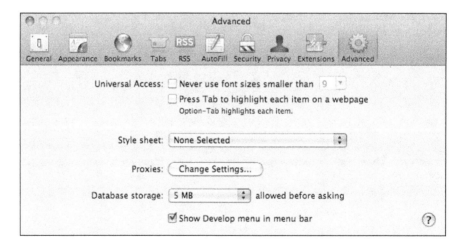

From this point on, you can right-click, as usual, on any web page and select **Inspect Element** to display the tools window.

If you were paying attention, you may notice that this console is almost identical to the console within Google Chrome. Of course, it has a command-line integration as we have seen in the other browsers.

Opera

Similar to Google Chrome, the developer tools in Opera can be easily accessed by right-clicking on a web page and selecting **Inspect Element**. Once the developer tools window opens at the bottom of the browser, select the **Console** tab to open the developer console. Initially, the console will be blank and clear of any interaction from the web page you are currently viewing.

Rather than having the console always active, Opera has decided to read console commands only when the console is actually open. Therefore, refreshing the page will reveal the console interaction:

Internet Explorer

As of Internet Explorer 9, Microsoft has begun including a developer's toolset directly within the browser. The **Developers Tools** window can be opened at anytime by pressing *F12* while viewing a page. Just like Opera, Internet Explorer requires a page to be refreshed to enable the usage of the console on the active page, as it stays inactive when it is closed.

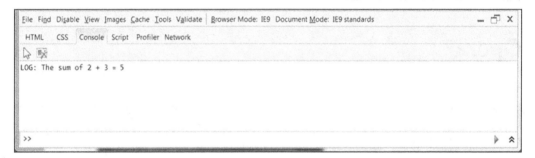

Of course, just like every other console, we can call our JavaScript methods and variables from the command line.

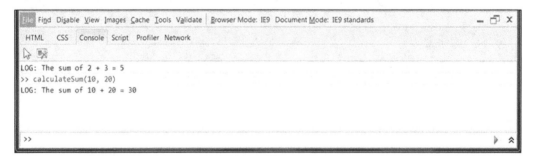

Syntax differences

Now that we have some media to work with and the browser tools at our disposal, let's start some more toying with JavaScript and compare its syntax to what you already know in ActionScript 3.

Variables

Unlike variables declared within ActionScript 3, JavaScript variables are not strictly typed. This takes the familiar ActionScript 3 variable declaration from:

```
var myVariable:String = 'abc123';
```

to a simpler syntax within JavaScript which looks as follows:

```
var myVariable = 'abc123';
```

This lack of strict typing is referred to as dynamic typing. Variables in JavaScript can be used as any type at any time. Consider this example:

```
var exampleVar;                    // A undefined variable
exampleVar = "Some example text";  // Variable is now a String
exampleVar = 12345;                // Variable is now a Number
```

Dynamic typing allows code to be writing faster by requiring less input from the developer, but this development ease comes at the cost of debugging large applications. ActionScript 3's strict typing allows the compiler to catch issues even before exporting a new version of your application. JavaScript will not do this natively, and it is probably one of the biggest complaints most developers with prior ActionScript 3 experience have when using the language.

Variable type conversion

Although variables in JavaScript are not strictly typed, there are methods to ensure that variable data is in correct form for the desired action. Type conversion can be used on variables to ensure they are formatted properly:

```
myString = String('12345');    // Convert to a String
myBoolean = Boolean('true');   // Convert to Boolean
myNumber = Number('12345');    // Convert to Number
```

Conditions and loops

We will cover these two aspects together as the syntax for conditions and loops in JavaScript are almost the same to what you are used to in ActionScript 3. If, `if...
else`, and `if... else if` conditions are no different than that in ActionScript:

```
if(cats > dogs) {
    // Code for cat people...
} else if (cats < dogs) {
    // Code for dog people...
} else {
    // Code for everyone else...
}
```

Also, the `switch` statements can be used and just like `if` statements; the syntax is exactly the same as that in ActionScript:

```
switch(animal) {
  case 'cat':
    // Code for cat people...
    break;
  case 'dog':
    // Code for dog people...
    break;
  default:
    // Code for everyone else...
}
```

Loops are no different to their counterparts in ActionScript. Consider these `for` and `while` loops:

```
for(var n = 0; n < myArray.length; n++) {
    // Code within loop...
}

while(n < 100) {
    // Code within loop...
}

do {
    // Code within loop...
} while(n < 100);
```

Functions

As in ActionScript 3, functions in JavaScript are blocks of code encased within curly braces ({ }). Every function is associated with a keyword that is used to call the function and run the encased code within it. As usual, functions may return values back to the point where the call was originally made. This is accomplished using the `return` statement.

The syntax of JavaScript function is very similar to ActionScript functions but is without the need for strict typing of expected parameters and the function return types. As a Flash developer, your ActionScript 3 functions probably looked something like the follows:

```
function getCoffee (owner:String, milks:int, sugars:int):void {
  // Code...
}
```

This syntax can be easily converted to JavaScript just by removing the variable and return type declarations so that the same function in JavaScript can be written as follows:

```
function getCoffee (owner, milks, sugars) {
  // Code...
}
```

Objects

Technically, everything declared in JavaScript is an object, however, time will come when you will need to create your own custom objects. This can be done in one of the following two manners. The first one, which should be very familiar to ActionScript developers is as follows:

```
player = new Object();
player.name = "John Smith";
player.lives = 5;
player.posX = 10;
player.posY = -30;
```

You can also create objects by defining them as a functions as follows:

```
function player(name, lives, posX, posY) {
  player.name = name;
  player.lives = lives;
  player.posX = posX;
  player.posY = posY;
```

```
  }

  var teddyBear = new player("Teddy", 5, 10, 10);
  console.log(teddyBear.name);
```

DOM events

Integrating DOM events allows you to use JavaScript to deal with events that occur within HTML documents.

Mouse events

The DOM exposes mouse events for basic user interactions with the mouse pointer. By using the onclick event parameter within an HTML tag, we can execute JavaScript when a user clicks on a specific element:

```
<img src="my-image.jpg" id="my-image"
  onclick="PLACE YOUR JAVASCRIPT HERE">
```

However, we can also target the element completely from JavaScript and deal with the event handler outside our HTML source code, to keep our project clean and easy to understand:

```
document.getElementById("my-image").onclick=function() {
  // Place your JavaScript here...
};
```

Of course, you are not limited to just clicks for mouse events. Events can also be handled for mouse over, mouse out, mouse down, and mouse up. In the examples within this book, we will utilize all of these events as well as methods to extend them even further.

Example JavaScript in action

With all of the JavaScript syntax specifications covered, let's use some of them into a working example and see what happens. Have a look at the following simple HTML document containing JavaScript to sort a randomized array of numbers:

```
<!DOCTYPE html>
<html lang="en">
  <head>
    <meta charset="utf-8" />
    <title>Insertion Sort - JavaScript Syntax Example</title>

    <script type="text/javascript">
```

```
// Number of elements to sort.
elementCount = 10000;
// The array which will be sorted.
sortlist = new Array();

/**
 * Called on button click.
 */
function init() {
  // Prepare random array for sorting.
  for(i = 0; i < elementCount; i++)
    sortlist.push(i);

  //shuffle(sortlist);
  sortlist.sort(function() {
    return 0.5 - Math.random();
  });

  // Display the random array prior to sorting.
  console.log(sortlist);

  // Start a timer.
  console.time('Iteration Sort Timer');

  // Sort the randomized array.
  insertionSort(sortlist);

  // Stop the timer.
  console.log('Sorted ' + elementCount + ' items.');
  console.timeEnd('Iteration Sort Timer');

  // Display the sorted array.
  console.log(sortlist);
}

/**
 * The popular Insertion Sort algorithm.
 */
function insertionSort(list) {
  // It's always smart to only lookup array size once.
  l = list.length;

  // Loop over supplied list and sort.
  for(i = 0; i < l; i++) {
```

```
        save = list[i];
        j = i;

        while(j > 0 && list[j - 1] > save) {
          list[j] = list[j - 1];
          j -= 1;
        }

        list[j] = save;
      }
    }
  </script>
</head>

<body>
  <p>
    Click the button below to begin.
    Be sure to open up your browsers developer console.
  </p>
    <button onclick="init()">Start Sorting</button>
</body>
</html>
```

This example covers many of the features and syntax specifications of JavaScript that we have just covered. Within our JavaScript block declared in the HTML document head tag, we have created two functions. The first function is our initiation method to prepare and run the application once it called. The second function contains the popular insertion sort algorithm, which will sort our randomized array of numbers. To enable both functions to use the same variable, we create elementCount and sortlist as global variables outside of each function's scope. Within the HTML body tag is a button element, which renders a typical form button element on the page and when a user clicks this button, the onclick handler calls the init function.

This example isn't flashy by any means but, as I mentioned above, it covers many of the different aspects of the JavaScript syntax specifications.

Timing JavaScript execution

One important point to note while dealing with JavaScript execution timing is to be sure that the entire page has finished loading prior to allowing the JavaScript to begin executing its code. The reason for waiting for page to load is to allow all of the assets and external references to load on the page before attempting to manipulate them. If your JavaScript attempts to perform an action on an element that doesn't exist, your application flow could fail. To avoid this issue, we can add an event listener to the DOM allowing it to run only once the page has been completely loaded and comes to display. Utilizing the DOM event for JavaScript offers an easy way to do just this as shown in the following code:

```
window.addEventListener("load", init, false);

var init = function() {
  // Start everything from in here.
}
```

Now, when the window has completed its load process the `init` function is called and the remainder of the application code can begin execution. JavaScript actually has a number of ways to accomplish execution of the code, specifically once the page has finished loading. The following chapters of this book will use and explain many of them using examples.

Summary

In this chapter, we spent some time to better familiarize ourselves with the process involved in preparing media assets for our HTML5 projects. Also, preparation and integration techniques for each of the typical multimedia formats as well as some popular pieces of software available to aid in getting this done were covered in this chapter. We took a quick jump right into ActionScript 3 versus JavaScript syntax in order to become more familiar with the small but important difference while writing JavaScript compared to ActionScript 3. This sets us up perfectly for *Chapter 3, Scalability, Limitations, and Effects*, where we will begin putting HTML5 to the limits in order to see what are its limitations and short comings as well as all of the surprising things it can do.

3
Scalability, Limitations, and Effects

With our media assets ready for HTML5 integration, let's continue this journey by looking over some of the new and exciting object manipulation features within CSS3 and JavaScript and how they relate to what you are familiar with as a Flash Developer. During the course of this chapter, we will review many of the specific features of HTML5 that have allowed it to gain extensive usage and popularity, becoming more like typical Flash development.

What we will cover in this chapter:

- Initial development limitations and ways to avoid them
- Some of the new and exciting CSS3 additions
- Developing responsive layouts for mobile and desktop
- Targeting CSS styles for specific displays with CSS Media Queries
- Controlling and streaming audio and video, and the limitations compared to Flash
- Client-side file integration and manipulation
- Sending heavy processes to the background with HTML5 Web Workers
- Introduction to server-side communication with WebSockets
- Understanding what the Canvas element is and why it's important
- Introduction to WebGL and its relation to Stage3D

HTML5 limitations

If you haven't noticed by now, many of the HTML5 features you will use either
have failsafes, multiple versions, or special syntax to enable your code to cover
the entire spectrum of browsers and supported HTML5 feature sets within them.
As time passes and standards become solidified, one can assume that many of these
failsafes and other content display measures will mature into a single standard
that all browsers will share. However, in reality this process may take a while and
even at its best, developers may still have to utilize many of these failsafe features
indefinitely. Therefore, a solid understanding of when, where, and why to use these
failsafe measures will enable you develop your HTML5 web pages in a way that
can be viewed as intended on all modern browsers.

To aid developers in overcoming these previously stated issues, many frameworks and
external scripts have been created and open sourced, allowing for a more universal
development environment saving developers countless hours when starting each
new project. Modernizr (`http://modernizr.com`) has quickly become a must-have
addition for many HTML5 developers as it contains many of the conditions and
verifications needed to allow developers to write less code and cover more browsers.
Modernizr does all this by checking for a large majority (more then 40) of the new
features available in HTML5 in the clients browser and reporting back if they are
available or not in a matter of milliseconds. This will allow you as the developer to
determine if you should display an alternate version of your content or a warning to
the user.

Getting your web content to display properly in all browsers is and always has been
the biggest challenge for any web developer and when it comes to creating cutting
edge interesting content, the challenge usually becomes harder. This chapter will not
only cover many of the new HTML5 content manipulation features, but demonstrate
them in code examples as well. To allow you to better understand how these features
look without the use of third-party integration, we will avoid using external libraries
for the time being. It is worth noting how each of these features and others look in all
browsers. Therefore make sure to test the examples as well as your own work in not
just your favorite browser, but many of the other popular choices as well.

Object manipulation with CSS3

Prior to the advent of CSS3, web developers used a laundry list of content
manipulation, asset preparation, and asset presentation techniques in order to
get their web page layout the way they wanted in every browser. Most of these
techniques would be considered "hacks" as they would pretty much be a work
around to enable the browser to do something it normally wouldn't. Features
such as rounded corners, drop shadows, and transforms were all absent from a

web developer's arsenal and the process of getting things the way you want could get mind numbing. Understandably, the excitement level surrounding CSS3 for all web developers is very high as it enables developers to perform more content manipulation techniques then ever before without the need for prior preparation or special browser hacks. Although the list of available properties in CSS3 is massive, let's cover some of the newest and most exciting of the lot.

box-shadow

It's true that some designers and developers say drop shadows are a part of the past, but the usage of shadowing HTML elements is still a popular design choice for many. In the past, web developers needed to perform tricks such as stretching small gradient images or creating the shadow directly into their background image to achieve this effect in their HTML documents. CSS3 has solved this issue by creating the box-shadow property to allow for drop shadow like effects on your HTML elements.

To remind us how this effect was accomplished in ActionScript 3, let's review this code snippet:

```
var dropShadow:DropShadowFilter = new DropShadowFilter();
dropShadow.distance = 0;
dropShadow.angle = 45;
dropShadow.color = 0x333333;
dropShadow.alpha = 1;
dropShadow.blurX = 10;
dropShadow.blurY = 10;
dropShadow.strength = 1;
dropShadow.quality = 15;
dropShadow.inner = false;
var mySprite:Sprite = new Sprite();
mySprite.filters = new Array(dropShadow);
```

As mentioned before, the new box-shadow property in CSS3 allows you to append these shadowing effects with relative ease and many of the same configuration properties:

```
.box-shadow-example {
   box-shadow: 3px 3px 5px 6px #000000;
}
```

Despite the lack of property names on each of the values applied to this style, you can see that many of the value types coincide with what was appended to the drop shadow we created in ActionScript 3.

This `box-shadow` property is assigned to the `.box-shadow-example` class and therefore will be applied to any element that has that classname appended to it. By creating a `div` element with the `box-shadow-example` class, we can alter our content to look something like the following:

```
<div class="box-shadow-example">CSS3 box-shadow Property</div>
```

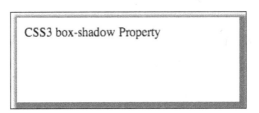

As straightforward as this CSS property is to add to your project, it declares a lot of values all in a single line. Let's review each of these values in order that we can understand them better for future usage. To simplify the identification of each of the variables in the property, each of these have been updated to be different:

```
box-shadow: 1px 2px 3px 4px #000000;
```

These variables are explained as follows:

- The initial value (`1px`) is the shadow's **horizontal offset** or if the shadow is going to the left or to the right. A positive value would place the shadow on the right of the element, a negative offset will put the shadow on the left.

- The second value (`2px`) is the **vertical offset**, and just like the horizontal offset value, a negative number would generate a shadow going up and a positive value would generate the shadow going down.

- The third value (`3px`) is the **blur radius** that controls how much blur effect will be added to the shadow. Declaring a value, for example, `0` would create no blur and display a very sharp looking shadow. Negative values placed into the blur radius will be ignored and render no different then using 0.

- The fourth value (`4px`) and last of the numerical properties is the **spread radius**. The spread radius controls how far the drop shadow blur will spread past the initial shadow size declaration. If a value `0` is used, the shadow will display with the default blur radius set and apply no changes. Positive numerical values will yield a shadow that blurs further and negative value will make the shadow blur smaller.

- The final value is the hexadecimal color value, which states the color that the shadow will be in.

Alternatively, you could use `box-shadow` to apply the shadow effect to the interior of your element rather then the exterior. With ActionScript 3, this was accomplished by appending `dropShadow.inner = true;` to the list of parameters in your `DropShadowFiler` object. The CSS3 syntax to apply `box-shadow` properties in this manner is very similar as all that is required is the addition of the `inset` keyword. Consider the following code snippet, for example:

```
.box-shadow-example {
  box-shadow: 3px 3px 5px 6px #666666 inset;
}
```

This would produce a shadow that would look like the following screenshot:

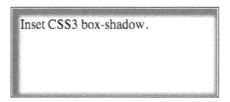

Inset CSS3 box-shadow.

 Included in the code examples for this chapter is a box-shadow tool that will allow you to better understand the affect each of the properties will have.

text-shadow

Just like the `box-shadow` property, `text-shadow` lives up to its name by creating the same drop-shadowing effect, specifically for text:

```
text-shadow: 2px 2px 6px #ff0000;
```

Like `box-shadow`, the initial two values for `text-shadow` are the horizontal and vertical offsets for the shadow placement. The third value, which is optional is the blur size and the fourth value is the hexadecimal color:

> Lorem ipsum dolor sit amet, consectetur adipiscing elit. Donec tristique malesuada nulla, at gravida lacus ele
>
> Lorem ipsum dolor sit amet, consectetur adipiscing elit. Donec tristi
>
> Lorem ipsum dolor sit amet, con gravida lacus eleifend eget.

border-radius

Just like element or text shadowing, adding rounded corners to your elements prior to CSS3 was a chore. Developers would usually append separate images or use other object manipulation techniques to achieve this effect on the typically square or rectangle shaped elements. With the addition of the `border-radius` setting in CSS3, developers can easily and dynamically set element corner roundness with only a couple of line of CSS all without the usage of vector 9 slicing like in Flash.

Since HTML elements have four corners, when appending the `border-radius` styling, we can either target each corner individually, or all the corners at once. In order to easily append a border radius setting to all the corners at once, we would create our CSS properties as follows:

```
#example {
  background-color:#ff0000; // Red background
  width: 200px;
  height: 200px;
border-radius: 10px;
}
```

The preceding CSS not only appends a 10px border radius to all of the corners of the `#example` element, by using all the properties, which the modern browsers use, we can be assured that the effect will be visible to all users attempting to view this content:

Lorem ipsum dolor sit amet, consectetu
malesuada nulla, at gravida lacus eleifei
amet mi semper dignissim. Nulla posue
condimentum quam in massa eleifend ii
tortor urna, mollis at ornare id, volutpat
enim nec consequat rhoncus, dolor lorei
tellus augue vitae nulla. Etiam luctus ul

As mentioned above, each of the individual corners of the element can be targeted
to only append the radius to a specific part of the element:

```
#example {
  border-top-left-radius: 0px; // This is doing nothing
  border-top-right-radius: 5px;
  border-bottom-right-radius: 20px;
  border-bottom-left-radius: 100px;
}
```

The preceding CSS now removes our #example element's left border radius by
setting it to 0px and sets a specific radius to each of the other corners. It's worth
noting here that setting a border radius equal to 0 is no different than leaving that
property completely out of the CSS styles:

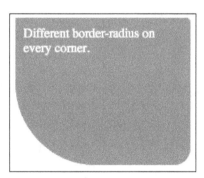

Fonts

Dealing with customized fonts in Flash has had its ups and downs over the years.
Any Flash developer who has needed to incorporate and use customized fonts in
their Flash applications probably knows the pain that comes with choosing a font
embedding method as well as making sure it works properly for users who don't
have the font installed on their computer viewing the Flash application.

CSS3 font embedding has implemented a "no fuss" way to include custom fonts into your HTML5 documents with the addition of the @font-face declaration:

```
@font-face {
  font-family: ClickerScript;
  src: url('ClickerScript-Regular.ttf'),
    url('ClickerScript-Regular .otf'),
    url('ClickerScript-Regular .eot');
}
```

CSS can now directly reference your TTF, OTF, or EOT font which can be placed on your web server for accessibility. With the font source declared in our CSS document and a unique font-family identification applied to it, we can start using it on specific elements by using the font-family property:

```
#example {
  font-family: ClickerScript;
}
```

Since we declared a specific font family name in the @font-face property, we can use that custom name on pretty much any element henceforth. Custom fonts can be applied to almost anything that contains text in your HTML document. Form elements such as button labels and text inputs also can be styled to used your custom fonts. You can even remake assets such as website logos in pure HTML and CSS with the same custom fonts used in the original asset creation.

Acceptable font formats

Like many of the other embedding methods for assets online, fonts needs to be converted into multiple formats to enable all common modern browsers to display them properly. Almost all of the available browsers will be able to handle the common True Type Fonts (.ttf file types) or Open Type Fonts (.otf file types), so embedding one of those two formats will be all that is needed. Unfortunately Internet Explorer 9 does not have support built in for either of those two popular formats and requires fonts to be saved in the EOT file format.

External font libraries

Many great services have appeared online in the last couple of years allowing web developers to painlessly prepare and embed fonts into their websites. Google's Web Fonts archive available at http://www.google.com/webfonts hosts a large set of open source fonts which can be added to your project without the need to worry about licensing or payment issues. Simply add a couple of extras lines of code into your HTML document and you are ready to go.

Another great site that is worth checking out is Font Squirrel, which can be found at `http://www.fontsquirrel.com`. Like Google Web Fonts, Font Squirrel hosts a large archive of web-ready fonts with the copy-and-paste-ready code snippets to add them to your document. Another great feature on this site is the `@font-face` generator which give you the ability to convert your preexisting fonts into all the web compatible formats.

Before getting carried away and converting all your favorite fonts into web ready formats and integrating them into your work, it is worth noting the End User License Agreement or EULA that came with the font to begin with. Converting many available fonts for use on the web will break license agreements and could cause legal issues for you down the road.

Opacity

More commonly known as "alpha" to the Flash developer, setting the opacity of an element not only allows you to change the look and feel of your designs, but allows you to add features like content that fades in and out. As simple as this concept seems, it is relatively new to the available list of CSS properties available to web developers. Setting the opacity of an element is extremely easy and looks something like the following:

```
#example {
    opacity: 0.5;
}
```

As you can see from the preceding example, like ActionScript 3, the opacity value is a numerical value between 0 and 1. The preceding example would display a element at 50 percent transparency. The opacity property in CSS3 is now supported in all the major browsers, so there is no need to worry about using alternative property syntax when declaring it.

RGB and RGBA coloring

When dealing with color values in CSS, many developers would typically use hexadecimal values, which would resemble something like `#000000` to declare the usage of the color black. Colors can also be implemented in their RGB representation in CSS by utilizing the `rgb()` or `rgba()` calls in place of the hexadecimal value. As you can see by the method name, the `rgba` color lookup in CSS also requires a forth parameter which declares the colors alpha transparency or opacity amount. Using RGBA in CSS3 rather than hexadecimal colors can be beneficial for a couple of reasons. Consider you have just created a `div` element which will be displayed on top of existing content within your web page layout.

If you ever wanted to set a background color to the div as a specific color but wish for only that background to be semi transparent and not the interior content, the RGBA color declaration now allows you to do this easily as you can set the colors transparency:

```
#example {
  // Background opacity
  background: rgba(0, 0, 0, 0.5); // Black 50% opacity

  // Box-shadow
  box-shadow: 1px 2px 3px 4px rgba(255, 255, 255, 0.8); // White 80%
  opacity

  // Text opacity
  color: rgba(255, 255, 255, 1);     // White no transparency
  color: rgb(255, 255, 255);   // This would accomplish the same
  styling

  // Text Drop Shadows (with opacity)
  text-shadow: 5px 5px 3px rgba(135, 100, 240, 0.5);
}
```

As you can see in the preceding example, you can freely use RGB and RGBA values rather than hexadecimal anywhere color values are required in CSS syntax.

Element transforms

Personally, I find CSS3 transforms to be one of the most exciting and fun new features in CSS. Transforming assets in the Flash IDE as well as with ActionScript has always been easily accessible and easy to implement. Transforming HTML elements is a relatively new feature to CSS and is still gaining full support by all the modern browsers.

Transforming an element allows you to manipulate its shape and size by opening up a ton of possibilities for animations and visual effects to assets without the need to prepare the source before hand. When we refer to "transforming an element", we are actually describing a number of properties that can be applied to the transformation to give it different characteristics. If you have transformed objects in Flash or possibly in Photoshop before, these properties may be familiar to you.

Translate

As a Flash developer used to primarily dealing with X and Y coordinates when positioning elements, the CSS3 Translate Transform property is a very handy way of placing elements and it works on the same principal. The `translate` property takes two parameters which are the X and the Y values to translate, or effectively move the element:

```
transform:translate(-25px, -25px);
```

Unfortunately, to get your transforms to work in all browsers, you will need to target each of them when you append transform styles. Therefore, the standard transform style and property would now look something like this:

```
transform:translate(-25px, -25px);
-ms-transform:translate(-25px, -25px);      /* IE 9 */
-moz-transform:translate(-25px, -25px);     /* Firefox */
-webkit-transform:translate(-25px, -25px);  /* Safari and Chrome */
-o-transform:translate(-25px, -25px);       /* Opera */
```

Rotate

Rotation is pretty self-explanatory and extremely easy to implement. The `rotate` properties take a single parameter to specify the amount of rotation, in degrees, to apply to the specific element:

```
transform:rotate(45deg);
-ms-transform:rotate(45deg);      /* IE 9 */
-moz-transform:rotate(45deg);     /* Firefox */
-webkit-transform:rotate(45deg);  /* Safari and Chrome */
-o-transform:rotate(45deg);       /* Opera */
```

It is worth noting that regardless of the fact that the supplied value is always intended to be a value in degrees, the value must always have **deg** appended for the value to be properly recognized.

Scale

Just like `rotate` transforms, scaling is pretty straightforward. The `scale` property requires two parameters, which declare the scale amount for both X and Y:

```
transform:scale(0.5, 2);
-ms-transform:scale(0.5, 2);      /* IE 9 */
-moz-transform:scale(0.5, 2);     /* Firefox */
-webkit-transform:scale(0.5, 2);  /* Safari and Chrome */
-o-transform:scale(0.5, 2);       /* Opera */
```

Skew

Skewing a element will result in the angling of the X and Y axes:

```
transform:skew(10deg, 20deg);
-ms-transform:skew(10deg, 20deg);        /* IE 9 */
-moz-transform:skew(10deg, 20deg);       /* Firefox */
-webkit-transform:skew(10deg, 20deg);    /* Safari and Chrome */
-o-transform:skew(10deg, 20deg);         /* Opera */
```

The following illustration is a representation of skewing an image with the preceding properties:

Matrix

The `matrix` properties combine all of the preceding transforms into a single property and can easily eliminate many extra lines of CSS in your source:

```
transform:matrix(0.586, 0.8, -0.8, 0.586, 40, 20);
/* IE 9 */
-ms-transform:matrix(0.586, 0.8, -0.8, 0.586, 40, 20);
/* Firefox */
-moz-transform:matrix(0.586, 0.8, -0.8, 0.586, 40, 20);
```

```
/* Safari and Chrome */
-webkit-transform:matrix(0.586, 0.8, -0.8, 0.586, 40, 20);
/* Opera */
-o-transform:matrix(0.586, 0.8, -0.8, 0.586, 40, 20);
```

The preceding example utilizes the CSS transform matrix property to apply multiple transform styles in a single call. The `matrix` property requires six parameters to rotate, scale, move, and skew the element. Using the matrix property is only really useful when you actually need to implement all of the transform properties at once. If you only need to utilize one aspect of element transforms, you will be better off using just that CSS style property.

3D transforms

Up until now, all of the transform properties we have reviewed have been two dimensional transformations. CSS3 now also supports 3D as well as 2D transforms. One of the best parts of CSS3 3D transforms is the fact that many devices and browsers support hardware acceleration allowing this complex graphical processing to be done on your video cards GPU. At the time of writing this book, only Chrome, Safari, and Firefox have support for CSS 3D transforms.

 Interested in what browsers will support all these great HTML5 features before you start developing? Check out http:// caniuse.com to see what popular browsers support in a simple, easy-to-use website.

When dealing with elements in a 3D world, we make use of the Z coordinate, which allows the use of some new transform properties.

```
transform:rotateX(angle)
transform:rotateY(angle)
transform:rotateZ(angle)
transform:translateZ(px)
transform:scaleZ(px)
```

Let's create a 3D cube from HTML elements to put all of these properties into a working example. To start creating our 3D cube, we will begin by writing the HTML elements which will contain the cube as well as the elements which will be making up the cube itself:

```
<body>
  <div class="container">
    <div id="cube">
      <div class="front"></div>
```

```
            <div class="back"></div>
            <div class="right"></div>
            <div class="left"></div>
            <div class="top"></div>
            <div class="bottom"></div>
        </div>
    </div>
</body>
```

This HTML creates a simple layout for our cube by not only creating each of the six sides, which makes up a cube with specific class names, but the container for the entire cube as well as the main container to display all of our page content. Of course, since there is no internal content in these containers and no styling yet, opening this HTML file in your browser would yield an empty page. So let's start writing our CSS to make all of these elements visible and position each to form our three dimensional cube. We will start by setting up our main containers which will position our content and contain our cubes sides:

```css
.container {
  width: 640px;
  height: 360px;
  position: relative;
  margin: 200px auto;

  /* Currently only supported by Webkit browsers. */
  -webkit-perspective: 1000px;
  perspective: 1000px;
}
#cube {
    width: 640px;
    height: 320px;
    position: absolute;

/*
Let the transformed child elements preserve
the 3D transformations:
*/
  transform-style: preserve-3d;
    -webkit-transform-style: preserve-3d;
    -moz-transform-style: preserve-3d;
}
```

The `container` class is our main element, which contains all of the other elements within this example. After appending a width and height, we set the top margin to `200px` to push the display down the page a bit for better viewing and the left and right margins to auto which will align this element in the center of the page:

```
#cube div {
   display: block;
   position: absolute;
      border: 1px solid #000000;
      width: 640px;
      height: 320px;
      opacity:0.8;
}
```

By defining properties to the `#cube div`, we set the styles to every `div` element within the `#cube` element. We are also kind of cheating the system of cube by setting the width and height to rectangular proportions as the intention is to add videos to each of the cube sides once we structure and position it.

With the basic cube-side styles appended, its time to start transforming each of the sides to form the three-dimensional cube. We will start with the front of the cube by translating it on the Z axis, bringing it closer to the perspective:

```
#cube .front  {
-webkit-transform: translateZ(320px);
   -moz-transform: translateZ(320px);
   transform: translateZ(320px);
}
```

In order to append this style to our element in all modern browsers, we will need to specify the property in multiple syntaxes for each browser that doesn't support the default `transform` property:

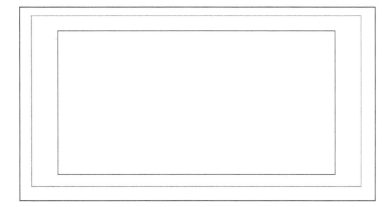

The preceding screenshot shows what has happened to the `.front` div after appending a Z translation of 320px. The larger rectangle is the `.front` div, which is now 320px closer to our perspective. For simplicity's sake, let's do the same to the `.back` div and push it 320px away from the perspective:

```
#cube .back   {
  -webkit-transform:
       rotateX(-180deg)
       rotate(-180deg)
       translateZ(320px);
  -moz-transform:
       rotateX(-180deg)
       rotate(-180deg)
       translateZ(320px);
  transform:
       rotateX(-180deg)
       rotate(-180deg)
       translateZ(320px);
}
```

As you can see from the preceding code, to properly move the `.back` element into place without placing it upside down, we flip the element by 180 degrees on the X axis and then translate Z by 320px just like we did for `.front`. Note that we didn't set a negative value on the translate Z because the element was flipped. With the `.back` CSS styles in place, our cube should look like the following:

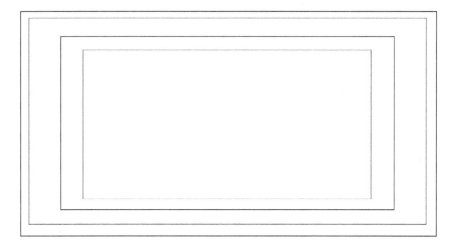

Now the smallest rectangle visible is the element with the classname `.back`, the largest is our `.front` element, and the middle rectangle is the remaining elements to be transformed.

To position the sides of our cubes we will need to rotate the side elements on the Y axis to get them to face the proper direction. Once they are rotated into place, we can translate the position on the Z axis to push it out from the center as we did with the front and back faces:

```
#cube .right {
    -webkit-transform: rotateY(90deg) translateZ( 320px );
    -moz-transform: rotateY(90deg) translateZ( 320px );
    transform: rotateY(90deg) translateZ( 320px );
}
```

With the right side in place, we can do the same to the left side but rotate it in the opposite direction to get it facing the other way:

```
#cube .left {
-webkit-transform: rotateY(-90deg) translateZ( 320px );
    -moz-transform: rotateY(-90deg) translateZ( 320px );
    transform: rotateY(-90deg) translateZ( 320px );
}
```

Now that we have all four sides of our cube aligned properly, we can finalize the cube positioning by aligning the top and bottom sides. To properly size the top and bottom we will set their own width and height to override the initial values set in the #cube div styles:

```
#cube .top {
    width: 640px;
    height: 640px;

    -webkit-transform: rotateX(90deg) translateZ( 320px );
    -moz-transform: rotateX(90deg) translateZ( 320px );
    transform: rotateX(90deg) translateZ( 320px );
}
#cube .bottom {
    width: 640px;
    height: 640px;

    -webkit-transform: rotateX(-90deg) translateZ( 0px );
    -moz-transform: rotateX(-90deg) translateZ( 0px );
    transform: rotateX(-90deg) translateZ( 0px );
}
```

To properly position the top and bottom sides, we rotate the .top and .bottom elements +-90 degrees on the X axis to get them to face up and down, and only need to translate the top on the Z axis to raise it to the proper height to connect with all of the other sides.

With all of those transforms appended to our layout, the resulting cube should look like the following:

Although it looks 3D, since there is nothing in the containers, the perspective isn't really showing off our cube very well. So let's add some content such as a video in each of the sides of the cube to get a better visualization of our work. Within each of the sides, let's add the same HTML5 video element code:

```html
<video width="640" height="320" autoplay="true" loop="true">
  <source src="cube-video.mp4" type="video/mp4">
  <source src="cube-video.webm" type="video/webm">
  Your browser does not support the video tag.
</video>
```

Since we have not added the element playback controls in order to display more visible area of the cube, our video element is set to *autoplay* the video as well as *loop* the playback on completion. Now we get a result that properly demonstrates what 3D transforms can do and is a little more visually appealing:

Since we set the opacity of each of the cube sides, we can now see all four videos playing on each side, pretty cool! Since we are already here, why not kick it up one more notch and add user interaction to this cube so we can spin it around and see the video on each side.

To perform this user interaction, we need to use JavaScript to translate the mouse coordinates on the page document to the X and Y 3D rotation of our cube. So let's start by creating the JavaScript to listen for mouse events:

```javascript
window.addEventListener("load", init, false);

function init() {
  // Listen for mouse movement
  window.addEventListener('mousemove', onMouseMove, false);
}

function onMouseMove(e) {
```

```
var mouseX = 0;
var mouseY = 0;

// Get the mouse position
if (e.pageX || e.pageY) {
  mouseX = e.pageX;
  mouseY = e.pageY;
} else if (e.clientX || e.clientY) {
  mouseX = e.clientX + document.body.scrollLeft +
    document.documentElement.scrollLeft;
  mouseY = e.clientY + document.body.scrollTop +
    document.documentElement.scrollTop;
}

console.log("Mouse Position: x:" + mouseX + " y:" + mouseY);
}
```

As you can see from the preceding code example, when the `mousemove` event fires and calls the `onMouseMove` function, we need to run some conditionals to properly parse the proper mouse position. Since, like so many other parts of web development, retrieving the mouse coordinates differs from browser to browser, we have added a simple condition to attempt to gather the mouse X and Y in a couple of different ways.

With the mouse position ready to be translated into the transform rotation of our cube, there is one final bit of preparation we need to complete prior to setting the CSS style updates. Since different browsers support the application of CSS transforms in different syntaxes, we need to figure out, in JavaScript, which syntax to use during runtime to allow our script to run on all browsers. The following code example does just that. By setting a predefined array of the possible property values and attempting to check the type of each as an element style property, we can find which element is not undefined and know it can be used for CSS transform styles:

```
// Get the support transform property
var availableProperties = [
    'transform',
    'MozTransform',
    'WebkitTransform',
    'msTransform',
    'OTransform'
    ];
// Loop over each of the properties
for (var i = 0; i < availableProperties.length; i++) {
  // Check if the type of the property style is a string (ie. valid)
  if (typeof document.documentElement.style[availableProperties[i]] ==
```

```
'string'){
    // If we found the supported property, assign it to a variable
    // for later use.
      var supportedTranformProperty = availableProperties[i];
    }
}
```

Now that we have the user's mouse position and the proper syntax for CSS transform updates for our cube, we can put it all together and finally have 3D rotational control of our video cube:

```
<script>
  var supportedTranformProperty;

  window.addEventListener("load", init, false);

  function init() {
    // Get the support transform property
    var availableProperties = ['transform', 'MozTransform',
      'WebkitTransform', 'msTransform', 'OTransform'];
    for (var i = 0; i < availableProperties.length; i++) {
      if (typeof document.documentElement.
        style[availableProperties[i]] == 'string'){
            supportedTranformProperty = availableProperties[i];
        }
  }

    // Listen for mouse movement
    window.addEventListener('mousemove', onMouseMove, false);
  }

  function onMouseMove(e) {
    // Get the mouse position
    if (e.pageX || e.pageY) {
      mouseX = e.pageX;
      mouseY = e.pageY;
    } else if (e.clientX || e.clientY) {
      mouseX = e.clientX + document.body.scrollLeft +
        document.documentElement.scrollLeft;
      mouseY = e.clientY + document.body.scrollTop +
        document.documentElement.scrollTop;
    }

    // Update the cube rotation
    rotateCube(mouseX, mouseY);
```

```
}

function rotateCube(posX, posY) {
  // Update the CSS transform styles
document.getElementById("cube").style[supportedTranformProperty] =
  'rotateY(' + posX + 'deg) rotateX(' + posY * -1 + 'deg)';
}

</script>
```

Regardless of the fact we have attempted to allow for multi browser use of this example, it is worth opening it up in each to see how something like 3D transforms with heavy internal content run. During the time of writing this book, all WebKit browsers were the easy choice when viewing content like this, as browsers such as Firefox and Internet Explorer render this example at a much slower and lower quality output:

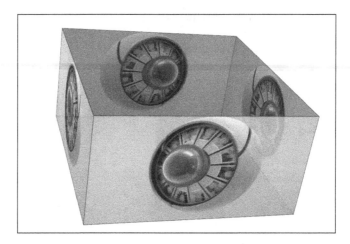

Transitions

With CSS3, we can add an effect when changing from one style to another, without using Flash animations or JavaScripts:

```
div {
  transition: width 2s;
  -moz-transition: width 2s;      /* Firefox 4 */
  -webkit-transition: width 2s; /* Safari and Chrome */
  -o-transition: width 2s;        /* Opera */
}
```

If the duration is not specified, the transition will have no effect, because the default value is 0:

```
div {
    transition: width 2s, height 2s, transform 2s;
    -moz-transition: width 2s, height 2s, -moz-transform 2s;
    -webkit-transition: width 2s, height 2s, -webkit-transform 2s;
    -o-transition: width 2s, height 2s,-o-transform 2s;
}
```

 It should be worth noting that Internet Explorer currently does not have support for CSS3 transitions.

Browser compatibility

If you haven't noticed yet, the battle of browser compatibility is one of the biggest aspects of a web developer's job. Over time, many great services and applications have been created to help developers overcome these hurdles in a much simpler manner than trial-and-error techniques. Websites such as http://css3test.com, http://caniuse.com, and http://html5readiness.com are all great resources to keep on top of HTML5 specification developer and browser support for all the features within.

Frame rate

One would assume since you, the reader, are coming from a Flash development background, a moment should be taken to talk about frame rates or frames per second when developing HTML5 applications. Since every asset in Flash applications is based on the timeline model, calculating how many frames of that timeline are displayed every second is a pretty simple calculation. However, all the technologies that make up HTML5 development do not rely on the use of a timeline during runtime. Therefore calculating the frames per second or FPS value of a webpage is not always an accurate measure of performance of your HTML5 projects.

 Our CSS 3D Transform example found in the chapter code examples includes the use of a great piece of JavaScript called **Stats.js** to monitor the frames per second as well as the ms. Stats.js is a open source project that can be found at https://github.com/mrdoob/stats.js.

Developing for mobile

Another one of the driving forces behind the popularity of HTML5 is the overwhelming support for it on most of the modern mobile browsers (`http://mobilehtml5.org`). With the loss of Flash Player on all mobile platforms now, the use of HTML5 to deliver content is at an all time high and the usage is growing daily. Applications, frameworks, and templates such as jQuery Mobile (`http://jquerymobile.com`), Phone Gap (`http://phonegap.com`), Appcelerator (`http://www.appcelerator.com`) and the Mobile Boilerplate (`http://html5boilerplate.com/html5boilerplate.com/dist/mobile`) all of which will be covered in detail in *Chapter 5, Code Once, Release Everywhere*, are all specifically built to aid web developers for building web content that is specifically targeted for mobile viewing. CSS can be set up in a responsive manner to allow the same page content to be displayed in an optimized format depending on the device and viewport configuration a user is viewing your content with.

Responsive layouts

The term "responsive layout" seems to get used on a more frequent basis as HTML5 development has grown in popularity. It has, to some, become a keyword to define one of the key features of good HTML5 development. Regardless of how the term is used, at the end of the day when we refer to "responsive layouts" in web development, we are referring to the usage of modern web development techniques to enable the same page content to transition its layout and content within it to adjust for the users device and viewing resolution. In other words, making sure your page content is set up in an optimized manner for all viewing resolutions and is able to transition between any one of the layouts without the need for content of page refreshing.

CSS Media Queries

One of the most important assets when creating responsive layouts is the use of CSS Media Queries. Media Queries allow you to target specific CSS styles depending on your user's device, resolution, rotation, and more. Knowing as much as possible about the device and software loading your HTML documents will allow you to not only specify how specific devices and browsers are to display your content, but it can also allow your code to monitor real-time changes to the viewing methods as well. For instance, the following Media Query example changes the background color depending on device rotation:

```
@media screen and (orientation:portrait) {
   background-color: #FF0000;
}
```

```
@media screen and (orientation:landscape) {
    background-color: #0000FF;
}
```

The list of CSS Media Queries properties is short but it is important to understand what is available to you when creating your conditions. Therefore, let's quickly review what properties you have at your disposal when writing your Media Queries:

- `width`: Describes the width of the targeted display area.
- `height`: Describes the height of the targeted display area.
- `device-width`: Describes the width of the rendering display of the output device.
- `device-height`: Describes the height of the rendering display of the output device.
- `orientation`: Is `portrait` when the value of the height media feature is greater than or equal to the value of the width media feature. Otherwise the orientation is `landscape`.
- `aspect-ratio`: Defined as the ratio of the value of the `width` media feature to the value of the `height` media feature.
- `device-aspect-ratio`: Defined as the ratio of the value of the `device-width` media feature to the value of the `device-height` media feature.
- `color`: Describes the number of bits per color component of the output device. If the device is not a color device, the value is zero.
- `color-index`: Describes the number of entries in the color look up table of the output device. If the device does not use a color look up table, the value is zero.
- `monochrome`: Describes the number of bits per pixel in a monochrome frame buffer. If the device is not a monochrome device, the output device value will be 0.
- `resolution`: Describes the resolution of the output device, that is, the density of the pixels. When querying devices with non-square pixels, in `min-resolution` queries the least-dense dimension must be compared to the specified value and in `max-resolution` queries the most-dense dimensions must be compared instead. A `resolution` (without a "min-" or "max-" prefix) query never matches a device with non-square pixels.
- **scan**: Describes the scanning process of "tv" output devices.
- **grid**: Used to query whether the output device is grid or bitmap. If the output device is grid-based (for example, a "tty" terminal, or a phone display with only one fixed font), the value will be 1. Otherwise, the value will be 0.

Audio and video playback control

As we saw in the last chapter, integrating audio and video assets with basic controls into and HTML5 document is extremely easy. But if you intend to use your multimedia in other forms than just a straightforward video playback element, you will need to understand the properties available for custom playback code integration.

Preloading

By default, when an audio or video element is displayed in a HTML5 document, the source asset declared within it will be preloaded to allow for instantaneous playback when the user initiates the player. Assets will be preloaded only as far as the browsers deems necessary to enable fluid uninterrupted playback. To override this setting, we can use the `preload` parameter within the audio element to declare what we would like to be preloaded when a user views our page.

Setting the preload parameter to `auto` will preload the entire audio upon page load and could be a useful addition to any audio you are almost certain a user will watch at some point after the page loads. With the `preload` parameter set, our audio element would look something like the following:

```
<audio controls preload="all">
  <source src="my-audio .mp3" type="audio/mpeg">
  <source src="my-audio.ogg" type="audio/ogg">
  Your browser does not support the audio element.
</audio>
```

Aside from preloading everything, we can also preload absolutely nothing by setting `preload="none"` rather than `auto`. Removing preloading from audio will allow users to surf your pages without the need for unnecessary audio downloads but will result in longer loading times for audio to player once the user initiates the audio playback. Finally we can also just load audio metadata when preloading by setting `preload="metatdata"`. This will allow the audio element to view what data it is about to load, which can be very useful when dynamically adding audio into an audio element and requiring the need to verify if it is fit for playback before attempting to do so.

Autoplay

As described in *Chapter 2, Preparing for the Battle*, with the `autoplay` setting appended to a video element, the video will begin to play the moment it is able to do so without the need to stop the video for further buffering. Unlike many of the other element parameters in HTML, the `autoplay` parameter does not require a value. So just appending `autoplay` to the element will be enough to do the job. It is worth keeping in mind that the `autoplay` setting will be ignored when loaded on almost all mobile browsers. Mobile browsers tend to ignore this setting in an attempt to conserve bandwidth on a wireless connection.

Looping

With the loop setting appended to the audio element, the video will restart every time is finishes. Like the `autoplay` parameter, the `loop` parameter does not require a value. If you only wanted a video to loop a specific number of times, you can either watch how many times its loops with the `loop` parameter set and then remove it when necessary, or control the entire playback from JavaScript to control the loop count without the loop parameter in the video element.

Sound effects

Playing a sound effect at a specific moment can be accomplished in a number of ways with the use of the HTML5 audio element and JavaScript. In its simplest form, playing sound effects can be implemented as done the following code example:

```html
<body>
  <audio src="audio/ping.mp3" preload="auto" id="audio-ping">
  </audio>

  <script>
    window.addEventListener("load", init, false);

    function init() {
      window.addEventListener(
          'mousedown',
          onMouseDown,
          false
      );
    }

    function onMouseDown(e) {
      document.getElementById('audio-ping').play();
    }
  </script>
</body>
```

When the audio element is created inside the HTML document body, we set the `preload="auto"` which will make sure the audio is preloaded completely as soon as possible. We do this so there is no latency when the sound is needed during the effect event. The audio element is also given an ID to enable referencing in JavaScript a couple line down. With the window load event listener, we wait for page load then apply an event listener to any `mousedown` event anywhere in the browser window. When this fires, we select our audio element by ID and call the built in `play()` method resulting in the audio playback on every click of the browser window.

Media playback manipulation

Aside from the `play()` method in the preceding example, JavaScript has the accessibility to control much more of the audio and video element directly. Audio volume can be set as a value between `0` and `1` as shown in the following example:

```
document.getElementById('audio-ping').volume = 0.5; // Set the volume
to 50%
```

We can also gather all the stats on the element by utilizing the following exposed objects within it:

```
var media = document.getElementById('audio-ping');
media.seekable.start(); // Start time (seconds)
media.seekable.end();    // End time (seconds)
media.currentTime = 20; // Seeks playback to 20 seconds
// Total amount of seconds the playback has displayed
media.played.end();
```

Reading local files with the File API

Another feature that brings HTML5 content into a more application-like feature set is the addition of the File API. Users can now interact with their local content on a much more in depth level than ever before. Users can import files in the traditional HTML form manner or now just drag the file into specified drop zones in your HTML5 layouts. Once a file has been submitted to the web page by the user, your JavaScript File API usage can allow you to view, edit, and manipulate the file data prior to ever submitting it to the server. We will dig deeper into the the File API in many of the examples in chapters to come.

Web Workers

In the past when executing processor intensive JavaScript, browsers would often tend to freeze until the processing had been completed and the results were returned. With the advent of HTML5 Web Workers, you can now execute your processor intensive JavaScript code as a background process that will not affect the performance of the active document. Users will be able to continue using the site as intended as they wait for the Web Worker to complete its jobs in the background.

To easily check if a user's browser has support for HTML5 Web Workers, we can check if the type of the `Worker` object is undefined or not:

```
if(typeof(Worker) == "undefined") {
    // This browser doesn't support Web Workers...
}
```

Depending on whether the browser supports the usage of Web Workers, we can easily create a new worker at anytime by instantiating a new `Worker` object and a reference to its JavaScript source:

```
worker = new Worker("worker.js");
```

In the preceding example, we created a new worker and referenced it to the source within the `worker.js` file. The next step is to create the event listener for when the worker posts an update. To create this listener, we create a function on the `onmessage` property and retrieve the message from the `event.data` property:

```
// Create an event listener for worker updates.
worker.onmessage = function (event) {
    console.log('New worker event - ' + event.data);
};
```

The code within the worker can be anything, although it makes the most sense for it to be something that would normally freeze the browser for a short period of time. Regardless of what your worker is doing, to enable the callback to your code you will use the `postMessage` built-in function:

```
postMessage(YOUR_DATA);
```

 Since your Web Worker code is located in external files, it will not have access to the window, document or parent object in its JavaScript source.

You will find more usage of Web Workers in this chapter's example files as well as some of the examples in chapters to come when we start building bigger JavaScript projects.

WebSockets

Adding server-side communication to your web pages to enable features such as multiuser interactivity or push notifications is becoming more and more popular with the advent of WebSockets. To put it in a nutshell, WebSockets fill the void when you need a server to communicate with the client without requiring the client's request.

When building Flash applications, typically one would use technologies and frameworks such as **Real-Time Media Flow Protocol (RTMFP)** or SmartFoxServer (`http://www.smartfoxserver.com`) to allow for server-based multiuser applications. This concept is now available with the use of WebSockets and is a true testament to how far the development of the HTML specification has come.

In the upcoming chapters, we will continue to look into more thorough examples of WebSockets in action, as well as some other interesting methods for connecting users viewing your HTML5 content, such as Socket.io (`http://socket.io`), Node.js (`http://nodejs.org`), and Google V8 (`http://code.google.com/p/v8`).

The Canvas element

We can't finish this chapter without at least beginning to make mention of the HTML5 Canvas element. The Canvas allows developers to use the Canvas 2D Drawing API to draw graphics on the fly into an empty controllable area. From the perspective of a Flash developer, the easiest way to understand the Canvas elements feature set is that it uses similar features to the ActionScript 3 Drawing and Graphics API within an empty area in the HTML layout which is very similar to the Flash Stage.

To better understand what all the fuss is about, let's create a simple drawing application with the use of the Canvas. To begin, we need to append the Canvas element into the body of our HTML document. There is no content required to be inside the element's tags, as it will only be viewable when the user is attempting to view this content from a browser without the support for the Canvas element:

```
<body>
  <canvas id="example" width="640" height="480" style="border:1px
    solid #000000;">
    Your browser does not support the HTML5 Canvas element.
  </canvas>
</body>
```

Two important additions have been appended to the Canvas in this example and they are the element ID, which will be used in JavaScript in the following steps, as well as the width and height declaration. Without the width and height set in the element, most browsers will render the Canvas at 300px x 150px. To aid us in the development of this application, a 1px border has been added to the Canvas to allow us to see exactly where its boundaries are within the browser window. Finally as mentioned, the internal content within the Canvas element will only display if the element is not supported within the browser rendering it. If the application has been also written as a Flash application, the object embed for the Flash SWF could be used in place of the text warning we are using in this example.

The next step is to set up the reference to our Canvas and its 2D context within JavaScript, and since we set an ID on our element, we can easily reference it to a variable within our code:

```
var canvas, context; // Variables to hold Canvas references

window.addEventListener("load", init, false);

function init() {
  // Set the canvas reference to a JavaScript variable.
  canvas = document.getElementById('example');

  // Get the 2D canvas context to allow for 2D Drawing API integration
  context = canvas.getContext('2d');
    if(!context) {
      alert("Failed to get canvas context!");
    return;
}

  canvas.addEventListener('mousemove', onMouseMove, false);
  canvas.addEventListener('mousedown', onMouseDown, false);
  canvas.addEventListener('mouseup', onMouseUp, false);
}

function onMouseDown(e) {
  isDrawing = true;
}
function onMouseUp(e) {
  isDrawing = false;
}
```

With our Canvas referenced and mouse event listeners set up to watch for when the user has the mouse button down, let us finalize this example by writing our onMouseMove function to draw a line when the isDrawing variable is true:

```
function onMouseMove(e) {
    var x, y;
```

```
    if (e.pageX || e.pageY) {
      x = e.pageX;
      y = e.pageY;
    } else if (e.clientX || e.clientY) {
      x = e.clientX + document.body.scrollLeft +
        document.documentElement.scrollLeft;
      y = e.clientY + document.body.scrollTop +
        document.documentElement.scrollTop;
    }

    if(!isDrawing) {
      // Since the mouse isn't down, just move
// the context to the latest mouse position.
        context.beginPath();
        context.moveTo(x, y);
    } else {
        // The mouse is down so draw the line to
// the current mouse position.
        context.lineTo(x, y);
        context.stroke();
    }
  }
}
```

If you notice, the initial code in our onMouseMove function is taken from our 3D Transforms example and allows us to read the mouse X and Y position on the different modern browsers. The condition following the mouse position lookup should look semi-familiar if you had used the Drawing API in ActionScript 3. Assuming the mouse is down, we draw a line to the current mouse position and set the default stroke on it. In this case, the default stroke is a 1px black solid line. When the mouse is not down, we simply move the context to the mouse position but do not draw any lines. This allows us to constantly reset and wait for a new line to be started. When tested in the browser, this example will look something like this:

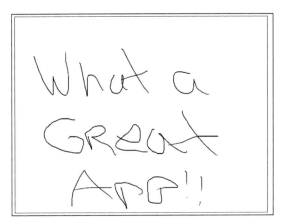

This example really is only the start of what is available to developers but hopefully gives you an idea of how it works. We will continue to look into the Canvas element in the next chapter.

Stage3D versus WebGL

Before we end this chapter, some mention should be made about the availability of WebGL and its similarities and differences to Stage3D in Adobe Flash. WebGL is a cross-platform web standard which allows developers to create and manipulate low-level 3D graphics, bringing plugin-free 3D development to the Web. WebGL can be implemented and viewed in all modern browsers, an exception is Internet Explorer.

Take note that it seems Microsoft is planning to release Internet Explorer 11 with WebGL support.

The key aspects of WebGL and Stage 3D are that they both support the use of hardware acceleration. This can drastically increase the performance of graphical processing loads when viewing content on devices and browsers with proper support. Although this book doesn't contain the room to dive too deep into the use of WebGL, we will look at a couple of frameworks and libraries which support and use it in *Chapter 6, HTML5 Frameworks and Libraries*.

For more information and to see if your current web browser supports the use of WebGL, head over to `http://get.webgl.org`, the WebGL public wiki (`http://www.khronos.org/webgl/wiki`), or view some intriguing examples at `http://www.khronos.org/webgl/wiki/Demo_Repository`.

Summary

Although we have covered a ton of interesting features during the course of this chapter, there are still many very cool additions to HTML5 we will be looking at in the upcoming chapters. The key thought to take away from what we have covered so far is how the relationships between features in Flash and HTML5 are similar yet different at the same time. Understanding what technology will be able to allow you to develop your applications in the best possible manner is a key trait for any good developer. In the next chapter, we will dig deeper into the use of JavaScript and how it relates to ActionScript 3 when programming in an object-oriented manner.

4

Building Robust Applications with HTML5

Since the advent of ActionScript 3, Flash developers have become accustomed to developing in an **object-oriented programming** (OOP) paradigm. When transitioning to JavaScript, many developers with an experience of OOP would initially be put off by the syntax JavaScript uses to accomplish the same functionality. However, a misunderstanding of the syntax may lead to a misunderstanding of the functionality. Therefore, in this chapter we will cover the use of JavaScript OOP, Events, and Event Listeners as well.

In this chapter we will cover the following:

- JavaScript class structure, usage, and syntax
- Object inheritance
- Class constructors
- Tools and frameworks to aid in development
- Creating custom events and listeners

Writing object-oriented JavaScript

In 2006, when Adobe released Flash Player 9 with the inclusion of ActionScript 3 support, the Flash development community saw a major paradigm shift in the way they developed their Flash applications. Prior to the use of ActionScript 3, developers were tasked with writing their applications in ActionScript 2, which is primarily used as a scripting programming language. ActionScript 3 was designed as a true object-oriented programming language with strict typing, which allows for code to be written in a reusable, more controlled manner.

With the use of ActionScript 3 and the new ActionScript Virtual Machine compiler released for Flash Player 9, the code within Flash applications was not only written in an OOP structure but could also run up to 10 times faster than the previous legacy Flash applications. Over time, Flash developers have become accustomed to writing proper OOP structured code, which has allowed them to easily transition their programming skill set to other languages such as Java, C++, or C#.

The use of the OOP paradigm in JavaScript is a bit tricky to understand at first, so let's create an example class structure in ActionScript 3 and port it directly to JavaScript to see the visual syntax differences. In this example, we will create a sample "Player" class that will emulate the basic functionality of a character in a game. Rather than setting up each Player in our game with a separate code, based on functionality, we will use the Player class to create as many players as we need in our game and alter their properties via constructors, getters, setters, and public variables. To get a better idea of this concept, consider the following code example:

```
package {
public class Player {
    // Private Variables
    private var lives:int; // How many lives our player has.
    private var xPosition:int; // The players X position.
    private var yPosition:int; // The players Y position.

    // Public Variables
    public var name:String = 'John'; // The players name.

    /**
     * The Player constructor.
     * This function is called when a new Player is        *
       instantiated.
     *
     * @param playerName: The name to give to our player.
     * @param lives: How many lives to give our player.
     */
    public function Player(playerName:String,
    playerLives:int = 5):void {
        // Update the player variables with
        // the supplied parameters.
        name = playerName;
        lives = playerLives;
    }

    /**
     * Return the current amount of lives the player has.
```

```
    */
    public function get lives():int {
        return lives;
    }

    /**
     * Move the players x and y position.
     *
     * @param    x: The new X position to move the player to.
     * @param    y: The new Y position to move the player to.
     */
    public function move(x:int, y:int):void {
        // Update the player position variables.
        xPosition = x;
        yPosition = y;

        updatePosition();
    }

    /**
     * The would be the function that actually moves the
     * displayed player display object on the stage.
     * This would get called every time a players X and Y
     * position values are updated.
     */
    private function updatePosition():void {
        // Code to update the players display object...
    }
  }
}
```

Although simplified for example purposes, this class example should look pretty familiar to any developer with the experience of coding in ActionScript 3. With this class within our Flash project, we can import it and instantiate it at any time within our application. Declared within the object are properties and methods that can be called by the parent object to manipulate the data for the specific Player object, and this is typical of any class. When you are ready to add a new Player into your application, we can instantiate a new object with the following ActionScript 3 code:

```
var player:Player = new Player('John', 10);
```

By appending the required values into the constructor, we give our Player a unique name as well as an initial value as to how many lives this Player will have. We now have our new Player, which we can manipulate in our imaginary game.

Now let's take a look at the same class that is rewritten in JavaScript:

```javascript
function Player(playerName, playerLives) {
  // Private variables
  var lives = playerLives;
  var xPosition = 0;
  var yPosition = 0;

  // Public variables
  this.name = playerName;

  // Return the current amount of lives the player has.
  this.lives = function() {
    return lives;
  }

  /**
   * Move the players x and y position.
   *
   * @param      x: The new X position to move the player to.
   * @param      y: The new Y position to move the player to.
   */
  this.move = function(x, y) {
    xPosition = x;
    yPosition = y;

    updatePosition();
  }

  /**
   * The would be the function that actually moves the displayed
   * player display object on the stage. This would get called
   * every time a players X and Y position values are updated.
   */
  function updatePosition() {
    //
  }
}
```

At first glance one can see that there is no class declaration, which one would be familiar with, as in many other programming languages. Instead, when creating "classes" in JavaScript, one uses a function to simulate the usage of a traditional class structure. Package declarations are removed from the equation as well as the inclusion of JavaScript is appended to the HTML document rendering the web page. By all means, pending it was logical; one could separate all one's JavaScript classes into separate files for ease of development. However, when publishing large amounts of JavaScript to a public-hosted environment, to conserve the amount of requests to the web server for data, JavaScript should be consolidated as much as possible. We will dig further into the preparation of your HTML5 projects for production environments in *Chapter 10, Preparing for Release*.

 One thing must be noted at this point of time. With the lack of strict typing and many other specific class structure rules, the same JavaScript functionality can be written in numerous ways. During the course of this chapter, I have written the examples to be as user-friendly as possible in order to allow us to examine the syntax better.

Class syntax

In the initial JavaScript class example, we examined the differences between ActionScript 3's class structure as compared to JavaScript when creating object-oriented code. The example used one of the more traditional methods of creating a class in JavaScript by using a function in place of the typical class declaration.

Functions

Many of the example JavaScript functions we have used in code examples so far have shown some of the different ways in which we can define a new function. As I just mentioned, depending on what the developers are comfortable with, they may choose to write their functions in JavaScript in one of the following ways:

```javascript
function isAlive1() { return true; }
var isAlive2 = function() { return true; };
window.isAlive3 = function() { return true; };

console.log(isAlive1());
console.log(isAlive2());
console.log(isAlive3());
```

Each of the three `console.log` outputs in the previous example would yield the proper Boolean return of *true*. It is also worth noting that the order of the function definitions and function usage is not required to be as demonstrated in the preceding sample of code. The following example would yield the exact same result:

```javascript
console.log(isAlive1());

function isAlive1() { return true; }
var isAlive2 = function() { return true; };
```

```
window.isAlive3 = function() { return true; };

console.log(isAlive2());
console.log(isAlive3());
```

When attempting to call a function that has not been defined, a `ReferenceError` error will be dispatched and displayed in the JavaScript console.

Although our application would continue running despite this runtime error, it would generally mean that there is an issue with our code. Rather than having the default `ReferenceError` error sent to the JavaScript console, we could use a simple condition to handle this issue within our code.

```
try {
    console.log(isAlive4());
} catch(error) {
    console.log('Failed to call isAlive4() - ' + error);
    // Run alternate code here...
}
```

Variable scope

Understanding properly how variables scope in JavaScript is a critical step in understanding the core aspects of the language. Scope refers to the accessibility that the variables have to other parts of the code when they are created somewhere within your code. Variables can be instantiated and referenced depending on the syntax used to declare them. JavaScript utilizes what many refer to as *function scope*, whereby all variables and functions scope in the same manner. At the top of the scope chain are the global variables and functions. As with all programming paradigms, global means everything, and a global variable or function is accessible anywhere else within your code.

```
var name = 'John';

function getName() {
```

```
      return name;
  }


  // Both calls return the name as it is accessible globally.
  console.log(name);
  console.log(getName());
```

This code demonstrates the use of a global variable. Since the variable name is declared above the scope of the function that uses it, there would be no errors when running this code. However, variables can also be locally declared from within a function.

```
  function getName() {
    var name = 'John';
    return name;
  }


  console.log(name);        // Error
  console.log(getName());   // Success
```

As the Player's name (which in this case is John) is created within the getName function, it is not globally accessible to any of the code outside of that function. As simple as the concept of global and local variables is, when you begin to consider the lack of strict typing and the use of exact variable names for global and local variables, your head may begin to spin. Not to worry, this is another one of the typical learning curve issues developers have with JavaScript. But as mentioned before, mastering variable scope in JavaScript is one of the essential skills every good HTML5 developer must have.

To demonstrate some of the issues presented, and to allow you to fully view scoping in action, let's review the following example:

```
  // We will start with a globally scoped variable which is
     accessible by everything.
  var alpha = 'a';

  // Global scope example.
  function a() {
      console.log(alpha); // Reference the global alpha variable.
  }

  // Local scope using a supplied variable.
  function b(alpha) {
      console.log(alpha); // Reference the supplied alpha variable.
  }
```

```
// Local scope using a variable created within the function.
function c() {
  var alpha = 'c';
  console.log(alpha);
}

// Update the global object property.
function d() {
    this.alpha = 'd'; // Create an internal object property.
}

function e() {
    var n = 'e';

    this.alpha = function() {
        console.log(n);
    }
};

function f() {};


a();     // A
b('b'); // B
c();     // C

console.log(new d().alpha); // D

var e = new e().alpha();     // E

f.prototype.alpha = 'f';
console.log(new f().alpha); // F
```

The previous example, although an illogical way to output the characters A to F,
demonstrates many of the ways in which variables and functions can be manipulated
to access data from specific areas in your application's scope chain.

Public and private variables and functions

The next step for understanding variables and functions within JavaScript is by
learning how to create and utilize public and private members. Unlike in ActionScript
3, variables are not typed as private or public, thus making the syntax a little harder
to understand.

Local or private variables

Private (or local) variables are declared by utilizing the `var` keyword when creating variables within an object. The resulting variable will only be accessible within that specific object and would require a getter and setter method to allow for external manipulation. This manner of variable declaration is similar to using the `private` keyword when creating variables in ActionScript 3. A general rule of thumb in OOP development is to use private variables whenever possible as it will lead to far less issues with variable corruption or other misusage.

```
function Example() {
   var foobar = 'abc'; // Only accessible within the Example
scope.
}
```

Public variables

Public variables or properties are declared by using the `this.myVariableName` syntax. Similar to the `public` keyword when creating variables in ActionScript 3, public variables in JavaScript are accessible not only to the code within the object's scope chain but also from outside of the object it was created in as well.

```
function Example() {
   this.foobar = 'abc'; // Accessible outside the Example scope.
}
```

Private functions

Private functions, which are only accessible within the object scope, can be written in a couple of different ways.

```
function Example() {
   function TestOne() {
     return true;
   }

   var testTwo = function() {
     return true;
   };
}
```

Both examples demonstrated previously yield a private function. Any attempt to call the function from outside of the object scope would result in a runtime error.

Public functions

Public or privileged functions, like public variables, are accessible from outside of the object they were created in, and are created using the `this.myFunctionName = function() {...}` syntax.

```
function Example() {
  this.test = function() {
    return true;
  }
}
```

Prototype

One of the more confusing aspects of a JavaScript object's syntax is the use of the prototype object. As we have seen in the examples and explanations up to this point, everything in JavaScript is an object, and within every JavaScript object is a prototype property.

 If you were using Flash back in the days of ActionScript 1 or ActionScript 2, you may be familiar with the concept of the prototype object (`http://help.adobe.com/en_US/as2/reference/flashlite/WS5b3ccc516d4fbf351e63e3d118ccf9c47f-7ec2.html`). This object was utilized in both programming languages, but dropped on the release of ActionScript 3.

To see this concept in action, let's start simple and work our way forward into more complex usages of the prototype object. We will start by looking at the prototype object for a new empty object.

```
var player = {}; // Create a new empty object.
console.log(Object.getPrototypeOf(player)); // Return the prototype
object.
```

Running this code in a web browser would result in a JavaScript log that would resemble something very close to the following code, if not the same:

```
Object
  __defineGetter__: function __defineGetter__() { [native code]
  }
  __defineSetter__: function __defineSetter__() { [native code]
  }
  __lookupGetter__: function __lookupGetter__() { [native code]
  }
  __lookupSetter__: function __lookupSetter__() { [native code]
  }
```

```
constructor: function Object() { [native code] }
hasOwnProperty: function hasOwnProperty() { [native code] }
isPrototypeOf: function isPrototypeOf() { [native code] }
propertyIsEnumerable: function propertyIsEnumerable() {
[native code] }
toLocaleString: function toLocaleString() { [native code] }
toString: function toString() { [native code] }
valueOf: function valueOf() { [native code] }
```

This output can give us a lot more sense of what the prototype object is really about. As you already know from previous ActionScript 3 development, object variable types come with many built-in methods to manipulate the content within it. Looking at the output of the prototype of our `Player` object, you may notice that many of these familiar methods and properties are listed.

We can use this prototype object to append new properties to an object at any time. Consider the following example where we create a simplified `Player` object and append the move functionality to it via the prototype object rather than directly within the object itself:

```
function Player(name) {
  this.name = name;
  this.lives = 0;
  this.xPosition = 0;
  this.yPosition = 0;
}

Player.prototype.move = function(x, y) {
  this.xPosition = x;
  this.yPosition = y;
}
```

The same concept could be used for overriding the default object behavior. By modifying the move properties via the prototype object, any further calls to the move method would result in a newly appended behavior.

```
function Player(name) {
  this.name = name;
  this.lives = 0;
  this.xPosition = 0;
  this.yPosition = 0;

  this.move = function(x, y) {
    this.xPosition = x;
    this.yPosition = y;
  }
```

```
    }

    Player.prototype.move = function(x, y) {
        this.xPosition = x + 5;
        this.yPosition = y + 5;
    }
```

Keep in mind that these changes are targeted to the object itself and not the instance. Therefore, these changes will affect each and every Player instance demonstrated as follows:

```
    function Player(name) {
        this.name = name;
        this.lives = 0;
        this.xPosition = 0;
        this.yPosition = 0;

        this.move = function(x, y) {
            this.xPosition = x;
            this.yPosition = y;
        }
    }

    function init() {
        var susan = Player('Susan');
        var john = Player('John');

        // Modify the move function for ALL Player instances.
        Player.prototype.move = function(x, y) {
            this.xPosition = x + 5;
            this.yPosition = y + 5;
        }
    }
```

So why is this important? While depending on how your application is built, by utilizing the prototype object, you can easily append shared code to objects directly, without the need for coding the same thing more than once. Less code means less memory, and it will always make your life easier when it comes to maintaining your projects.

Instance types

As you begin to float around all of this new JavaScript code and syntax in these examples and in your own, adding checks and conditions for instance types will prove to be an important addition. The lack of strict typing will require you to write and maintain clean and optimized code to get your applications working properly. Consider some of the following code snippets for acquiring information on the instance type of our `Player` object:

```
// Create a player instance
var player = new Player('John');

// Check the type of player.
console.log(typeof(player));

// Output the constructor data from the player.
console.log(player.constructor);

// Check if the player is a Object - returns a Boolean.
console.log(player instanceof Object);
```

Each of these calls to the `console.log` method are performing different ways to look up the instance of the `Player` object. When we run this code in a web browser and open up the developer console, we get the following output:

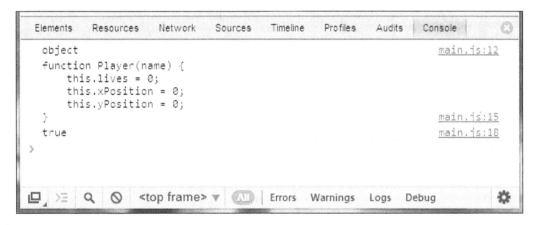

The initial `object` output is a result of the `typeof()` function call made on the `Player` object. The second output is the code block returned when calling the constructor of the `Player` object. Finally, the conditional console call (`console.log(player instanceof Object)`) results in the Boolean return in the console letting us know that the `instanceof` condition is true.

Object literals

Literals are simply a shorter method to define arrays and objects within JavaScript. We are already creating new objects in JavaScript with the following syntax:

```
var player = new Object();
var player= Object.create(null);
var player = {};
```

We can further extend the preceding syntax by creating the internals of the object directly within the variable declaration.

```
var player = {
   name: "John",
   lives: 5,
   xPosition: 0,
   yPosition: 0,
   move: function(x, y) {
     xPosition = x;
     yPosition = y;

     // Update the position display...
   }
}
```

This `Object` syntax, however, creates major issues with its lack of reusability as its instance already will have existed when it is created. Since there is no need to instantiate the object, we can continue our code by referencing its properties.

```
player.name = "Susan";
player.move(5, 5);
```

Constructors

As we have seen in some of the previous examples, in comparison to ActionScript 3, the object constructor syntax is a bit different than one would typically be used to. Since classes are just functions, we can just place the code typically found within the constructor directly within the class.

You can easily look up the reference to the function that initially created an object, by calling the `constructor` property on it.

```
console.log(player.constructor);
```

When attempting to look up the constructor of a built-in object type such as an array, string, or date, the output will conceal the inner code and display a warning of the use of native code as follows.

```
var test = Array();
console.log(test.constructor);
```

This would generate the following in the browser's JavaScript console:

```
function Array() { [native code] }
```

Inheritance

By using the `call()` method on a pre-existing object, we can update the reference to `this` from the object itself to somewhere else in the code.

```
function Player(name) {
  this.name = name;
  this.age = 20;
}

function John() {
  Player.call(this, 'John');

  this.age += 35;
}

function Jill() {
  this.age += 20;
}
Jill.prototype = new Player('Jill');

function init() {
  var john = new John();
  console.log(john.name + ' is ' + john.age);

  var jill = new Jill();
  console.log(jill.name + ' is ' + jill.age);
}
window.addEventListener("load", init);
```

This example demonstrates a simple inheritance of the `Player` object within the new `John` object. This allows us to access the internal values within `Player` and use them externally within the `John` class. In this example case, we make John 35 years older than the default `Player`. We can also use the prototype object to declare object inheritance.

```
function Player(name) {
  this.name = name;
  this.age = 20;
}

function Jill() {
  this.age += 20;
}
Jill.prototype = new Player('Jill');

function init() {
  var jill = new Jill();
  console.log(jill.name + ' is ' + jill.age);
}
window.addEventListener("load", init);
```

When the new `jill` object is created, it inherits all of the base properties and functions from `Player` as the prototype reference has declared object inheritance. The resulting output for this example on page load would display the following:

```
John is 55
Jill is 40
```

Listing object properties

At any point you can look up the available properties within an object by using the `Object.getOwnPropertyNames()` method. Keeping private and public syntax in mind, let's review the following example to view the output when looking up an object's properties:

```
function Player() {
  // Private variables
  var _this = this;      // Reference to this object
  var lives;
  var positionX = 0;
  var positionY = 0;
  var playerElement;

  // Public variables
```

```
    this.name = '';        // The players name.
    this.age = 10; // The players age (default = 10).

    this.move = function(x, y) {
      positionX = x;
      positionY = y;

      // Move the player...
    };

    function blink() {
      // Blink players eyes...
    }
  }

  var player = new Player();
  var properties = Object.getOwnPropertyNames(player);

  console.log(properties);
```

Again, with public and private variables in mind, only variables created with the keyword this are visible outside of the object scope. Executing the preceding code example would provide the following array of properties' names as the output:

```
["name", "age", "move"]
```

Making OOP in JavaScript easier

To many developers, the culmination of all of these workarounds and syntax changes that come with developing object-oriented JavaScript may seem just like a laundry list of "hacks". Regardless of your point of view on the matter, there are many options available to aid in building large-scale JavaScript-based applications with a more traditional development flow. In *Chapter 6, HTML5 Frameworks and Libraries*, we will dig into many of the popular JavaScript libraries and frameworks available, and how they can be used to not only speed up your development time but also provide a more solid end result on all modern browsers and devices.

JavaScript events

As with most languages, events are what really brings an application to life. Without the use of events, programs would usually just run from start to finish without the need for human interaction. JavaScript events are built around the asynchronous event model. Rather than checking continually to see if a condition is met, events can use call-back structures, like in ActionScript, to execute code once an event has been fired. A great example of this, which you may have already seen in many other examples thus far:

```
window.addEventListener("load", init, false);
```

We use this Event Listener on the `window` object to allow our code to determine when the `window` object will finish loading, so that we can call our initial method to begin JavaScript manipulation of our document.

Keyboard and mouse events

Mouse events are another one of the core elements almost all JavaScript projects contain. Although we will be using these events within the examples all throughout this book, it's worth reviewing a consolidated list of not only the mouse, but keyboard and touch events as well, so that you can have a better understanding of what is easily available to you for input event listening. The different keyboard and mouse events are listed as follows:

*   **mousedown:** A mouse button has been pressed down
*   **mouseup:** A mouse button has been released
*   **click:** A mouse button has been clicked
*   **dblclick:** A mouse button has been double-clicked
*   **contextmenu:** Some action to trigger a context menu has occurred
*   **scrolling:** The context has been moved on the scroll axis
*   **keydown:** A keyboard key has been pressed into the down state
*   **keypress:** A keyboard key has been pressed and released
*   **keyup:** A keyboard key has been released

Touch events

Touch event support is growing closer to a set standard; however, you will notice support and feature set differences depending on what device and browser you are testing on. It's worth noting that just like Flash applications running on a touch interface, you can use the mouse events with no issues, and still support the use of an actual mouse. However, as a mouse can only click on one point at a time, if your application will need multitouch support, you will have to begin utilizing the touch event structure. In the next two chapters, we will look further into the use of HTML on touch devices and how the development differs. The touch events supported are as follows:

- **touchstart:** A user has started to touch an element
- **touchmove:** A user has moved the touch position since touchstart
- **touchend:** A user has removed his/her finger from the element

Custom events

Having the ability to create custom events and dispatch them to waiting Event Listeners allows you to further extend your application's OOP syntax and structure. Typically, as a Flash developer using ActionScript 3, you would utilize the flash events class to create custom events so as to create the flow of communication from class to class. In its simplest form, it would look like the following:

```
import flash.events.Event;
import flash.events.EventDispatcher;

var myEvent:Event = new Event("myEvent", false);
dispatchEvent(myEvent);
```

As with most of the functionality in ActionScript 3, to optimize the application's file size and execution speed, packages must be directly imported into the project when utilizing extended internal functionality. Therefore, when creating and dispatching events in ActionScript 3, we should always import the Event and EventDispatcher classes, after which we can instantiate a new event with our custom event type that is supplied as a string. When the event is dispatched, there will need to be an Event Listener to execute further code to complete the event sequence within your application. I am sure you are well aware that the typical Event Listener in ActionScript 3 is described in the following syntax:

```
addEventListener("myEvent", myCustomEventHandeler, false, 0,
true);
```

Using the same ActionScript 3 syntax like all Event Listener setups, the custom event type, which is again in the form of a string, is supplied to the identifier. The second parameter supplied is always the function to be called once this listener has fired. The final three parameters control bubbling and weak referencing for event control and memory cleanup.

Fortunately, the customized events' setup and structure in JavaScript are extremely similar with some obvious differences. Consider this working example in comparison to what we just reviewed and what you already know about events in ActionScript 3.

```
function init() {
    // Create an event listener
    document.addEventListener("myEvent", myEventHandeler, false);

    // Create our custom event
    var myEvent = document.createEvent("Event");

    // initEvent(event type, allow bubbling, allow prevented)
    myEvent.initEvent("myCustomEvent", true, true);
    myEvent.customData = "We can add more data into our event
    easily!";
    document.dispatchEvent(myEvent);
}


function myEventHandeler(event) {
    console.log('The custom event has been dispatched - ' +
    event);
    console.log('And retrieve our appended data - ' +
    event.customData);
}

window.addEventListener("load", init);
```

Apart from the lack of imported classes, this event example should look pretty familiar in the eyes of any Flash developer. As with majority of the examples in this book, we wait for the window to load with an Event Listener that we have often seen up to this point. Within the `init` function, we start by creating our Event Listener. In this case, we append the listener to the document; however, this could be appended to any object within your code. Note that not only is the method to create a new Event Listener exactly the same (`addEventListener`), but the syntax of the initial two parameters is the same as well. The final Boolean value supplied controls event bubbling, which we will refer back to in a while. The remaining code within the `init` function contains our event instantiation as well as the dispatching of that event. Again, thanks to the glory that is, ECMAScript, the syntax and structure of the custom event is nearly identical.

While creating our event type in JavaScript with the `createEvent()` method, the availability of event modules depends on the DOM Level support that the viewing browser has. At the time of writing this book, majority of the browsers are moving towards full support of the DOM Level 3 Events, which include UIEvent, DOMFocus, DOMActivate, Event, MouseEvent, MutationEvent, TextEvent, KeyboardEvent, and HTMLEvent. You can always check out the complete list of currently available or future specified DOM Level 3 Events by heading over to `http://www.w3.org/TR/DOM-Level-3-Events/`.

The third parameter of the `addEventListener` method specifies whether the registered Event Handler captures the specified event or not. If the Event Handler captures an event, then each time the event occurs on the element or its descendants, the Event Handler will be called.

Event bubbling

When an event is dispatched, it will follow the object's parent tree to the absolute parent object until it is either handled or stopped. This behavior is known as event bubbling and is found in ActionScript 3 as well as JavaScript event structure. In Flash projects, an event will bubble all the way to the main object or in most cases, the Stage. In JavaScript, the event will bubble to the document object.

In the following example, we will examine dealing with the `mousedown` event on the document and object by controlling the propagation of the event:

```
function init() {
  // Add a mouse click listener to the document.
  document.addEventListener("mousedown", onDocumentClick,
  false);

  // Add a mouse click listener to the box element.
  var box = document.getElementById('box');
  box.addEventListener("mousedown", onBoxClick, false);
}

function onDocumentClick(event) {
  console.log('The document has been clicked - ' + event);
}

function onBoxClick(event) {
  console.log('The box has been clicked. - ' + event);

  // Stop this event from reaching the document object
  // and calling the document level event listener.
```

```
        event.stopPropagation();
    }

    window.addEventListener("load", init);
```

This JavaScript snippet applies a `mousedown` Event Listener to both an element within the document as well as the document itself. If the user was to click on the element within the page, both Event Listeners would be called, resulting in two different handlers handling the same mouse click. Although this may be handy in some applications, the natural way to deal with this issue and only allow a single handler to be called is by stopping the flow of the event bubbling with the `stopPropagation()` method.

Dealing with event propagation in JavaScript is identical to what you are used to in ActionScript 3. At any point in the event flow, you can easily stop the traversal of the event by calling either the `stopPropagation()` or `stopImmediatePropagation()` method. If you are familiar with these methods from ActionScript 3 development, you will already know that they are almost identical by nature. The only difference is that the `stopImmediatePropagation()` call stops the event flow from reaching any further Event Listeners in the current node.

Putting it all together

At the end of the day, all of these code examples only define each of the individual pieces of JavaScript's functionality. Continuing with our `Player` class concept that we have been using throughout this chapter, we then put some finishing touches to our example "Player in a game" class structure.

```
function Game() {
    // An array to hold all our player objects
    var players = new Array();

    // Game Constructor
    // Reference to the game element in the document.
    var gameElement = document.getElementById('game');

    // Get the game element size.
    var gameElementWidth = gameElement.offsetWidth;
    var gameElementHeight = gameElement.offsetHeight;

    // Be sure to update these values if the window is
    // to ever be resized.
    window.onresize = function() {
        console.log("NOTICE: Browser Resize: " +
```

```
gameElementWidth + " x " + gameElementHeight);
    gameElementWidth = gameElement.offsetWidth;
    gameElementHeight = gameElement.offsetHeight;
  };

  // Player Class.
  function Player(name) {
    this.name = name;

    // Create the element for the player.
    var playerElement = document.createElement("div");
    playerElement.class = 'element';
    playerElement.style.position = "absolute";
    playerElement.style.left = Math.floor((Math.random() *
    gameElementWidth - 100) + 1) + 'px';    // Random position within
    viewabled bounds
    playerElement.style.top = Math.floor((Math.random() *
    gameElementHeight - 100) + 1) + 'px';
    playerElement.style.color = "#000000";
    playerElement.style.display = "block";
    playerElement.style.padding = "5px";
    playerElement.style.border = "1px solid #000000";
    playerElement.style.width = "100px";
    playerElement.style.height = "100px";
    playerElement.innerHTML = this.name;
    gameElement.appendChild(playerElement);

    // Move this players X and Y positions.
    this.move = function(x, y) {
      playerElement.style.left = x + "px";
      playerElement.style.top = y + "px";
    }

    // Return the current position of this player
    // as a object.
    this.getPostion = function() {
      var position = {};
      position.x = parseInt(playerElement.style.left);
      position.y = parseInt(playerElement.style.top);
      return position;
    }
  }

  // Public Methods
```

```
    this.addNewPlayer = function(name) {
      // Check if this player name is already created
      var l = players.length;
      for(var i = 0; i < l; i++) {
        if(name == players[i].name) {
          console.log('Error: Player with the name ' +
          name + ' already exsits.');
          return;
        }
      }

      // Create the new player instance
      var player = new Player(name);

      // Add a reference to the global players array.
      players.push(player);
    }

    this.getPlayer = function(name) {
      // Check if this player name is already created
      var l = players.length;
      for(var i = 0; i < l; i++) {
        if(name == players[i].name) {
          return players[i];
        }
      }

      return false;
    }
}

function init() {
  // Create the game instance.
  var game = new Game();
```

```
// For this game we will automatically create two players.
game.addNewPlayer('Jack');
// Try to add another Jack to view name check.
game.addNewPlayer('Jack');
game.addNewPlayer('Jill');

document.addEventListener('keydown', onKeyDown);

// Called when the user presses a key on the keyboard.
function onKeyDown(event) {
    // The key that was just pressed (ID).
    var key = event.keyCode;

    // Lookup the player to reference.
    var player = game.getPlayer('Jack');

    // Make sure the player exsists.
    if(player == false) return;

    // Get the players current position.
    var position = player.getPostion();

    // Forward
    if(key == 38) player.move(position.x, position.y - 10);

    // Backwards
    if(key == 40) player.move(position.x, position.y + 10);

    // Left
    if(key == 37) player.move(position.x - 10, position.y);

    // Right
    if(key == 39) player.move(position.x + 10, position.y);
  }
}

window.addEventListener("load", init);
```

Though still a simple example of what all this could look like in a single package, this example encompasses many of the features we have looked at within this chapter:

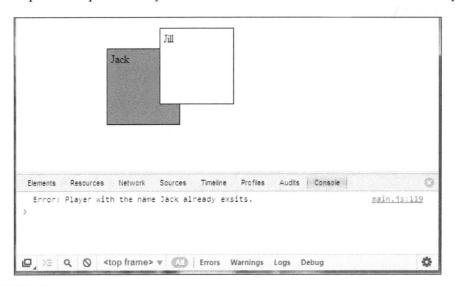

Summary

Although this chapter covers the main concepts surrounding the syntax and structure of objects in JavaScript development, in reality we could write a whole book on the topic. That being said, we will continue to cover these and more aspects of the more advanced side of JavaScript development throughout this book. As mentioned in the introduction of this chapter, many of the differences and paradigm changes presented with advanced JavaScript development may seem a bit daunting to some Flash developers. However, once you get your head wrapped around most of these core concepts, the rest of the puzzle pieces begin to fit together with ease. In the next chapter, we will be looking into some of the tools available for porting pre-existing Flash content to HTML5.

 Looking for even more advanced JavaScript syntax and structure tips and techniques? You can check these books from Packt Publishing, *Object-Oriented JavaScript* by *Stoyan Stefanov*, *Learning jQuery, Third Edition* by *Jonathan Chaffer* and *Karl Swedberg*, and *jQuery for Designers: Beginner's Guide* by *Natalie MacLees*.

5
Code Once, Release Everywhere

As I am sure you may have noticed by now that although all the modern browsers support many aspects of the specified HTML5 feature set, in many cases, developers have to write their code in specific ways to enable proper cross-browser support for their projects. Not only is this a time consuming task that requires a lot of redundancy and conditioning, but it requires developers to stay caught up on the cutting edge of the current browser support of the HTML5 specification; not only for every browser targeted, but every update for each browser as well. With the popularity of HTML5 development growing at an extremely fast rate, many developers have created libraries and frameworks to aid in targeting all platforms with a single instance of code.

In this chapter, we will learn:

- An overview of the CreateJS Toolkit, a Flash developer's best friend for HTML5 development as well as its internal libraries, EaselJS, SoundJS, PreloadJS, and TweenJS
- Using Modernizr to detect clients' browser features
- Looking deeper into CSS3 media queries

Covering all your bases

One of the biggest differences in the development paradigm between Flash and HTML5 is the expectation a developer has from the user who will be viewing the end product. Typically, a Flash developer will preset the publish settings for the project, when starting a project to the Flash Player that will best support the feature set to be built into the application. Of course, this means that the user's Flash Player installed on their computer must be up-to-date in order to fill the prerequisite version. When developing any HTML-based web project, this issue is exponentially greater because the developer loses control over how a user is exactly able to view their content. Although some browsers are more common than others, there is a massive range of Internet Browser software available today, not only for desktops and mobiles, but for devices such as televisions as well. Unfortunately, each of these browsers is not built to the exact same specification and if you ignore testing your project in each and every one of them, you cannot guarantee that your content will be displayed and will act as you had created it to.

With the release of Microsoft's Internet Explorer Version 10, long gone are the days of web developers complaining about developing web pages for Internet Explorer Version 6. However, a new set of issues have been born with the advent of HTML5. Web pages and web-based applications are now gaining accessibility to many of the features you have become accustomed to with native desktop applications. New system integration, such as file accessibility, peripheral support, as well as hardware acceleration have required that modern web browsers implement support for these features to enable proper support for users viewing this new HTML5 content.

So which browser is the best? Well, from the developer's perspective, as nice as it is to have a favorite, this really doesn't matter if you want everyone to view your content. Understanding the differences and how they have changed, and will change, will keep your HTML5 skill set up-to-date and ahead of the curve. As mentioned before, if you are using any of the popular and modern web browsers available today, most of your bases will be covered. At the time of writing this book, upcoming features such as **WebRTC**, which we will cover later in this book, are only supported in browsers such as Google Chrome.

CreateJS

Since this book is written specifically for Flash developers extending their skill set with HTML5, the first library we cover to aid in JavaScript development has to be CreateJS. CreateJS is a collection of open source, modular JavaScript libraries that can work separately to enable a more seamless transition from ActionScript 3 to JavaScript. CreateJS has been specifically created to easily allow web developers to create, embed, and manipulate media assets into their HTML5 projects with relative ease. This point is especially true if you come from a Flash development background.

The latest versions of all of the elements within CreateJS as well as the full documentation can be found at http://www.createjs.com.

CreateJS focuses on the asset integration and manipulation end of things to enable you, the developer, to spend more time making sure your project is pixel perfect. There have been some great examples of some amazing projects in the recent past that have made use of this library, producing some stunning HTML5 experiences, such as http://www.findyourwaytooz.com, http://www.atari.com/arcade, and http://shinobicorp.com/retro-soccer.

Although we could go into great detail about each of the exciting features within the CreateJS package, we would probably end up filling half this book. Therefore, to make sure you can at least get your feet wet and understand what CreateJS has to offer, let's review each of the elements within the package and how they can be utilized in your HTML5 projects.

EaselJS

EaselJS is a JavaScript library which aims at mimicking the Flash Display List syntax within ActionScript 3 into JavaScript. It does this by using the HTML5 Canvas element like a stage within Flash. As a newcomer to HTML5 and JavaScript syntax, EaselJS may be a library that will not only allow you to continue creating applications in a similar manner as what you have been developing up to this point but also allow you to easily port your preexisting Flash applications to HTML5 with relative ease.

 The most up-to-date EaselJS documentation can easily be found at http://www.createjs.com/Docs/EaselJS.

EaselJS can be used to handle all your graphical elements such as bitmaps, vectors, and sprite sheets for your HTML5 project. One of the best use cases of EaselJS is porting an existing ActionScript 3 class into JavaScript. Since EaselJS is set up to emulate the display list in Flash, once our ActionScript 3 class has been converted, we can begin to use it in our JavaScript project almost the same way we did in our Flash project.

Every project using EaselJS, or any other CreateJS library, needs to import the library source into their HTML5 project. Once you have acquired the necessary JavaScript source files from the CreateJS website, set up your HTML document as demonstrated in the following example:

```html
<!DOCTYPE html>
<html lang="en">
  <head>
    <meta charset="utf-8" />
    <title>CreateJS - EaselJS Example</title>

    <!-- Import the EaselJS Library -->
    <script src="easeljs-0.5.0.min.js"></script>

    <script>
      function init() {
        // We can place our custom code here.
      }
    </script>
  </head>

  <body onload="init()">
    <canvas id="exampleCanvas" width="800" height="600">
  </body>
</html>
```

As you can see from the preceding example, the EaselJS library is imported into our document within the `<script>` tag. We have also added an empty Canvas element to the body of our document. Since EaselJS uses the HTML5 Canvas element in replacement of the Stage in Flash, this will be a requirement in this example and all projects using this library.

To kick things off in our example, we will start by reviewing a basic ActionScript 3 class, which could be used in any Flash project. This class is a simple demonstration to apply a bitmap graphic to the position of the mouse over the stage and update the graphic's position as the mouse moves. This example encompasses not only the use of external graphic references but mouse- and time-based events as well:

```actionscript
package {

  import flash.display.*;

  public class MouseLine() {

    private var oldX:int;
```

```
    private var oldY:int;

    public function MouseLine() { }

    public function update(container:Sprite, x:int, y:int):void {
        container.graphics.setStrokeStyle(1);
        container.graphics.moveTo(oldX, oldY);
        container.graphics.lineTo(x, x);

        oldX = x;
        oldY = y;
    }
  }
}
```

All of this should look very familiar provided you have spent any time working with ActionScript 3 classes, so let's jump right into the conversion process. As we have seen in the examples throughout the book so far, when creating classes in JavaScript, there are some immediate differences in syntax, layout, and usage from ActionScript 3. First and foremost are the package declaration as well as the import statements. Packages do not exist in JavaScript; therefore, that code can be removed. The code directory and the file structure you have grown accustomed to can still be utilized; however, there will be no reference needed in code to distinguish what code is in what package. Import statements can also be completely removed as they are not used in JavaScript as well. Instead, any further external code required within the project should be imported within a <script> tag element inside the HTML document.

Since we intend to keep all of our classes as separate files within the project source structure, we can replace the typical package syntax in ActionScript 3 classes with the following self-executing anonymous function:

```
(function(window) {
   // Place Your Code here
}) (window);
```

When our class source code is placed within this function, it will automatically be executed when it has been loaded, allowing us to utilize this class from the rest of our project's code. After the strict typing on functions and variables has been removed, as well as the public and private variables converted into JavaScript syntax, our class will look something as the following:

```
(function(window) {

  function MouseLine() {
    this.oldX = 0;
```

```
      this.oldY = 0;
   };

   MouseLine.update = function(container, x, y) {
      container.graphics.setStrokeStyle(1);
      container.graphics.moveTo(this.oldX, this.oldY);
      container.graphics.lineTo(x, y);

      this.oldX = x;
      this.oldY = y;
   }

   window.MouseLine = MouseLine;

})(window);
```

Notice the final line appended within the self-executing anonymous function, `window.MouseLine = MouseLine;`

This final addition to the class allows us to instantiate a new `MouseLine` object from our application base and utilize the functionality within the class. But before we can start using this class, we need to import it into our project as follows:

```
<script type="text/javascript" src="MouseLine.js"></script>
```

With our class saved as `MouseLine.js`, we can now import it into our HTML document as usual by using the `<script>` tag in the head of our HTML5 document. For this example, we will also open another `<script>` tag within the document *head*, where we will place our custom JavaScript code that utilizes our new class:

```
<script type="text/javascript">
   var stage;
   var line;

   function init() {
      stage = new createjs.Stage("exampleCanvas");
   }
</script>
```

In the preceding example, we start constructing the `stage` for our EaselJS project. We begin by creating two global variables, one for our `stage` element and the other for our mouse graphic element. Following the global variables is our `init()` function, which will be called on page load. The next step within our `init` function is to set up the Canvas element we applied to the body of this HTML document. We use the `new.createjs.Stage('canvas-element')` syntax to tell EaselJS that our Canvas with the ID of `exampleCanvas` is our intended stage.

With EaselJS applied into our project and referencing our Canvas element, the next step is to apply a ticker to allow us to emulate the `onEnterFrame` event in ActionScript 3. Since we intend for the graphic in our `MouseGraphic` class to follow our mouse when on the Canvas, we will need to constantly check the position of the mouse to translate those values into the x and y position values of the graphic. As mentioned, in ActionScript 3, one would traditionally use an `onEnterFrame` event; however, without the concept of MovieClips and frames in JavaScript, the setup uses a `Ticker` object from EaselJS instead.

Still within our `init()` function we have just created, we can now apply the following code to set up our `Ticker` object:

```
createjs.Ticker.setFPS(60);
createjs.Ticker.addListener(window);
```

Not only have we created a new event listener for our `Ticker` object with the preceding lines of code, but we are also setting the intended frames per second of our Canvas rendering by utilizing one of the many internal CreateJS object methods. However, with our event listener created, we need a function to be called every time a new frame has been rendered. When using the `Ticker` object in CreateJS, we can simply append a `tick()` function in the same scope as the `Ticker` object, which will be called upon every interval:

```
function tick() {
    stage.update();
}
```

Within this tick function, we also add the call to our global variable reference to our Stage object created in our `init()` function. This, as you may assume, is the call that actually tells the `stage` object to update itself by rendering the next interval in the stage progression. Therefore, any of the code one would typically append inside of an `onEnterFrame` event in ActionScript 3 would be placed before calling the `stage.update()` method.

With our basic EaselJS structure in place, our example should now look something as the following:

```
<!DOCTYPE html>
<html lang="en">
  <head>
    <meta charset="utf-8" />
    <title>CreateJS - EaselJS Example</title>

    <script src="easeljs-0.5.0.min.js"></script>
    <script src="MouseLine.js"></script>
```

```
<script>
  var stage;
  var mouseImage;

  function init() {
    stage = new createjs.Stage("exampleCanvas");

    createjs.Ticker.setFPS(60);
    createjs.Ticker.addListener(window);
  }

  function tick() {
    stage.update();
  }

</script>
</head>

<body onload="init()">
  <canvas id="exampleCanvas" width="800" height="600">
</body>
</html>
```

Finally, we need to import our custom class and read the mouse position property at each interval of the `Ticker` object in order to reposition the image:

```
<!DOCTYPE html>
<html lang="en">
  <head>
    <meta charset="utf-8" />
    <title>CreateJS - EaselJS Example</title>

    <style>
      canvas {
        border:1px solid #000;
      }
    </style>

    <!-- Import the EaselJS library. -->
    <script type="text/javascript" src="../js/easeljs-0.5.0.min.js">
    </script>

    <!-- Import our custom classes. -->
    <script type="text/javascript" src="MouseLine.js"></script>
```

```
<script type="text/javascript">
  // A global reference to our stage object.
  var stage;
  var line;

  /**
   * Called on body load.
   */
  function init() {
    // Initialize the stage.
      stage = new createjs.Stage("exampleCanvas");
      line = new createjs.Shape();
      stage.addChild(line);

      // Create our ticker (ie. onEnterFrame).
      // Sets the target frames per second.
      createjs.Ticker.setFPS(60);
      createjs.Ticker.addListener(window);
  }

  /**
   * The 'tick' function is continuously called on the
   specified interval set by Ticker.setFPS()
   */
  function tick() {
  line.graphics.beginStroke(createjs.Graphics.getRGB(0, 0, 0));

    MouseLine.update(line, stage.mouseX, stage.mouseY);

    stage.update();
  }

</script>
</head>

<body onload="init()">
  <!— Canvas element to be used as our Stage. -->
  <canvas id="exampleCanvas" width="800" height="600">
</body>
</html>
```

This simple example is only the tip of the iceberg when it comes to using EaselJS, but it shows off the core of how the flow of using the Canvas element as a stage can be done. EaselJS is really the core of the CreateJS bundle, as when it is utilized with any or all of the other libraries within the bundle, everything comes to life. Let's continue with the list of libraries within CreateJS by looking into the next library, TweenJS.

TweenJS

For a Flash developer, the concept of tweening an object should be nothing new. However, dealing with object animations in ActionScript 3 is far easier than using CSS3 animations or writing your own tweening engine. This is where TweenJS comes into play. TweenJS (http://www.createjs.com/#!/TweenJS) uses the common tweening syntax used in ActionScript and libraries such as TweenMax (http://www.greensock.com/tweenmax) to allow you to easily create HTML5-ready animations by allowing TweenJS to do all the object property manipulation over a specific period of time. Although TweenJS is a very simple library, the time it may be able to save you while developing a new project or converting your preexisting Flash project can be priceless. As with all the CreateJS package elements, TweenJS works extremely well with the EaseJS library, as we can demonstrate in the following code example:

```html
<!DOCTYPE html>
<html lang="en">
  <head>
    <meta charset="utf-8" />
    <title>CreateJS - TweenJS Example</title>

    <style>
      canvas {
        border:1px solid #000;
      }
    </style>

    <!-- Import the TweenJS library. -->
    <script type="text/javascript" src="easeljs-0.6.1.min.js">
    </script>
    <script type="text/javascript" src="tweenjs-0.4.1.min.js">
    </script>
<!-- Import the TweenJS Ease library as well. -->
    <script type="text/javascript" src="Ease.js"></script>


    <script type="text/javascript">
      var canvas, stage;
```

```
// Called on body load.
function init() {
  stage = new createjs.Stage("exampleCanvas");

  var circle = new createjs.Shape();
  circle.graphics.beginFill("#00FF00").drawCircle(100, 100,
  100);

  stage.addChild(circle);

  createjs.Tween.get(circle, {loop:true})
    .to({
      x:600,
    }, 1000)
    .wait(500)
    .to({
    scaleX:0.2,
      scaleY:0.2
    }, 500)
    .to({
      x:600,
      y:400
    }, 1000)
          .to({
      scaleX:1,
      scaleY:1
    },1000)
    .to({
      x:0,
      y:0
    }, 1000);

  createjs.Ticker.setFPS(30);
  createjs.Ticker.addEventListener("tick", stage);
  }
    </script>
  </head>

<body onload="init()">
  <!-- Canvas element to be used as our Stage. -->
  <canvas id="exampleCanvas" width="800" height="600">
  </body>
</html>
```

As you can see in the preceding example code, tweening elements within the stage created by EaselJS is extremely straightforward and familiar to any Flash developer. As with all the elements within CreateJS, TweenJS can be used with or without the remainder of the CreateJS suite. Therefore, if you are in need of a simple but powerful tweening engine to save massive amounts of time and overhead while animating elements in your HTML5 projects, TweenJS is definitely worth a look.

PreloadJS

Just as in Flash applications, preloading your assets within your HTML5 projects can be a critical step to ensure your content is being delivered in the proper manner to your end users. PreloadJS (`http://www.createjs.com/#!/PreloadJS`) allows for easy set up of multiple assets preloading with real-time progress feedback and queue support. As we saw with the EaselJS example, CreateJS has set up its own asset management system which easily integrates into the PreloadJS API (`http://www.createjs.com/Docs/PreloadJS/modules/PreloadJS.html`). Consider the following simplified example, which loads external audio and image assets from the Web.

```html
<!DOCTYPE html>
<html lang="en">
  <head>
    <meta charset="utf-8" />
    <title>CreateJS - PreloadJS Example</title>

    <!-- Import the PreloadJS library. -->
    <script type="text/javascript"
    src="../js/preloadjs-0.3.1.min.js">
    </script>
    <!-- Import the SoundJS library. -->
    <script type="text/javascript"
    src="../js/soundjs-0.4.1.min.js">
    </script>

    <script type="text/javascript">

      // Called on body load.
      function init() {
        var loadCount = 0;

        var queue = new createjs.LoadQueue(false);
        queue.installPlugin(createjs.Sound);
        queue.addEventListener("complete", handleComplete);
        queue.addEventListener("fileload", handleFileLoad);

        // We can load a specific external file...
```

```
queue.loadFile({id:"sound",
src:"http://www.w3schools.com/html/horse.mp3"});

// Or create a manifest which lists all of the files to load.
queue.loadManifest([
// Load some Google Doodles from the Google Servers.
        { id: "doodle1",
        src:"http://www.google.com/logos/2013/first_day_of_
        summer_2013-1536005-hp.gif" },
        { id: "doodle2",
        src:"http://www.google.com/logos/2013/first_day_of_
        winter_2013-1985005-hp.gif" },
        { id: "doodle3",
        src:"http://www.google.com/logos/2013/140th_
        anniversary_of_the_rcmp-1580006-hp.jpg" }
]);

// Called on LoadQueue file load complete.
function handleFileLoad(event) {
  var item = event.item;
      console.log("File Loaded: " + item.id);

  loadCount++;
      console.log((loadCount / 4) * 100 + "% completed.");
}

// Called on LoadQueue load complete.
function handleComplete() {
    console.log("File Loading Completed!");

    createjs.Sound.play("sound");

    var d1 = queue.getResult("doodle1");
    document.body.appendChild(d1);

    var d2 = queue.getResult("doodle2");
    document.body.appendChild(d2);

    var d3 = queue.getResult("doodle3");
    document.body.appendChild(d3);
    }
  }

</script>
</head>

<body onload="init()">
</body>
</html>
```

As we have seen in the previous examples in this book, waiting for all of the document and its assets to load prior to interacting with them is a critical step almost every JavaScript application will utilize. However, when your assets are being downloaded during a page load, there is no easy way to monitor the download or completion process. Although our typical `onload` calls will still wait until our assets are ready to be used, in many applications, the use of a progress bar can greatly enhance the end user experience during longer application load times.

Reviewing the preceding example again, you can see that we have added event listeners for each file when it is loaded as well as when all assets have completed loading. Combining the numerical value of how many assets are to be loaded with the number of assets that have been loaded, we can easily find the current preload completion percentage. To avoid a long code example, I have supplemented the use of some preload user interfaces by just using the developer console:

SoundJS

At the time of writing this book, dealing with audio and audio interaction support on all the modern HTML5 compatible browsers is unfortunately still pretty difficult. The current level of HTML5 audio support can be extremely varying from browser to browser and even more so on most mobile platforms. Properly conditioning your audio interactions and manipulations to work on every device and browser can almost seem like an impossible task. Thankfully, SoundJS is here to help and solve many of the common issues that arise with HTML5 audio development. SoundJS allows you to easily query the client's browser capabilities to ensure you are delivering audio with the proper features and plugins that the user's device supports:

```
<script>
  var preload;

  function init() {
    if (window.top != window) {
      document.getElementById("header").style.display = "none";
    }

    createjs.FlashPlugin.BASE_PATH = "../src/soundjs/"
    // Initialize the base path from this document to the Flash Plugin
    if (!createjs.SoundJS.checkPlugin(true)) {
      document.getElementById("error").style.display = "block";
      document.getElementById("content").style.display = "none";
      return;
    }

    document.getElementById("loader").className = "loader";
    var assetsPath = "assets/";
    var manifest = [
        {src:assetsPath+"Game-Break.mp3|"+assetsPath+"Game-Break.ogg",
        id:1, data: 1},
        {src:assetsPath+"Game-Spawn.mp3|"+assetsPath+"Game-Spawn.ogg",
        id:2, data: 1},
        {src:assetsPath+"Game-Shot.mp3|"+assetsPath+"Game-Shot.ogg",
        id:3, data: 1},

        {src:assetsPath+"GU-StealDaisy.mp3|"+assetsPath+"GU-
        StealDaisy.ogg", id:4, data: 1},
        {src:assetsPath+"Humm.mp3|"+assetsPath+"Humm.ogg", id:5, data:
        1},
        {src:assetsPath+"R-Damage.mp3|"+assetsPath+"R-Damage.ogg",
        id:6, data: 1},

        {src:assetsPath+"Thunder1.mp3|"+assetsPath+"Thunder1.ogg",
        id:7, data: 1},
        {src:assetsPath+"S-Damage.mp3|"+assetsPath+"S-Damage.ogg",
        id:8, data: 1},
```

```
        {src:assetsPath+"U-CabinBoy3.mp3|"+assetsPath+"U-CabinBoy3.
        ogg", id:9, data: 1},

        {src:assetsPath+"ToneWobble.mp3|"+assetsPath+"ToneWobble.ogg",
        id:10, data: 1},
        {src:assetsPath+"Game-Death.mp3|"+assetsPath+"Game-Death.ogg",
        id:11, data: 1},
        {src:assetsPath+"Game-Break.mp3|"+assetsPath+"Game-Break.ogg",
        id:12, data: 1}
          ];

    preload = new createjs.PreloadJS();
    //Install SoundJS as a plugin, then PreloadJS will initialize it
    automatically.
    preload.installPlugin(createjs.SoundJS);

    //Available PreloadJS callbacks
    preload.onFileLoad = function(event) {
        // Show the icon on loaded items.
        var div = document.getElementById(event.id);
        div.style.backgroundImage =
        "url('assets/audioButtonSheet.png')";
    };
  preload.onComplete = function(event) {
    document.getElementById("loader").className = "";
  }

    //Load the manifest and pass 'true' to start loading
    immediately. Otherwise, you can call load() manually.
    preload.loadManifest(manifest, true);
}

function stop() {
  if (preload != null) { preload.close(); }
  createjs.SoundJS.stop();
}

function playSound(target) {
    //Play the sound: play (src, interrupt, delay, offset, loop,
    volume, pan)
    var instance = createjs.SoundJS.play(target.id,
    createjs.SoundJS.INTERRUPT_NONE, 0, 0, false, 1);
  if (instance == null || instance.playState ==
  createjs.SoundJS.PLAY_FAILED) {
  return; }
  target.className = "gridBox active";
  instance.onComplete = function(instance) {
    target.className = "gridBox";
  }

  }
}
</script>
```

CreateJS Toolkit

One of the greatest aspects of CreateJS is the CreateJS Toolkit created by *Grant Skinner* (http://www.gskinner.com) and Adobe. This Toolkit is an Adobe Flash Professional plugin that enables you to easily create CreateJS-ready animations and elements from within the Flash Professional environment, something every Flash developer is already used to.

 You can get the latest news and documentation for the CreateJS Toolkit at http://www.adobe.com/devnet/createjs.html.

Setting up the Toolkit

To begin, you will need to head over to the Adobe CreateJS Toolkit page on the Adobe website (http://www.adobe.com/devnet/createjs.html) to download the latest version of the plugin to install on your machine. One of the easiest ways to find this page is by clicking on the link that may already be displayed when opening Flash CS6:

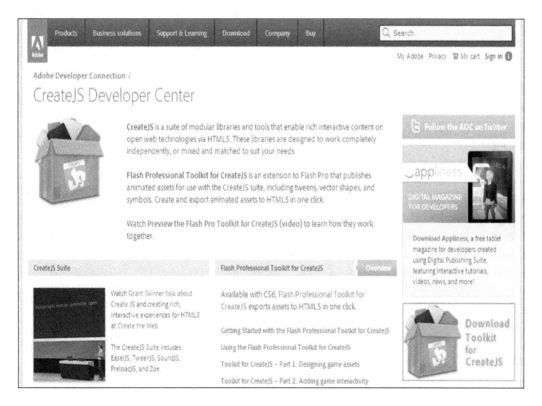

Once you have downloaded the extension, be sure to have quit any running instances of Flash CS6 and open the downloaded file within the Adobe Extension Manager CS6 application to install it into your machine's Creative Suite setup. Read over and accept the terms and conditions to finish the installation.

Once the installation is finished, you should be able to see the CreateJS Toolkit extension listed under the Flash extensions, and that's it, we are ready to start using the Toolkit back again inside Flash:

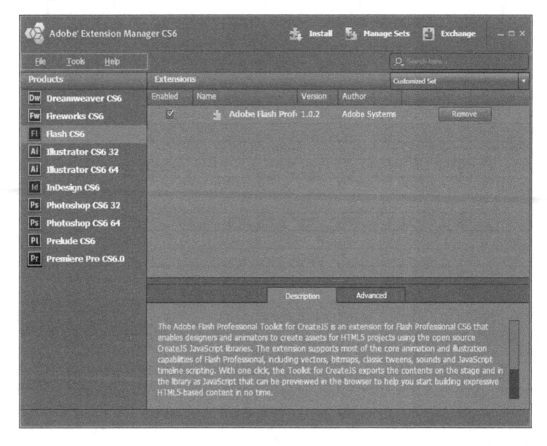

With the extension installed and Flash reopened, start a new ActionScript 3 project and open the CreateJS Toolkit window by selecting it from the **Window** dropdown. The resulting Toolkit window will look similar to the following image. From this window, you will be able to configure and publish your current project within Flash Professional with the CreateJS Toolkit rather than the traditional export to the SWF setup:

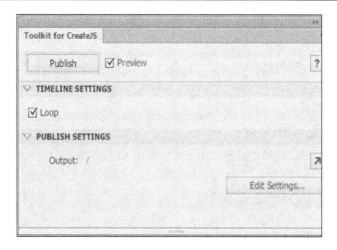

Before we dig into publishing content, it is worth looking into the configuration settings within the Toolkit window. Click on the **Edit Settings** button within the Toolkit window to open the **Publish Settings** window of the CreateJS Toolkit:

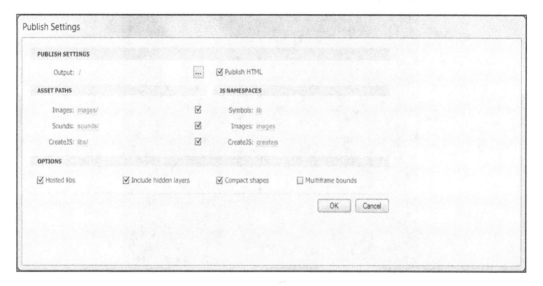

The configuration settings for publishing your content from within your Flash project is relatively straightforward. The default **Output** value will be in the same directory where the FLA file your project is saved within and asset paths are set up. The final values within the **Options** section are again pretty straight forward apart from the following values:

- **Compact Shapes**: This value compacts the code into a minimal version for drawing API class
- **Multiframe bounds**: This value calculates `boundsRect` for assets

Publishing your assets

Once your assets are all ready within your library and timelines, you can click on the **Publish** button within the Toolkit window. The result will be the typical application output but rather than being compiled into a SWF, the result is set up completely within HTML5:

The best part of this CreateJS Toolkit compiler is the ability to easily grab a piece of the exported source code and use it in a specific part of your application. This process dramatically improves the ability for designers and developers to easily work on HTML5 content and assets and update preexisting media with ease.

Reviewing the CreateJS Toolkit output

Before we finish up with the toolkit, it's worth reviewing some of the code that has been exported from its compiler. Let's check out what it has created for our space game example:

```html
<!DOCTYPE html>
<html>
<head>
<meta charset="UTF-8">
<title>CreateJS export from SpaceAssets</title>

<script src="http://code.createjs.com/easeljs-0.5.0.min.js"></script>
<script src="SpaceAssets.js"></script>

<script>
var canvas, stage, exportRoot;

function init() {
    canvas = document.getElementById("canvas");
    exportRoot = new lib.SpaceAssets();

    stage = new createjs.Stage(canvas);
    stage.addChild(exportRoot);
    stage.update();

    createjs.Ticker.setFPS(30);
    //createjs.Ticker.addListener(stage);
}
</script>
</head>

<body onload="init();" style="background-color:#D4D4D4">
    <canvas id="canvas" width="800" height="600"
    style="background-color:#ffffff">
</canvas>
</body>
</html>
```

As you can see, by all the examples and libraries above, CreateJS is a big collection of JavaScript functionality packaged into a couple of very well-maintained open source JavaScript libraries. As mentioned before, there is far more to get into than we have time to cover in this book, so be sure to head over to the CreateJS website (http://www.createjs.com) and read the documentation of the latest build.

Modernizr

An important feature we saw within the CreateJS bundle was the ability to easily check whether the client's web browser supports the intended HTML5 functionality to be used on your web page. However, only CreateJS has the ability to check for functionality compatibility for the features it uses within the libraries. If you are in need of digging deeper into checking whether your users have the appropriate functionality in their web browsers, the Modernizr project is definitely worth a look. Modernizr allows you to easily check for every feature within the HTML5 feature set with only a couple of lines of code and an external JavaScript file that is only a couple of kilobytes.

Using Modernizr

To start, you will need to head over to http://modernizr.com and download the latest version of the library. As with many JavaScript libraries, you will have the option of downloading the production or the development version of the code in order to conserve file size and bandwidth:

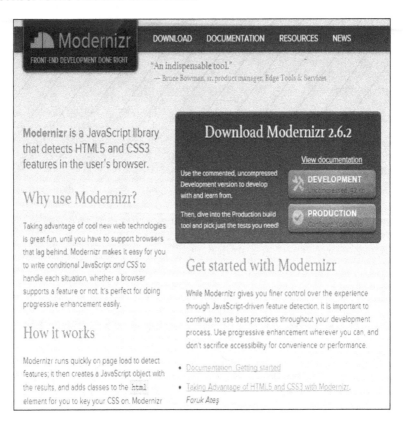

For ease of example and the sake of learning, we will download the development version of the code, which will include the entire Modernizer library. Once the JavaScript file has been downloaded, it can be included into your HTML document as you would include any JavaScript reference.

> If you are still having issues finding Modernizr setup, head over to the official installation documentation present at `http://modernizr.com/docs/#installing`.

Understanding Polyfills

The concept of a Polyfill in web development is pretty straightforward once you deal with it in an actual project. Fortunately, even if you are coming from a 100 percent Flash development background, you may have had an experience with this concept before. When embedding Flash content within an HTML page, even with the automated publish setting within Flash Professional, the resulting code will have created an HTML object element with references to the compiled SWF file. However if you look closely, or disable Flash in your web browser, you will notice there will still be a warning displayed alerting you to the fact that you need to download the Flash player as well as a link to the Flash player download page. This content is only displayed while the Flash content cannot be displayed and is an example of a Polyfill in its simplest form.

Using Polyfills in HTML5 may be a necessity in order to reach the intended audience on specific browsers and platforms. However, using Polyfills should not always be necessary. If you are trying to deliver the best experience possible, it may not be worth attempting to target browsers like IE7 with your cutting-edge HTML5 functionality.

Modernizr.load()

The `load` method within Moderizr may be one of the most powerful, yet easy-to-use utilities within the library. In a nutshell, the `load` method allows you to selectively choose which scripts and data should be loaded based on a simple condition that the user has the ability to utilize a specific piece of the HTML5 feature set. Consider the following example:

```
Modernizr.load({
  test: Modernizr.geolocation,
  yep : 'geo.js',
  nope: 'geo-polyfill.js'
});
```

This simple example shows how we can easily select which JavaScript file to load depending on whether the user has the ability to use the geolocation functionality within their browser. If the client has the ability to use geolocation API within their browser, the `geo.js` file will be loaded and the script will continue on. If the user is unable to use geolocation, the `nope` value is used and the `geo-polyfill.js` file will be loaded instead.

As you can see by this demo, Modernizr is a simple library with one main goal: to ease the mess of dealing with multiple browsers and platforms attempting to view your HTML5 content, and it does it very well.

What Modernizr can detect

Thanks to the contribution by many JavaScript developers around the world, Modernizr boasts the fact that it is able to detect and create a Polyfill for every HTML5 feature currently specified. With so many features to be listed, I will leave the researching on the Modernizr API documentation to you and give you this following code example to demonstrate some further use of this great library:

```html
<!DOCTYPE html>
<html lang="en">
  <head>
    <meta charset="utf-8" />
    <title>Modernizr Example</title>

    <!-- Import the Modernizr library. -->
    <script type="text/javascript"
    src="modernizr-latest.js">
    </script>

    <script>
      function init() {
        // Touch
        if(Modernizr.touch){
          console.log('You are on a touch enabled device.');
        } else {
          console.log('You are not on a touch enabled device.');
        }

        // WebGL
        if(Modernizr.webgl){
          console.log('You are on a WebGL enabled browser.');
        } else {
          console.log('You are on a WebGL enabled browser.');
```

```
      }

      // Display all values
      console.log(Modernizr);
    }
  </script>
</head>

<body onload="init()">
</body>
</html>
```

As you can see in the example above, the implementation of Modernizr is extremely straightforward. Conditions are easy to recognize as their naming conventions almost directly match the feature set which can be tested. To get a better understanding of the ever-growing API that Modernizr offers, head over to the official project documentation at `http://modernizr.com/docs`.

CSS media queries

Although we have already touched on CSS3 media queries in the previous chapters, it is worth stopping to make note of them in this chapter as well. If the active viewport was to change size while dealing with setting up your content to be viewable on all devices and to have a responsive layout and display set up, CSS3 media queries can easily allow you to avoid manipulating any of your site content and only manipulate the styles appended to them. This concept is great not only for implementing it on all your desktop and mobile projects but can be utilized for much more. Consider the following list of some of the properties that can be queried directly from within your CSS source:

- **All**: This property allows *all* the devices to listen to this property
- **Braille**: This property is used for braille-tactile feedback devices
- **Embossed**: This property is used for paged braille printers
- **Handheld**: This property is used for handheld devices (smartphones and tablets do *not* listen to this!)
- **Print**: This property is used for paged material and for documents viewed on screen in print preview mode
- **Projection**: This property is used for projected presentations, for example, projectors
- **Screen**: This property is used primarily for color computer screens and smartphones

- **Speech**: This property is used for speech synthesizers
- **tty**: This property is used for media using a fixed-pitch character grid such as teletypes, terminals, or portable devices with limited display capabilities
- **Tv**: This property is used for television-type devices such as low resolution, color, limited-scroll-ability screens with available audio

Properly utilized media queries can easily allow you to target a broad range of devices by allowing your content to respond to the specific size, platform and setup of the browser viewing it:

```
#mycontent {
    background-repeat: no-repeat;
    background-image:url('image.gif');
}

@media screen and (min-width: 1200px) {
    # mycontent {
        background-image:url('large-image.gif');
    }
}

@media print {
    #mycontent {
        display: none;
    }
}
```

Summary

In this chapter, we have covered some of the options available to you when converting or porting your existing Flash applications to HTML5 as well as methods to enable users to properly view their content on any device. We dug into each of the great libraries that make up CreateJS, from emulating the Flash Display List in JavaScript, to animating elements with the traditional ActionScript 3 tweening syntax. We checked out how useful the CreateJS Toolkit is to anyone with any prior knowledge of the Adobe Flash Professional IDE, and how assets can be compiled directly from the stage and library ready for use in web documents. We also learned about unifying your development experience by using libraries such as Modernizr. By querying browser feature support, you can easily decide whether an alternate display method or shim is necessary to enable the user to have a proper experience.

6
HTML5 Frameworks and Libraries

One of the most exciting aspects of working with any programming language is discovering new libraries and frameworks which can be utilized to extend and simplify the code that drives your applications. With the rise in popularity surrounding HTML5 development on many different platforms and devices, the amount of code that has been made publicly available to aid anyone with their HTML5 development has grown at an outstanding rate. In this chapter, we will overview some of the most popular libraries and frameworks, which you can utilize at any time to not only save you time, but also allow you to focus more on your user experience rather than writing complex JavaScript to work within every modern browser.

In this chapter, we will cover the following things:

- How frameworks and libraries can make your life easier
- Things we can create with a framework or library
- An overview of the ever-popular jQuery library and jQuery mobile framework
- Building **HTML** pages with the **HTML5** Boilerplate template
- Creating responsive unified page layouts with Bootstrap
- Animating your content using familiar tweening engines with GreenSock's Animation Platform
- Developing your JavaScript in the popular **MVC** structure with `Backbone.js`
- Programming hardware-accelerated 3D graphics with WebGL and `Three.js`
- An overview of JavaScript compilers by checking out Google's V8 project
- Pushing JavaScript to the limits of application development with `Node.js`

How frameworks and libraries can make your life easier?

From an outsider's or non-developer's perspective, the idea of using someone else's code within your project may bring up many negative connotations. If you're using the code that has been created and freely distributed by someone you don't know, how can you trust that it performs as advertised and won't show malicious functionality? Traditionally, when importing libraries and using frameworks in any programming language, only a small fraction of the entire code base will be utilized. This results in a larger overhead and possible implication on application runtime execution speeds. As valid as all of these arguments are, many of the popular concerns around using external libraries and frameworks have been solved. The concept of using external resources within **HTML5** projects has become so common that JavaScript has easily become the most popular programming language shared on the social coding website GitHub (`https://github.com/languages`).

Thanks to sites such as GitHub (`http://github.com`), the concept of sharing and contributing to open source projects has exploded. With the aid of external libraries and frameworks, developers can easily move from a concept or an idea in their mind to having a prototype built in a matter of minutes to hours. Developers can also focus more on the actual concept integration rather than dealing with small issues such as browser optimization and platform support. Therefore, as the environment around developers expands and the open source projects that back your projects grow, upgrading your external dependencies will result in having the latest and greatest support for your applications' feature set.

What can I do with JavaScript frameworks and libraries?

As you have seen in the chapters up to this point in the book, the support for JavaScript within modern web browsers is getting better every day. The idea of moving the entire typical application flow for all application types to the Web is becoming more of a reality as time passes. JavaScript is now starting to make its way into operating system applications on both desktop and mobile. With this new reach to so many platforms, JavaScript can do many things you may not even be aware of at this point in time. As a developer with experience in creating Flash applications, you may find that you will have another upper hand in terms of moving to **HTML5** when it comes to understanding and implementing many of the new and interesting JavaScript APIs. From microphone and camera integration to multi-touch gestures on a touch-enabled device, the amount of things you can do with JavaScript is growing every day. To get you a little more excited about what is possible, here is a short list of some of the great things the HTML5 applications can do:

- Dynamically control **CSS** properties to create 2D and 3D animations
- Real-time audio and video streaming from the client camera and microphone
- Render 3D graphics and high frame rate with hardware acceleration
- Compile the JavaScript directly to the machine code to be run as a server or application

Finding the right library or framework for your project

When it comes to finding the right external resources to include into your project, it can become a tedious task of sorting through projects as all seem to do the same thing. With the current popularity of JavaScript development, one can only expect that this issue will continue to worsen as more and more developers publish their projects. Thankfully the development community is on your side! So where does one go to find the latest and great open source projects to use within their **HTML5** projects? Well, as with anything on the Internet, there is no one-stop shop for finding all of these available projects. However, as the time passes, more and more projects are being hosted on GitHub (`http://github.com`), which easily allows the developers to share and contribute to projects while utilizing the Git version control system.

The best aspect of social coding websites such as GitHub when attempting to find new projects is not only the ability to sort projects by specific programming language, but by the current popularity of the project as well (`https://github.com/explore`). GitHub ranks project popularity by the number of other users who watch, fork, and contribute to the project in question. So just by sorting those values, countless popular and up-to-date projects will be displayed. Of course, using the site search will only refine your results when looking for specific topics and platforms:

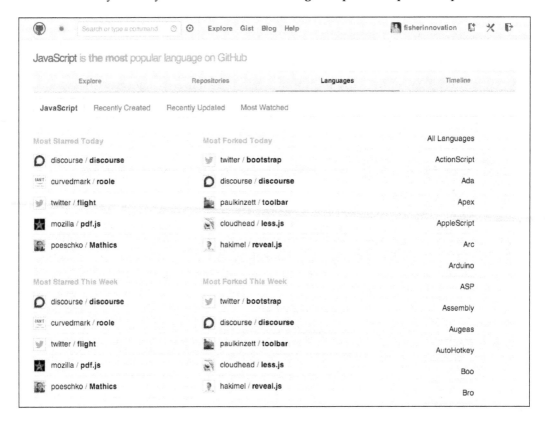

So after some digging around, you may have found a couple of libraries or frameworks that you consider to be an appropriate solution to your needs. The next decision is narrowing down the selection to something you can start with. So how do you choose? Well, obviously there is no simple answer to this question either. However, there are some important considerations worth making prior to downloading and implementing the library or framework you have located. The first consideration should always be what your expected end result is. If you are just having fun writing the code for yourself to learn about new frameworks, you pretty much have free rein to download and test anything you wish. If you are considering using this code for professional use or a project that may be open to public, spending some time on researching some more specifics about the project in question will help you keep out of trouble down the road. If you happen to find an open source project of interest but the project contains little or no development activity, be it bug fixes or updates, chances are the development team behind it has moved on to new projects. Therefore, the version of code you will download and use will require you to maintain and update it in order to implement and use it without any issues. Chances are if the developer who created the project in the beginning has abandoned it, they won't be coming back anytime soon to specifically help you with your issues. On the other hand, if you are looking at a project that has just been born or is still in early development, chances are if you implement the project into yours, you will need to manually correct any critical issues in the dependencies back into your project whenever they are made. Although this is typical of most development situations, it is always worth keeping in the back of your mind during the early stages (picking and choosing external assets) that you may use this code in the lifetime of your project.

In order to keep you updated with some features of what is out there, let's overview some of the great open source projects waiting to be used by you in your next project.

jQuery

There is no way we can start off with the list of JavaScript libraries without starting with jQuery. Up to this point in this book, we have yet to use jQuery in any of our examples. However, if you have spent any time looking into web development prior to reading this book, chances are you have already heard of this project. Originally released in 2006, jQuery has risen up to easily become the most popular JavaScript library in use as (at the time of writing this book) more than 55 percent of the top 10,000 most visited websites on the Internet. Due to the overwhelming use of jQuery in projects from big to small scattered all over the Internet, it has become an almost essential skill in the **HTML5** developer's arsenal.

 To keep you updated with everything related to jQuery, head over to the project website `http://jquery.com`.

Of course with the overwhelming popularity jQuery has had, comes the overwhelming amount of documentation, examples, and tutorials for using it. Therefore, rather than dedicating a vast amount of time looking at all of the features in jQuery, we will just overview the fundamentals of how it works and what you can do with it.

As with all the topics in this book, if you are so inclined to learn more, a quick Google search will be extremely helpful:

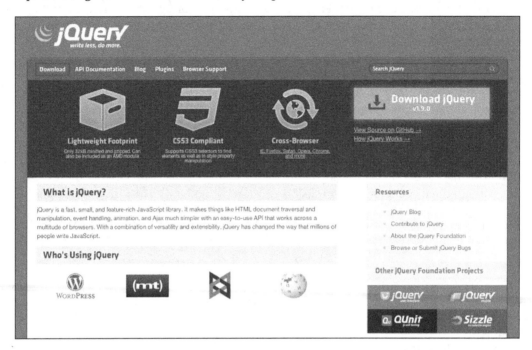

So what actually is jQuery? Well, jQuery is a relatively small JavaScript library to aid in all sorts of common JavaScript development tasks and issues. With easily selecting elements within your document, creating and handling events of all sorts, animating elements within your document, calling and retrieving external data with Ajax, jQuery can give you a much simpler, easy-to-use, and unified syntax that will work across a ton of web browsers. The best part about jQuery is that it can do all of this work with only the cost of importing a JavaScript file that is less than 50 KB.

Putting jQuery into action

As with all JavaScript projects, the best way to understand jQuery is by example. So let's quickly touch on how to properly add jQuery into your project as well as how to start using its functionality within your code.

It all starts by heading over to the jQuery project website to obtain the latest stable version of the project (http://jquery.com). It is probably worth noting that with almost all the actively developed open source projects, you will find a number of different build types available for you to download and use. Generally, when visiting a project website such as the jQuery website, you will usually find a link to download the latest stable release of the project. Stable releases of the actively developed projects are generally not the latest versions, but the stable version is one that is tested and approved to be used by the public. As the contributions to the project continue to roll in from the developers, they will continue to roll in until the development team has approved the current code base to be ready for public usage. Therefore, the entire time between each version release of the software, there will be a development version of the project, which in many cases you can also download and use, of course with the known possibility of encountering new and undocumented issues.

After reaching the jQuery download page (`http://jquery.com/download`), you will have the option of downloading either the compressed or uncompressed version of the current releases. The reason for compressing the code is to keep file size down and allowing for faster load times when requested by your web server. Compressing or condensing JavaScript is actually something you can easily do with your code and we will continue to dig deeper into that topic in the later chapters. For now, you can go ahead and save either of those jQuery source JavaScript files on your computer, preferably within the directory you will be creating your **HTML5** project. Once you have created an empty HTML document, importing jQuery is as simple as importing any other external JavaScript document:

```
<!DOCTYPE html>
<html lang="en">
  <head>
    <meta charset="utf-8" />
    <title>jQuery Importing Example</title>
    <script src="jquery.min.js"></script>
  </head>

  <body>
  </body>
</html>
```

With that hard work completed, you can now utilize all of jQuery's functionality within your project. However, there is a key place you will usually need to start from and that is controlling the point at which your code is ready to be executed. Up to this point, we have used a number of common techniques to accomplish this task such as setting the `body onload` parameter to a JavaScript function.

```
<body onload="init()">
```

Or setting an `onload` event on the `window` object:

```
window.onload = function() {
    // Start executing your code here...
}
```

One issue with this way of calling your JavaScript is the fact that this way of waiting for your document to load includes waiting for all the image assets to be loaded including uncontrolled external assets such as banner ads. Therefore, jQuery has created its own document-ready event handler syntax for circumventing this issue. Generally with all jQuery-based projects, the first snippet of code to append will be the document ready handler:

```
$( document ).ready( function() {
  // Start executing your code here...
});
```

Selecting elements with jQuery

One of the greatest aspects of jQuery is its selector engine, otherwise known as Sizzle (`http://sizzlejs.com`). What makes the selector engine so great is how easy it makes the entire development process when dealing with interacting elements within your HTML document. Consider our working example with some simple content additions within the body:

```
<!DOCTYPE html>
<html lang="en">
  <head>
    <meta charset="utf-8" />
    <title>jQuery Importing Example</title>

    <!-- Always import external libraries before your custom
    site code. -->
    <script src="jquery.min.js"></script>

    <script>
      $( document ).ready( function() {
        // Start executing your code here...
      });
    </script>
  </head>

  <body>
    <div>
        <p>
```

```
        <a href="http://www.google.com">Go to Google</a>
        </p>
    </div>
  </body>
</html>
```

As simple as this page layout is, each of the elements that make up the page can be easily controlled through the code by using jQuery selectors. To append an event listener to our link to Google, we can add it within our document ready callback function:

```
$( document ).ready(function() {
  $("a").click(function(event) {
    alert("Tell Google I said hello!");
  });
});
```

Although the preceding example is very simplistic, there are a couple of key aspects, which should be covered right off the bat. jQuery selector syntax relies on the `$()` syntax. In case of our example, within the selector syntax brackets, we supply the parameter "a" to select all of the `<a>` element tags within the body of our document. Just selecting an element isn't going to get you too far; therefore, the next step in the example is to chain a click event listener to the selected elements. Of course the click event is far from being the only available event you could apply to an element, you can reference the event documentation to see the entire list (`http://api.jquery.com/category/events`). The final step is to define the method to be used on event callback, and in our example, we have simply defined the function directly into the callback parameter.

With this change appended, saved, and then reloaded within a browser, the resulting action will be an alert dialog displayed when the link is clicked, followed by the page location (`http://google.com`). As you can see, our event listener has been fired before the predefined action of moving to the referenced **URL** in the anchor tag. The selector engine used in tandem with the vast amounts of jQuery events allows you to control a ton of user and web interactions that can occur within your pages.

Overriding the predefined actions is easily done as well. As you can see within the callback function defined in our example, when it is called, it passes the event variable into the method. This event property is used to control the event and can easily be manipulated or completely overridden:

```
$(document).ready(function() {
    $("a").click(function(event) {
            alert("You're not going anywhere!");
            event.preventDefault();
    });
});
```

By calling the preventDefault() method on the event object, we can disable the default action of the event and use our own code to control the result.

Controlling CSS via jQuery

Another great aspect of jQuery is the ability to easily control the look and feel of your elements with CSS3 properties. Getting and setting CSS values on any elements is a breeze when using jQuery selectors and CSS methods:

```
$("#example").css("width", 200);
$("#example").css("height", 300);
```

As you can see in the preceding example, setting the CSS properties for the width and height of a specific element is pretty straightforward. We could simplify these two lines of CSS property updates into one by passing the CSS properties to an object rather than passing them independently:

```
$("#example").css({ width:200, height:300 });
```

It is the equivalent of appending the following within your document's CSS structure:

```
#example {
  width:200px;
  height:300px;
}
```

CSS manipulation in jQuery isn't just for setting the width and height of an element in your document. jQuery now has full support for CSS3 properties, which include properties such as rounded corners, text effects, opacity, shadowing 2D and 3D transformations, and filters.

CSS animations

Since controlling CSS properties for pretty much any element via jQuery is possible, so is the ability to easily animate them as well.

Before looking at some examples, there are some important points to note. As mentioned in *Chapter 2*, *Preparing for the Battle*, and *Chapter 3*, *Scalability, Limitations, and Effects*, when covering CSS properties and their values in comparison to the ActionScript 3 API, the values when positioning elements within the document are not based on the traditional x and y value set. Rather when animating the position of an element, the element position value should be noted to properly define the right values to move an element when you intend for it to move around:

```html
<!DOCTYPE html>
<html lang="en">
  <head>
    <meta charset="utf-8" />
    <title>jQuery CSS Animation Example</title>

    <style>
      html, body {
        margin:0;
        padding:0;
        height:100%;
      }
      #example {
        width:200px;
        margin:auto;
        background-color:#EFEFEF;
        border:1px solid #000;
        text-align:center;
        cursor:pointer;
      }
    </style>

    <script src="jquery.min.js"></script>
    <script>
      $( document ).ready( function() {
        $('#example').click(function(event){
          // Animate the #example element
          $("#example").animate({
              marginLeft: '0',
              width:'100%',
              height:'100%',
              fontSize:'40px'
```

```
        }, 500, function(event) {
        // Update the element paragraph inner HTML.
          $("#example p").html('Animation Complete!');
        });
      });
    });
  </script>
</head>

<body>
  <div id="example">
    <p>Click To Begin Animation</p>
  </div>
  </body>
</html>
```

Requesting external data with jQuery Ajax

Thanks to the built-in `URLLoader` and `URLRequest` classes available in ActionScript 3, requesting external data either local to your project or external on the Web is pretty straightforward. A `URLLoader` is created, along with a `URLRequest` object containing the path reference to the data. Finally the `URLRequest` object is passed into the loader object and the `load` method is called:

```
Var loader:URLLoader = new URLLoader();
var request:URLRequest = new URLRequest("data.xml");
loader.load(request);
```

Of course to finish this example properly, you would need to add event handlers to catch the return of the data and know when you can begin manipulating or utilizing it. Nevertheless, the concept of calling and retrieving external data from your application is probably not new to you.

When developing your applications in JavaScript, the goto for this type of functionality is **AJAX**. **AJAX (Asynchronous JavaScript and XML)**, is the concept of exchanging data with your web server while the client is using your web page without the need for ever reloading the page. The use of **AJAX** on the Web today is so widespread that it is almost impossible to go a day without utilizing it in one of the many websites or services you reply on. A perfect example of this is the infinite scrolling when viewing your Facebook Timelines or Twitter Feeds. As you scroll down the page viewing content, the JavaScript running under the hood detects you are getting to the bottom of the page and calls the server for more data to continually populate the list. Traditionally, this would be done by applying the data to multiple pages and requiring the user to refresh the page for each view.

So what can jQuery do to aid in the development of your application's **AJAX** functionality? Well, within the jQuery library are a number of methods specifically designed to deal with the **AJAX** requests and request types.

In its most basic form, the jQuery `load` method can retrieve external data and place it within a selected element all in a single line of JavaScript:

```
$('#myElement').load('example.html');
```

Of course the external asset does not need to be an **HTML** document. **XML**, JavaScript, JSON, Plain Text, and HTML documents are all supported within AJAX requests.

Understandably you probably don't always want to just place the incoming data from your **AJAX** request right into your document, so a response handler is usually commonly placed amongst these types of calls. This can be achieved by using the **AJAX** method itself in a self-instantiating jQuery syntax:

```
$.ajax({
    url: 'example.html'
}).done(function(data) {
  if(data != '') {
    $("body").append(data);
  }
});
```

Now with the data returned, you can easily manipulate and verify the returned data from the **AJAX** call before assuming it is ready to include within your document.

Data can also be supplied with the call for external data. Depending on the requirements by the script in the referenced document, you can choose to send data over an **HTTP** GET request:

```
$.get("getmyphotos.php", { user:"johnsmith", id:"200" })
.done(function(data) {
    console.log(data);
});
```

Alternatively, you can choose to send data over an HTTP POST request:

```
$.post("getmyphotos.php", { user:"johnsmith", id:"200" })
.done(function(data) {
    console.log(data);
});
```

jQuery Mobile

In the recent past, the team behind jQuery has released jQuery Mobile (http://jquerymobile.com), which creates a unified **HTML5** user interface for developers to build the content on, and will be properly displayed over a wide range of modern mobile devices. Just like jQuery itself, jQuery Mobile is extremely lightweight and even comes with prebuilt packaged themes to be used within the themeable element designs. jQuery Mobile aims to ease your mobile development process by allowing you to focus more on your application content rather than writing special shims and conditional code for browser support. Updates are released from the development team at a pace that is able to keep up with the astounding speed of the mobile device marketplace. Therefore, you can write mobile web applications that will run on the maximum number of devices possible, without having to target each device specifically:

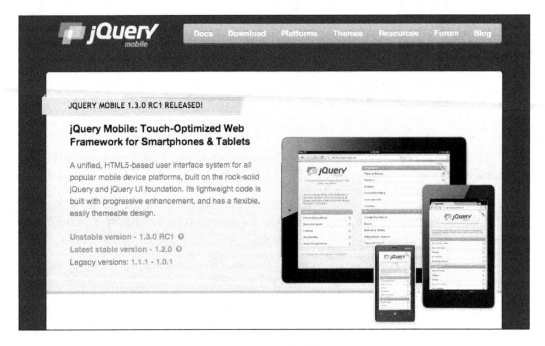

Since its initial release, jQuery Mobile has grown to be used by big and small websites throughout the Web. The core aspects of the jQuery Mobile framework include the usage of pages, dialogs, toolbars, listviews, and buttons. By developing your web pages and content around these core elements within the framework, you can layout your pages for mobile without ever needing to open Photoshop.

jQuery Mobile makes great use of Custom Data Attributes, a new feature within **HTML5**. If you examine the example multipage jQuery Mobile layout below, you will see many element properties that use the data-* syntax. These are the Custom Data Attributes that anyone can now implement into their **HTML5** project. They can have any string, which is at least a single character and can be utilized to easily declare values when setting element properties:

```
<body>
  <div data-role="page" id="one">
    <div data-role="header">
      <h1>Page 1</h1>
    </div>
    <div data-role="content" >
      <h2>Page One</h2>
      <p><a href="#two" data-role="button">Show Page 2</a></p>
      <p><a href="page3.html"
      data-role="button">Show Page 3</a></p>
    </div>
    <div data-role="footer" data-theme="d">
      <h4>Page Footer</h4>
    </div>
  </div>

  <div data-role="page" id="two" data-theme="a">
    <div data-role="header">
      <h1>Page 2</h1>
    </div>

    <div data-role="content" data-theme="a">
      <h2>Page Two</h2>
      <p><a href="#one" data-direction="reverse"
      data-role="button" data-theme="b">Back to Page 1</a></p>
    </div>

    <div data-role="footer">
      <h4>Page Footer</h4>
    </div>
  </div>
</body>
```

As you can see, this single **HTML** file is actually two pages long separated into DIV elements with the `data-role="page"` element. Now when the jQuery Mobile framework loads the **HTML** file containing these two pages, only the initial page will display and the second will wait for user interaction to slide into view. Within the first page you can see that the link to our second page is actually just an anchor tag, as it uses the # character prior to referencing the ID of another page within the current **HTML** document. To further demonstrate this difference, there is a second link to the third page within the initial pages navigation, which links out to an external **HTML** document in the traditional manner.

By default, when a new page is requested, the data is loaded (if it hasn't been already) and displayed within a DIV element, which is actually out of view to the end user. When the loading of data and document preparation is completed, the new page then animates from right to left into the visible display of the user. This content animation is typical of many modern mobile device application user interfaces therefore making your application more familiar to your end user:

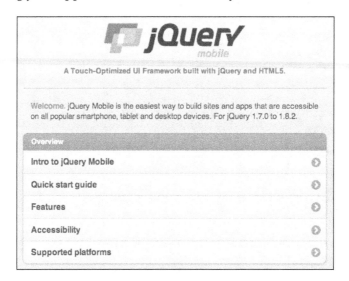

One of the easiest and most refined examples of jQuery Mobile in action is the documentation for the framework. As you can see in the preceding screenshot, by default, jQuery Mobile's user interface looks very mobile-friendly. The buttons are big and easily stretch to fit the page, allowing the users to easily select menu items without worrying about a misclick. Header and paragraph text is easy to read and positioned in a pixel perfect manner. Icons are added to specific elements within the documentation navigation. What isn't visible in a printed screenshot is the responsiveness of the layout. To better illustrate the importance of responsiveness on mobile, here is a screenshot of the same jQuery Mobile documentation webpage in an even larger window size:

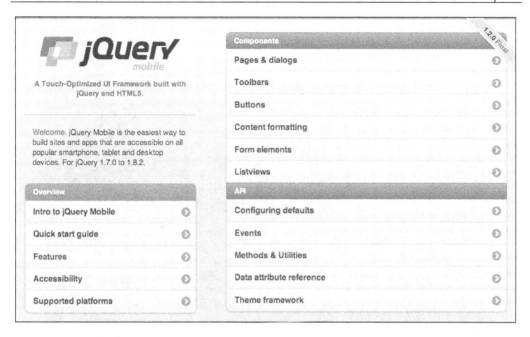

As you can see, the same page has now responded to the larger browser window size and reoriented the page layout to better fit the visible display area. Rather than have multiple designs for the same page to have displayed on different browser sizes, jQuery Mobile uses **CSS** Media Queries to define the current viewport size and orient the page content to fit properly. The greatest part of this process when building a site with jQuery Mobile is the fact that you don't need to bother writing a single line of **CSS** or define special **CSS** Media Queries yourself.

HTML5 Boilerplate

Libraries like jQuery are great for aiding you in coding your JavaScript with ease but getting your project up and running is a different question. Page layouts, browser failsafes, and tracking codes are usually all the things you will eventually add to your project and these are just some of the great features within the **HTML5** Boilerplate (`http://html5boilerplate.com`). The HTML5 Boilerplate isn't technically a library or a framework, as at its core, it is simply a starting point for creating HTML5 documents.

However, because of its simplicity, eagerness to stay up-to-date with all the changes around the Web, and a large group of open source contributions behind it, this **HTML5** template is a great start when working on any project big or small:

Upon downloading the latest version of the **HTML5** Boilerplate from the project website, you will find a collection of files that not only includes your basic ready-to-go `index.html` file and the file's references within, but a group of other common files usually found within the base level website directory on the public web server.

To understand exactly what this template looks like and what it actually does for you, let's take a quick glance at the following default `index.html` file:

```
<!DOCTYPE html>
<!--[if lt IE 7]>        <html class="no-js lt-ie9 lt-ie8 lt-ie7">
<![endif]-->
<!--[if IE 7]>          <html class="no-js lt-ie9 lt-ie8">
<![endif]-->
<!--[if IE 8]>          <html class="no-js lt-ie9"> <![endif]-->
<!--[if gt IE 8]><!--> <html class="no-js"> <!--<![endif]-->
    <head>
        <meta charset="utf-8">
        <meta http-equiv="X-UA-Compatible"
        content="IE=edge,chrome=1">
        <title></title>
        <meta name="description" content="">
        <meta name="viewport" content="width=device-width">

        <!-- Place favicon.ico and apple-touch-icon.png in the
        root directory -->
```

```
        <link rel="stylesheet" href="css/normalize.css">
        <link rel="stylesheet" href="css/main.css">
        <script src="js/vendor/modernizr-2.6.2.min.js"></script>
    </head>
    <body>
        <!--[if lt IE 7]>
            <p class="chromeframe">You are using an
            <strong>outdated</strong> browser. Please <a
            href="http://browsehappy.com/">upgrade your browser</a> or
            <a href="http://www.google.com/
            chromeframe/?redirect=true"> activate Google Chrome
            Frame</a> to improve your experience.</p>
        <![endif]-->

        <!-- Add your site or application content here -->
        <p>Hello world! This is HTML5 Boilerplate.</p>

        <script
        src="//ajax.googleapis.com/ajax/libs/jquery/1.9.0/jquery.min.
        js"></script>
        <script>window.jQuery || document.write('<script
        src="js/vendor/jquery-1.9.0.min.js"><\/script>')</script>
        <script src="js/plugins.js"></script>
        <script src="js/main.js"></script>

        <!-- Google Analytics: change UA-XXXXX-X to be your site's
        ID. -->
        <script>
            var _gaq=[['_setAccount',
            'UA-XXXXX-X'],['_trackPageview']];
            (function(d,t){var g=d.createElement(t),s=d.
            getElementsByTagName(t)[0];
            g.src=('https:'==location.protocol?'//ssl':'//www')
            +'.google-analytics.com/ga.js';
            s.parentNode.insertBefore(g,s)}(document,'script'));
        </script>
    </body>
</html>
```

As you can see, this template HTML file is doing quite a bit and thankfully it is extremely well documented. From top to bottom, this example is full of browser checks and failsafes, references to website icons for web and mobile platforms, references to Modernizr to clean and set the development environment to a unified platform to start from, and references to jQuery and default code including Google Analytics visitor tracking.

HTML5 Boilerplate is developed under the MIT license and even includes some refined and optimized web server configurations to use if you are interested in streamlining the way your web server delivers its content.

Bootstrap

If you're like me and enjoy writing code rather than dealing with designing and creating pages in Photoshop, you may be very interested in Bootstrap, created by two Twitter employees. Bootstrap is an HTML5 framework designed to allow developers to easily create powerful and responsive page layouts and designs based on a 12-column grid system. With support for rendering your page layouts properly on all modern devices and browsers, Bootstrap cuts out much of the need to write hours of CSS and JavaScript in order to properly get your content displayed in a universal manner for all the users, no matter how they are attempting to view your content:

Getting up and running with a new project developed with Bootstrap, like many of the projects covered in this chapter, is painfully simple. Simply head over to the project website at `http://twitter.github.com/bootstrap` and download the latest version. Once downloaded and unarchived, move the downloaded directory contents into the root of your project directory. You will notice that the downloaded Bootstrap files do not contain an HTML file for you to begin working from, rather it expects you to generate your own. The reason for this is due to the fact that pages are not defined to a specific layout template. Bootstrap utilizes the grid layout system to allow developers to easily place their site content in the format of a grid to easily allow a properly defined layout that can easily respond to dynamic browser window sizes:

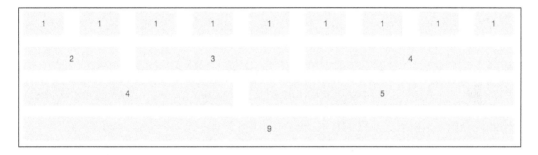

The default bootstrap layout is built on a 12-column grid layout with an infinite amount of rows, as an overflow of rows will just result in typical web page scrolling. Reviewing the example grid layouts in the preceding image, you can pretty much visualize every website you use on a daily basis and how it is arranged within a grid like this. Because this grid layout system is so valuable for almost any web page design, it can be of use to you on almost every HTML5 project you encounter in the future.

If you are still not convinced that Bootstrap is a viable solution for your website, head over to the **Examples** section of the Bootstrap project website to check out the latest list of popular websites that are using this project `http://twitter.github.com/bootstrap/getting-started.html#examples`.

Bootstrap add-ons

With the popularity of Bootstrap growing at such a fast rate, the amount of user contributions has begun to follow suit. Many of these third-party external plug-ins and features can be added on to the existing Bootstrap setup, to extend its base functionality. Let's take a quick glance at some of the most popular of these projects to give you some sense of what is available.

StyleBootstrap.info

Although Bootstrap comes packaged with a number of different color choices to choose from when creating elements, the chance you would want to further that level of customization is pretty high. `StyleBootstrap.info` (`http://stylebootstrap.info`) is a great online resource to easily customize the look and feel of your Bootstrap setup with a simple click and select user interface. Once you have completed your design, the site will generate the necessary **CSS** files for you to download and include within your project.

Font Awesome

Another great library that extends the already existing feature set within Bootstrap is Font Awesome (`http://fortawesome.github.com/Font-Awesome`). Although it may sound like this is a new font addition to the framework, it is actually an additional icon set, which can be easily implemented into your design. The reason for the referencing to the idea of a font is that the icon set is actually implemented within a packaged font to enable a scalable vector graphic rather than the typical bitmap graphic found in **HTML** documents. Since you're coming from a Flash background you probably already understand how important vector graphics can be when scaling images, you can probably see why using the font packaging concept makes for an extremely easy-to-use library. All of the icons within the package have specific names and can be easily implemented into your page by calling that unique icon name as a class in an **HTML** element:

icon-adjust	icon-edit	icon-magic	icon-share
icon-asterisk	icon-envelope	icon-magnet	icon-share-alt
icon-ban-circle	icon-envelope-alt	icon-map-marker	icon-shopping-cart
icon-bar-chart	icon-exchange	icon-minus	icon-signal
icon-barcode	icon-exclamation-sign	icon-minus-sign	icon-signin
icon-beaker	icon-external-link	icon-mobile-phone	icon-signout
icon-beer	icon-eye-close	icon-money	icon-sitemap
icon-bell	icon-eye-open	icon-move	icon-sort
icon-bell-alt	icon-facetime-video	icon-music	icon-sort-down
icon-bolt	icon-fighter-jet	icon-off	icon-sort-up
icon-book	icon-film	icon-ok	icon-spinner
icon-bookmark	icon-filter	icon-ok-circle	icon-star
icon-bookmark-empty	icon-fire	icon-ok-sign	icon-star-empty
icon-briefcase	icon-flag	icon-pencil	icon-star-half
icon-bullhorn	icon-folder-close	icon-picture	icon-tablet
icon-calendar	icon-folder-open	icon-plane	icon-tag

As you can see in the preceding screenshot, which displays only a small section of the available icons in the package, each icon has a specific name. As specified by the project documentation, the best way to append an icon into your document is to call the unique icon name within the class attribute of the `<i>` or italics **HTML** tag. As an example, if we wanted to place a book icon beside the word "Books" in our document, the HTML syntax would be represented as follows:

```
<p><i class="icon-book"></i> Books</p>
```

Since the italics tag can be placed within almost any HTML element, this allows you to place the icon wherever you need, like inside a Bootstrap customized button:

```
<a href="books.html" class="btn">
<i class="icon-book"></i> Books
</a>
```

Again, it is worth noting that since font packages are saved in vector formats to allow for dynamic font sizes, the icons within the default Bootstrap setup as well as this project are all in vector format as well. To change the size of an icon within your document, you can just set the `font-size` property or append it into an element that already has the font styles configured.

bootstrap-wysihtml5

If you're planning on building web applications that require large amount of text-based user input, the Bootstrap **WYSIWYG** (What You See Is What You Get) library is worth a look (`http://jhollingworth.github.com/bootstrap-wysihtml5`). With only a few lines of code, you can easily implement elegant tool-based input forms for your users to construct formatted **HTML**-based text content:

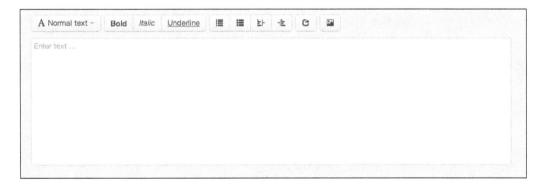

Although simple, this is just another one of the many great examples of what is freely distributed on the Internet and ready for you to use in your projects at any time.

Hammer.js

If you are planning on moving into the fast moving world of mobile web development, dealing with new events such as touch interaction is going to be a must. Although traditional JavaScript mouse events will translate directly to the basic touch events when used on a touch-enabled device, events such as swiping and pinching are not common to traditional desktop user interaction (`http://eightmedia.github.com/hammer.js`).

Hammer.js currently supports tap, double tap, swipe, hold, pinch (transform), and drag events, and is easily implemented into any preexisting website regardless of whether you are using jQuery or not. Due to the library's simplicity, the resulting file size is only 2 KB when minified and compressed:

```html
<!DOCTYPE html>
<html lang="en">
  <head>
    <meta charset="utf-8" />
    <title>Hammer.js Example</title>

    <style>
      body {
        padding:10px;
      }
          #touch-area {
              border: 5px dashed #000;
              text-align: center;
              width: 100%;
              line-height:10px;
              padding-top:200px;
              padding-bottom:200px;
          }
          #touch-area p {
          font-size: 30px;
          }
          #touch-area p.subtext {
                  font-size:12px;
                  color:#666;
          }
      </style>
```

```
        <script type="text/javascript"
        src="http://code.jquery.com/jquery-1.9.1.min.js">
        </script>
      <script type="text/javascript" src="lib/hammer.js"></script>
      <script type="text/javascript"
      src="lib/jquery.specialevent.hammer.js">
      </script>
      <script>
        function hammerLog(event){
            event.preventDefault();
            $('#output').prepend( "Type: " + event.type + ", Fingers: "
            + event.touches.length + ", Direction: " +
            event.direction + "<br/>" );
        }

        $(document).ready(function() {
          var events = ['hold', 'tap', 'swipe', 'doubletap',
          'transformstart', 'transform', 'transformend',
          'dragstart', 'drag', 'dragend', 'swipe', 'release'];

          $.each(events, function(key, val) {
            console.log('NOTICE: Applying Touch Event: ' + val);
            $('#touch-area').on(val,  hammerLog);
          });
        });
      </script>
  </head>

  <body>
    <div id="touch-area">
      <p>Touch here to see results<p>
      <p class="subtext">For best results, open this page on a touch
      enabled device.</p>
    </div>

    <p id="output"></p>
  </body>
</html>
```

GreenSock Animation Platform

If you have spent enough time developing Flash applications, chances are that you have ran into the GreenSock TweenMax or TweenLite library before. The TweenMax and TweenLite library easily allows you to tween your Flash objects around your stage with support for ActionScript 2 and ActionScript 3 projects. GreenSock has now produced and released a pure JavaScript implementation of their library with no dependencies that brings many of the great familiar features to your HTML5 projects.

So after looking at the jQuery animation methods and what they can do, why would you need to use a library like this? Well, unlike jQuery, GSAP JS is built to do one and only one thing very well. Features like sequencing animations to enable properly timed animations, overwrite control to stop running animations at anytime, and the ability to animate pretty much anything will extend your web application's visual appeal with relative ease.

Like the ActionScript companion, the GreenSock JavaScript library (http://www.greensock.com/v12) contains a ton of great up-to-date documentation and examples that will guide you in the right starting direction. In fact, they have specifically created a visual jump start guide to easily get you up and running with the library and demonstrate the results of the code right in the browser:

The best addition to the GSAP JS documentation is the Interactive Jump Start Guide that can be found at http://www.greensock.com/jump-start-js/. This simple-to-use, interactive application takes you from never using the library before, to understanding exactly what it can do in a matter of minutes; I can't stress how great of a feature this is.

Again, if you have had any experience using the GreenSock TweenMax or TweenLite libraries in any of your previous Flash projects, you are going to have an extremely easy time moving over to GSAP JS. As mentioned, the main issue most ActionScript 3 developers will face when using this library, is properly dealing with the **CSS3** properties, which are supplied for the Tweens to properly run.

Three.js

If the world of hardware accelerated 3D graphics is to your liking, `Three.js` (`http://mrdoob.github.com/three.js`) is definably worth a look. This lightweight 3D library is extremely easy to get up and running, and has loads of examples and documentation scattered all over the Web. `Three.js` uses not only the `<canvas>` element for rendering but `<svg>`, `CSS3D`, and `WebGL` as well allowing it to support a wide range of modern browsers and devices.

To give you some appreciation of what `Three.js` can do in print, check out some of these beautiful screen captures I took while viewing some example projects found on the `Three.js` project website:

As you can see from the preceding screenshots, JavaScript and WebGL have come a long way in a very short period of time. Again, all of these screenshots were taken from the examples found on the `Three.js` project website, so be sure to head over there and try these out for yourself to get a sense of how well they run on your machine and browser. Keep in mind that many of the modern mobile device web browsers are begging to have more robust WebGL support, so try it out on your phone or tablet as well.

Before starting the development of your `Three.js` project, it would be wise to make sure you are familiar with many of the common aspects and principals of 3D programming. At its core, a typical `Three.js` application will include a scene, a renderer, a camera, and an object. Each of these elements will work with one another to enable the creation of a 3D environment. One of the best introductory tutorials to learn about `Three.js` online is the *Getting Started with Three.js* article by *Paul Lewis* (`http://www.aerotwist.com/tutorials/getting-started-with-three-js`). In it, he covers all of the principals of 3D programming and how to utilize them within the `Three.js` framework.

Without getting into too much detail, as there are already many great books and online resources to learn Three.js development, here is a very simple code layout for rendering a scene in `Three.js`:

```
// Scene sizes
var WIDTH = 500;
var HEIGHT = 300;

// set some camera attributes
var VIEW_ANGLE = 45,
    ASPECT = WIDTH / HEIGHT,
    NEAR = 0.1,
    FAR = 10000;

// get the DOM element to attach to
var $container = document.getElementById('example');

// create a WebGL renderer, camera
// and a scene
var renderer = new THREE.WebGLRenderer();
var camera = new THREE.PerspectiveCamera(  VIEW_ANGLE,
                            ASPECT,
                            NEAR,
                            FAR  );
var scene = new THREE.Scene();
```

```javascript
// the camera starts at 0,0,0 so pull it back
camera.position.z = 300;

// start the renderer
renderer.setSize(WIDTH, HEIGHT);

// attach the render-supplied DOM element
$container.append(renderer.domElement);

// create the sphere's material
var sphereMaterial = new THREE.MeshLambertMaterial({ color:
    0xCC0000 });

// Set up the sphere vars
var radius = 50, segments = 16, rings = 16;

// Create a new mesh with sphere geometry -
// we will cover the sphereMaterial next!
var sphere = new THREE.Mesh(
    new THREE.SphereGeometry(radius, segments, rings),
    sphereMaterial);

// Add the sphere to the scene
scene.add(sphere);

// and the camera
scene.add(camera);

// create a point light
var pointLight = new THREE.PointLight( 0xFFFFFF );

// set its position
pointLight.position.x = 10;
pointLight.position.y = 50;
pointLight.position.z = 130;

// add to the scene
scene.add(pointLight);

// draw!
renderer.render(scene, camera);
```

Starting from the top of the preceding `Three.js` code example, we can see that initially the stage size is appended to a `WIDTH` and `HEIGHT` variable. These properties, which are familiar to every Flash developer define the viewable area where the content will be rendered. Following the stage configuration comes the initial camera configuration. As the 3D scene is created, the resulting view in the rendered frontend will be from the perspective of a camera that has been placed in the scene. Just like any other object, the camera can be moved around based on x, y and, z values as well as properties such as viewing angle, camera aspect and, zooming abilities. After the camera configuration, we need to target a specific element within the document to set as our stage, and a `document.getElementById` lookup to an element we have already created in our HTML document will do the trick. With the configuration values set, and an element selected ready to set our scene in, we can actually begin initializing our `scene` element.

Of course `Three.js` projects are not required to be 100 percent JavaScript. Once your scene is set up and ready for viewing, moving over to a 3D modeling software such as Blender or Maya will allow you to create extremely detailed 3D objects, which can be easily imported back into your HTML5 project. As you have seen in some of the example images previously, the level of detail that can be obtained can be simply amazing.

One final note about working with 3D or WebGL in JavaScript:. the current support for WebGL in the browser has been widespread in the desktop environment. You should have little or no issue viewing or testing your projects in almost every modern desktop web browser; however, you may still find many limitations on mobile browsers. Google's Chrome Browser on desktop and mobile is attempting to push the limits of WebGL with the advent of the Chrome Experiments site (`http://www.chromeexperiments.com/webgl/`). Containing a ton of great examples and projects, this site can easily let you test whatever browser, device, or platform you are running to see how well it copes with hardware accelerated graphics.

Compiling JavaScript

Long gone are the days of considering JavaScript just as a frontend development language used for HTML element manipulation. With the advent of JavaScript compilers, some pretty unimaginable things can be done by just writing some JavaScript code. Just like the methods you were used to in Flash, where ActionScript is compiled into binary packages, JavaScript compilers convert pure JavaScript into machine code, which can be run on a computer just like any other application. As far out as a concept this may seem, there are actually many great reasons for it and the best being for use in the Web browser.

Google's V8 Engine

In late 2008, Google released the initial version of Chrome and with it came the initial release of the V8 engine as well. V8 compiles JavaScript directly to native machine code and even optimizes the code when doing so. The result is applications that can run just like applications that are written in Python or C++. V8 is written in C++ and has been open source and freely available to the public since its original release. You can find out more about the Google V8 project by visiting the project website at `http://code.google.com/p/v8`.

Node.js

Easily one of the coolest new projects to be born from the Google V8 Engine is Node. js (`http://nodejs.org`). `Node.js` allows you to write server-side applications (usually web servers) in 100 percent JavaScript, something typically done in programming languages such as **PHP**, **Perl**, **Python**, and even **C** or **C++**.

Like many of the frameworks and libraries covered in this chapter, `Node.js` has a massive amount of great documentation and examples all over the Web. However, with the speed at which some of the projects are being developed, the documentation available can easily become outdated. One of the best resources for `Node.js`, which is constantly updated to the current stable release of the project, is `http://nodeguide.com` created by *Felix Geisendörfer*, one of the early core contributors to the `Node.js` project.

Since `Node.js` is made to run server side, rather than including it into your **HTML5** project, you must install it on a computer to be run as an application. So after downloading and installing the `Node.js` files on the machine of your choice, you can now run your `Node.js`-ready JavaScript files from the command line as you would any other command-line application.

To demonstrate the basic usage of how to start a `Node.js` application, we will use the popular `Node.js` web server example, which can be found within the official documentation. Create a new JavaScript file with the filename `example.js` and populate it with the following JavaScript:

```
var http = require('http');

http.createServer(
  function (request, response)
  {
    response.writeHead(200, {'Content-Type': 'text/plain'});
    response.end('Hello World\n');
  }
```

```
).listen(8000);

    console.log('Server running at http://localhost:8000/');
```

The first line of the example code is importing the **HTTP** module within the Node. js framework. With the HTTP module included, the createServer method is called with a success function supplied. The function contains a simple "Hello World" greeting and has the Content-Type set to text/plain, so the browser viewing it knows it is just plain text. Finally, the listen method is chained into the server declaration to specify the port, which the **HTTP** server will listen for requests on.

With the example.js file saved, open the command line on your system running Node.js and point the current working directory to the location of your new JavaScript file and type the following command. Executing the file with Node.js is as easy as referencing the JavaScript file with the *node* application:

% node example.js

Executing this command will result in the following response:

Server running at http://localhost:8000/

The command line will sit waiting for physical termination. Before stopping the server, we have to test to make sure it works. So head over to the URL stated in the response after executing the node command:

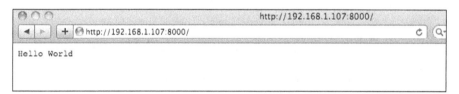

As simple as this output is, the reality is you just created a simple custom web server only using JavaScript. This is just the beginning of what Node.js has to offer and the best part is many of the great things that can be done with Node.js, have been, and are available for you to locate and use anytime you wish. Rather than spending hours on Google searching for modules to include in your project, Node.js uses its own system for finding and installing further functionality into your Node.js server.

Node Package Manager

If you are still unsure as to what Node.js could do for you, the **NPM (Node Package Manager)** may be able to help you out. A package manager is an online collection of packages available to be downloaded and utilized within your node projects with ease. Since Node.js is installed on your machine, the package manager can do all of the hard work when it comes to checking for dependencies, versions, and platform support. To easily search the current `Node.js` **NPM** directory, head over to `https://npmjs.org` and browse around until you find what you are interested in installing:

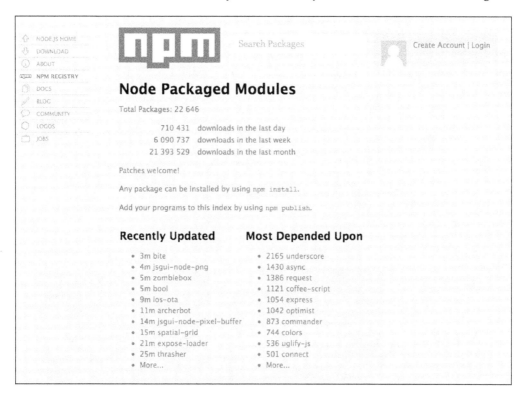

Any package that is located in the registry can easily be installed on your system by running the install command in the command line:

```
% npm install PACKAGE-NAME
```

As mentioned before, if the package you have requested to be installed requires other packages within the registry, they will automatically be downloaded and installed as well without you having to dig around to find the proper version yourself. As developers work on the packages you may be using and release updates, the NPM registry will automatically take care of updating you with the release information as well as allow for easy updating of any out-of-date packages you may have installed.

Hosting a public Node.js server

Since you are required to have a server to run your `Node.js` projects, you will need to set up a public facing server to host any projects you wish to be open to the Internet. Since installing `Node.js` on your computer for testing won't accomplish this, you will need to either setup your own, with the proper networking in place, or pay for this service from a `Node.js` hosting company. Since the company you use for your web hosting usually won't allow you to accomplish this, looking into services such as Nodejitsu (`http://nodejitsu.com`) may be of use:

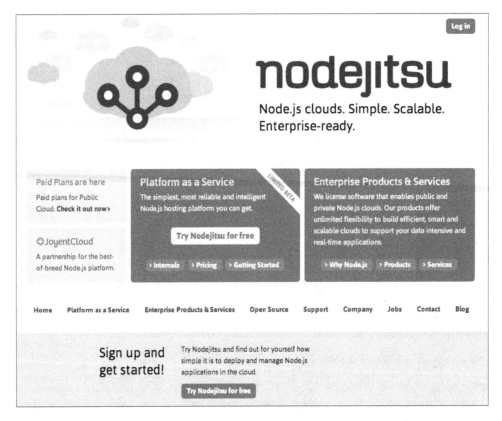

Just like a traditional web hosting company, Nodejitsu offers your own public facing `Node.js` server, which can be used from any of your web projects online. You can always start with a free trial account to get a sense of how the service allows you to use your `Node.js` server from anywhere in the world and then move into paid accounts if your needs continue.

Summary

This chapter has only dusted the surface of what is available to you as an **HTML5** developer. What has been presented here is a collection of some of the most popular libraries and frameworks currently available. The vast amount of amazing code that has been publicly released and actively developed on by developers all around the world is growing at what seems beyond an exponential rate. Allocating and utilizing external assets like those listed in this chapter require you, the developer, to understand the implications and benefits of using the library or framework prior to implementing them into a publicly available website.

Spending the time to dig around, test, and contribute too many of these projects that interest you will not only benefit your existing development skill set, but allow you to utilize the best tool for the job at hand. As time passes and the landscape of web development continues to evolve, keeping up-to-date with as many of these popular libraries and frameworks will always aid in keeping you updated with the entire **HTML5** development environment.

In the next chapter, we will extend this newly acquired knowledge of HTML5 frameworks and libraries into the realm of directly porting your preexisting Flash applications into HTML5 web-ready projects.

7
Choosing How You Develop

Moving into the HTML5 development flow will require you to move away from the applications which become familiar during the Flash development cycle. Applications such as Flash Professional, Flash Builder, and Flash Develop are all specifically designed to work with Flash content and Flash content alone. As great as these applications are, there are many similar HTML5 development applications that allow you to build rich web experiences in a very similar manner that you are used to. This chapter will cover the process of moving away from using the Adobe Flash Professional development environment and beginning the hard decision of what new development software to use when creating your HTML5 projects. Although there is an endless variety of great software that you could use, this chapter will cover many of the new and popular applications that the web developers are using right now.

In this chapter, we will cover the following:

- Understanding what is needed in an HTML5 IDE
- Tools for asset creation and manipulation
- Creating interactive animated HTML5 elements with Adobe Edge
- An overview of some of the most popular HTML5 code editors
- Tools for code execution and run time testing

Replacing the Flash development environment

The best part of developing applications in the Flash environment is the fact that Adobe has put in a ton of time building the tools and applications contained in the Creative Suite which allow you to create your entire application within their application set. Although, there is an argument that this system is confining and slow to update. The fact of the matter is, when all of the right tools are available to help you build your applications, jumping into your next project is that much easier. Since it's not regulated or controlled by one specific company, HTML5 development is a much more open development platform as developers can freely choose how and what they use to build their projects.

I must emphasize, in this chapter we will overview many of the common methods and applications that HTML5 developers are using to get the job done. Of course, none of these applications or methods are the absolute right way to build HTML5 projects, hopefully you will find an application that fits what you are looking for. As time progresses and you build more and more HTML5-related projects, be sure to always put in the extra effort when researching the best tool for the job at hand. The rapidly changing environment leads many projects to rise and fall in a short period of time. Staying on top of what is out there will help to keep you on top of the game, as well as continue to extend your HTML5 development skill set.

Requirements of HTML5 development environments

When it comes to writing HTML, CSS, and JavaScript all within the same code editor, there are some general considerations that most developers usually make to ensure that they acquire a feature set that suits their needs. Since the entire HTML5 stack is rendered as plain text documents, technically any text editor will get the job done. Although every developer has their own unique setup and development style, there are many common pieces of functionality that are always worth looking out for.

Asset and file management

Having the ability to preview and even manipulate assets that are included into your projects, such as images, video, audio, and other external assets, directly within your development environment can allow you to speed up the development flow by containing your focus within a specific application. Applications such as Adobe's Dreamweaver, which we will cover in a moment, are a great example of a software that has been designed to marry the process of design and development. It's worth noting that many of the plain and simple code editors, which will be overviewed in this chapter, may not contain features which support easy file and asset management. However, when large feature integrations like this are not included within code editors, the general end result is a much faster, light-weight application.

Code highlighting

As with any programming language, code highlighting or coloring is an essential feature to have within your code editor. The ability to easily understand what parts of your code are doing what, will allow you to not only develop your applications with greater ease, it will also help you understand other developer's code with far fewer issues. Code highlighting is also the key in making sure you're writing your code in the proper language syntax. For a code editor to be able to properly color or highlight your code, the applications must be able to properly recognize and parse the specific language that your code has been written in. Therefore, keeping an eye out for code-editing applications that have support for the specific programming language you intend to use it for is critical when attempting to find the best fit. Luckily, in our case, HTML5 development or HTML, CSS, and JavaScript development is widely supported by many code-editing applications available, so the amount of choice you have is extremely substantial.

Code completion

Having good code completion built into the code editor you choose to use can be a huge help with attempting to learn a new programming language. If you have spent time using Flash Builder in your Flash development career, I am sure that you have already seen how much faster you can write good, working code. Although, some developers argue that code completion just creates a lazy developer who avoids remembering the specifics of anything in the language syntax. The reality is that code completion is used by developers from new to seasoned veterans to avoid delays while writing code and to just generally speed up the time it takes to write long snippets of code.

When developing Flash applications with development environments such as Flash Builder (http://www.adobe.com/products/flash-builder.html) or Flash Develop (http://www.flashdevelop.org), you are presented with one of the best case scenarios for utilizing code completion. Since these code editors are specifically built for writing ActionScript 3, they can optimize this development experience by focusing on what is available in the ActionScript 3 API.

In reality there are two forms of code completion when developing HTML5 or many other languages for that matter. The obvious form of this is auto completing text as you type. An example of this would be when you have typed a declared variable name and hit the . key to get ready to specify a property on that object. Some editors will generate a dropdown menu below the active line of code with a list of available properties you can append on the current object. This form of code completion can be super handy when learning a new language as it is laying out the available possibilities right in front of you as you develop. The second form of code completion is the generation of larger snippets of code. For example, when you attempt to declare a new function by typing the word `function` in your code editor some editors will recognize this and automatically generate the default function layout for you. All you have to do is fill in the internal code and you're done. Some developers have issues with this feature as it may not generate the code to their exact specification, but many editors now support the ability to modify the pre-existing code snippets and even add your own.

Creating and manipulating assets

As a developer with previous experience creating applications in Flash, you may have grown accustomed to using the Flash Professional development environment to not only store your application asset files in SWC files for project inclusion, but to build entire projects as well. The ability to work with project assets within a feature-rich development environment such as Flash Professional is one of the reasons why Flash became so popular in the first place. When moving to HTML5 development, it would be a shame to lose such a great development environment for building and manipulating assets. Luckily, with the popularity of HTML5 booming, many new exciting projects and applications have been released to bring this type of asset control to the web development cycle.

Adobe Edge Animate

As Adobe grows its products into a fully cloud-based software setup, they have also introduced a number of HTML5-based projects allowing web developers to easily create HTML5 content in the traditional Adobe user-friendly environment. One of the newest and exciting pieces of software in this collection is Adobe Edge. Edge allows for easy creation of interactive and animated HTML5 content, all within a point and click user interface. In essence, you can think of Edge as the replacement for the Flash IDE when developing with HTML, CSS, and JavaScript in the HTML5 stack. Although this software has nowhere near the current power that the Flash IDE supports, its feature support has been growing on an exponential scale since it has been released.

Adobe Edge can be downloaded for free by signing in to Adobe's Application Manager. Head over to `http://html.adobe.com/edge/animate` to download Edge and sign up for an Adobe account if you haven't done so already. Once you have set up your account, locate the **Edge Tools & Services** section within the Application Manager and download the software to your computer. It's worth noting that, as mentioned, this new cloud-based software delivery system is the new direction Adobe is heading in to enable easier access to the software in their catalogue. You can easily test out any other product by Adobe by clicking on the **Try** link under each of the available software descriptions as shown in the following screenshot:

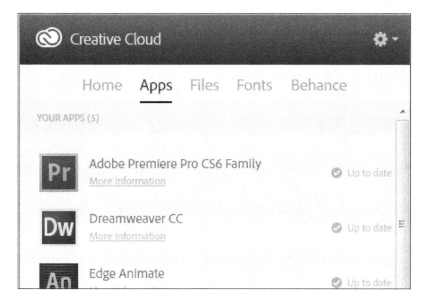

Once you have managed to get Edge downloaded and installed, fire it up, and you can get your first glance at the user interface. Although, it is not exactly like the Flash Professional user interface you may be used to, you can probably see many similarities that will easily allow you to integrate your existing Adobe user interface skills you gained from Flash, Photoshop, and so on:

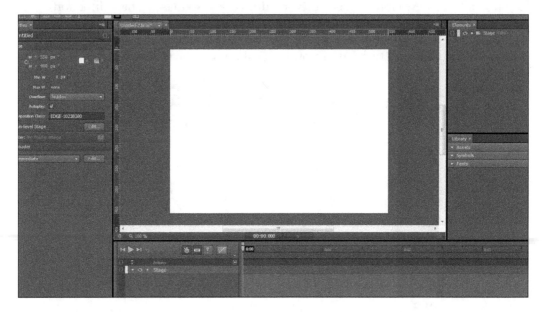

Let's take a moment to overview some of the exciting features and support Edge has for unique features such as CSS3 filters and animations. We can start, as most do, with a simple blue box, our Hello World of the user interface realm. The main toolbar by default is located on the top of the window and the square shape tool is easily found within:

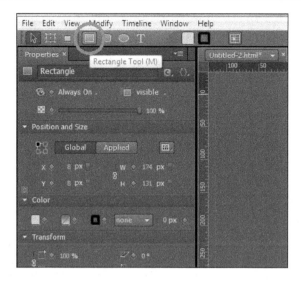

It's worth glancing at some of the other tools within the toolbar as they will be pretty familiar and self-explanatory. Regardless, we will come back and check those out shortly. For now we will select the square shape tool and draw a decently-sized rectangle on the stage presented in the user interface. Take notice of how similar this process is to creating content in Flash:

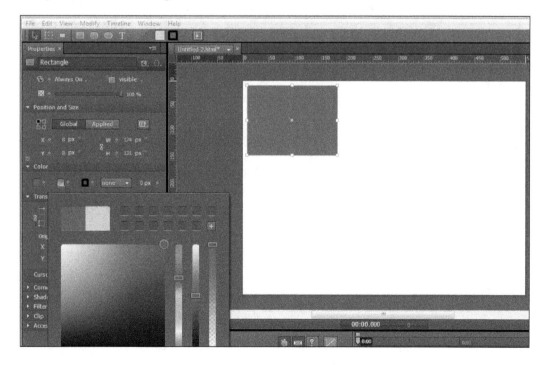

By default your shape won't be blue, so after it has been placed on the stage, head over to the **Properties** panel located on the left side of the application window by default and modify the color of the shape by using the color selector.

With our box ready to be animated, let's move our focus down to the **Timeline** panel displayed on the bottom of the application window by default. As mentioned, if you spent any time with Flash Professional and timeline-based animations, this feature within Edge will not only be familiar, but should probably excite you as well. If the concept of timeline animations is new to you, it is the process of controlling an element within the application view over a set amount of time. By defining how your assets animate over time, you can easily control their behavior on a specific playback interval. To demonstrate this, we will use the timeline to animate our new blue rectangle around the stage, applying different effects and properties to it as it moves around.

To start, we will enable the Toggle Pin which will easily allow us to set the new state of an element within a key frame of the animation timeline. The Toggle Pin is located in the **Timeline** panel in the top button navigation. It is represented with a blue pin marker:

With the Toggle Pin activated, when the timeline is set to a new position, any update to the element will only be applied within that new key frame. The resulting action will be an automatically created motion tween over a given period of time.

By dragging the play head on the timeline to 1 second, we have now told Edge to start applying new properties to any element on the stage. So, let's drag our blue box from the top-left corner of the stage to the top-right corner and then hit the Space bar to view the resulting animation:

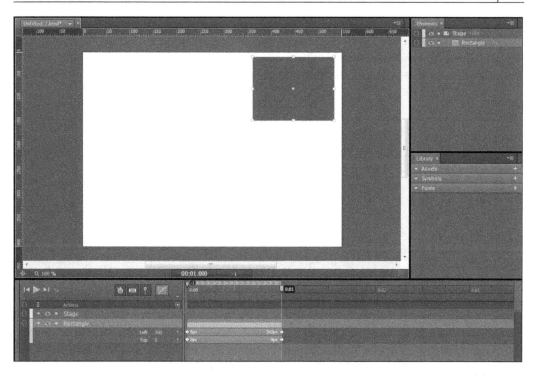

Of course, in text you will have to take my word, but the resulting action is that of what you are used to when tweening elements in Flash. As the play head travels from 0 seconds to our new keyframe at 1 second, the position of the blue box is automatically updated to animate the position from start to finish. As simple as this example is, it not only presents many of the extremely similar aspects Edge has with Flash Professional, but it highlights the core of what Edge has been made to do.

Let's spend a bit more time checking out what else can be done to our blue box by checking out what is available within the **Properties** panel. Without getting into too much detail of every bit of the **Properties** panel, the easiest way to sum it up is that it is obviously inspired by the **Properties** panel in Flash Professional. Although some of the properties available to you within Edge are different than that of Flash, the layout and style is almost identical. If Adobe Edge interests you, it would be worth spending some time and checking out some of the available properties that are available in the current release. I also recommend that when testing, open the published files in as many of the browsers you have at your disposal, from desktop to mobile. Get an idea as to how different devices and platforms react to the load of HTML5 animations to better judge how far to push your applications in the future.

Of course, at any time during your development or testing phase, you can select the **Preview in Browser** option in the **File** menu to view how your current project looks and feels within an actual web browser. This is also a perfect time to dig into the generated source code to get a better idea as to what the Edge compiler has actually done for us.

Edge builds the application source into HTML, CSS, and minimized JavaScript files and saves the JavaScript data with the filename of `YOUR-PROJECT-NAME_ edgePreload.js`. Although this minimized JavaScript is hard to read or understand, it is set up to be as small of a filesize as possible to optimize the loading when retrieved over the Internet by your end users.

Adobe Edge also contains a built-in code editor to allow you to easy append code into your Edge projects further extending what your web application can do. This code editor, though used in a slightly different manner, is an extremely recognizable panel to anyone who has written any ActionScript within the Flash IDE. Within the code editing panel, you will find a collection of code snippets that can be appended to your project with a single click. From adding features as simple as a play method call on one of your elements, to dynamically creating and destroying new instantiations of your elements, the built-in code snippets can easily get you on your feet. The code editor also can simplify the code display by only displaying what is needed for you to manipulate your elements. This can be toggled by selecting the **Full Code** tab available on the top-right corner of the code window and will result in the entire project JavaScript document source being displayed.

Coding environments

Generally, the bulk of the work to create an HTML5 project is going to take place within an environment set up to allow you to write HTML, CSS, and JavaScript all within the same location. Since all of these different development languages are all contained in plain text files, there is no specific requirement when choosing what editor you could use. However, as HTML5 grows into a more evolved web and application development platform, the need for platforms that support features such as media integration, code formatting and completion, device testing and debugging have pretty much become a must. Many software titles that have been around since before HTML5 have updated their feature set to include support for HTML5 development and have added new features to make developing for the Web easier. A perfect example of this in action is the latest version of Adobe's Dreamweaver included in the latest version of the Creative Suite.

Adobe Dreamweaver CS6

Since the Adobe Creative Suite should already be somewhat familiar to you, we will start the overview of HTML5 code editors with Adobe's Dreamweaver. Dreamweaver has been a part of the Creative Suite since Version 3. Although you may find that many web developers have a love or hate relationship with Dreamweaver, because of its ease of accessibility if you have purchased the Creative Suite, many web developers have used it at one point or another. The important thing to note now, regardless of if you have used Dreamweaver before or not, is that Adobe has added a ton of new features specifically related to HTML5 web development to aid in your entire development cycle:

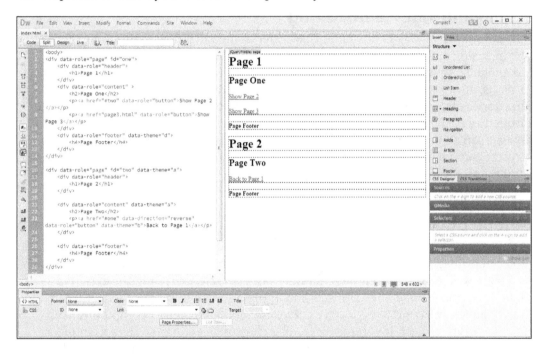

I won't dive too deep into the use of Dreamweaver, as there are many great books and tutorials available all over the Web to aid you when starting to learn its feature set and user interface. I will, however, overview some of the new and exciting features that Dreamweaver CS6 has included to allow web developers to integrate HTML5 elements and features into their web projects with ease. It is worth noting that many of these features, at the time of writing this book, are only available in the second update to Dreamweaver CS6 on the Creative Cloud. Users who have the natively installed version of Dreamweaver are currently out of luck. If you are interested in testing some of these features yourself, download the 30-day trial of Dreamweaver from the Creative Cloud and give it a go.

Audio and video embedding

The latest update to Dreamweaver CS6 added some great new features surrounding the inclusion and manipulation of HTML5-ready audio and video files into your documents. As with many forms of media that can be imported into your HTML5 projects, audio and video can now be easily selected from your project source directories and placed into your document with a couple of clicks. Setting element properties such as auto play, enabling playback controls, and even setting poster images can all be done directly from within the Dreamweaver user interface. This process can not only ensure you are developing your media playback code to proper syntax specification, but easily allows you to set playback alternatives for browsers and platforms that only support specific file types.

Adobe Edge support

As you have already learned about some of the power of Adobe Edge Animate, you can probably understand why direct Adobe Edge integration into Dreamweaver is a huge win for web developers. Rather than manually stripping the exported data from your Adobe Edge projects and applying them into your own, you can now seamlessly integrate your interactive and animated elements right into your Dreamweaver project. If you have ever been fortunate enough to save a couple hours with the **Import From Photoshop** feature in Flash Professional, you will easily understand how this cross-application communication can save you countless hours of development.

PhoneGap and jQuery Mobile support

You may be surprised to learn that Adobe actually played a major role in the development of the jQuery Mobile framework. It seems the relationship is still strong, as Adobe has continued its full jQuery Mobile support from Dreamweaver CS5.5 into CS6. The newest jQuery Mobile feature updates have made it incredibly easy to theme your jQuery Mobile projects:

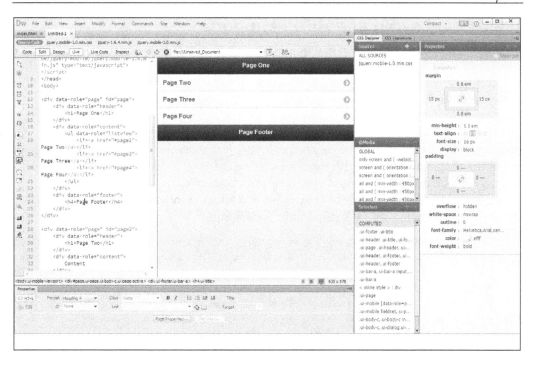

As you can see in the previous screenshot, the jQuery Mobile **Swatches** panel allows us to easily select specific elements within the live view of our project, and apply new theme properties to that element with a click of the mouse. The resulting code update is presented as the highlighted change showing you what has been modified in your existing document. This feature moves far beyond supporting just the default jQuery Mobile themes. Dreamweaver will automatically detect any customized themes that have been appended into your project and allow you to continue to manipulate and implement that theme within the Dreamweaver jQuery Mobile **Swatches** panel. You can drill your selection down to specific elements within your webpages and modify assets such as icons and fonts as well. The most popular HTML5 mobile framework just became a lot easier to use.

PhoneGap users are not left out in the cold either. If you are looking to build your mobile projects into native applications Dreamweaver has made it extremely user friendly from a developer's perspective. The new PhoneGap **Build Service** panel allows you to build your current working project for any of the support mobile platforms with a couple clicks of the mouse. Your PhoneGap builds can be sent and downloaded from the PhoneGap build server all from within Dreamweaver. Building native applications in HTML5 for five different popular mobile platforms has never been easier or more user friendly.

Fluid Grid Layout and HiDPI support

The new **Fluid Grid Layout** system in Dreamweaver allows you to easily target and customize your webpage layouts for specific devices right from project creation. With the grid system activated in your page layouts, you can begin specifying exactly how many columns a specific element can take up. If the browser window is resized or the page is loaded on a display that is above or below the targeted screen resolutions, the grid system will automatically respond to the change by updating how many columns will be displayed. The concept of laying out elements within your webpages is not a new one. However, with the release of so many devices which can now access your content, the requirements to stay on top of modern display specifications can be draining. Adobe has enabled Dreamweaver users to easily integrate an optimized condition set allowing for easy responsive web design:

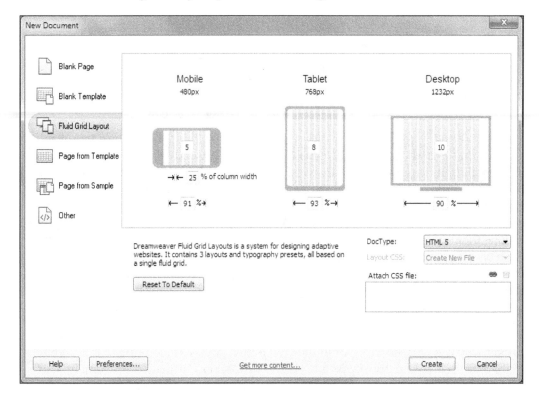

Today we are seeing mobile and desktop screens getting higher in pixel density. The need for proper environments that will allow developers to test on these displays, even if they do not have access to one, has become a must. Dreamweaver has now integrated **HiDPI** support into an easy to use user interface making testing for specific display types a breeze.

Aptana

If you're coming from a Flash development background that mainly existed in Flash Builder, then Aptana (`http://www.aptana.com`) may be worth a look. Built on the same Eclipse (`http://www.eclipse.org`) editor that Flash Builder has been created with, Aptana brings an extremely recognizable code development user interface to many Flash developers:

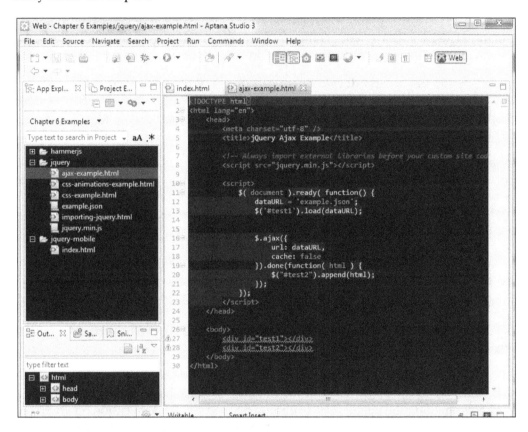

Aptana includes a ton of great features specifically designed to aid with web development. Code-assist features are in place to aid with HTML, CSS, and JavaScript syntax and deployment wizards can easily integrate automated file updating to your public web server. Aptana also contains built-in support for Git integration so you can easily integrate version control support for your projects. Like Flash Builder, Aptana allows you to easily add multiple projects into the application at the same time. Having the code from multiple projects in front of you can easily save you time when referencing source code from a feature you added elsewhere. Aptana is free to use, open source, and actively developed on by a large group of contributors.

Brackets

One of the newest and the most exciting HTML5 code editors in the works is Brackets by Adobe (`http://brackets.io/`). This open-source editor is not only designed specifically for HTML5 developers, but the application itself is actually written with the HTML5 stack, allowing you to easily customize your editing experience.

Brackets is actually an amazing representation as to how far HTML development has come in the last couple years. The ability to create such a rich interactive environment to manipulate local files on your computer with web technology is just another step in moving towards a completely web application-based lifestyle.

Brackets is still in the early development process but is already in a useable state to be used by anyone today. Despite being written in HTML, CSS, and JavaScript, since it is packaged and run as a desktop application, it can easily create and manipulate file on your local machine.

To start using Brackets, you will need to head over to the project website to get the links to the latest builds (`http://download.brackets.io/`). As with many open source projects, as the end user, you will be presented with the choice to download a pre-packaged build of the software which is usually the most stable. Or you can download the nightly, or latest development build which the contributors to the project are actively working on. Development builds are, as you may assume, unstable and may result in some issues upon usage. However, if you are willing to brave the storm of buggy software, the information and experiences you have while using it can be extremely important to the development team working on the project. Submitting issues and bugs that you may have encountered during your usage should be logged within the Brackets **Issue Tracker** on their GitHub project account (`https://github.com/adobe/brackets/issues`).

For the purpose of example, I will download the latest pre-packaged stable build of the software to show you some of the exciting features that Brackets has to offer. After downloading the installer and running it, open up the application on your Windows or OS X-based machine. On the initial boot up of the application, you will be presented with a default example setup that will look something like the following screenshot:

As you can see in the previous screenshot, the interface, though familiar to many of you, is extremely simplistic yet elegantly styled and laid out.

Inline editing

One of the coolest features currently built into Brackets is its easy to use inline code editing system. As a web developer, you will find yourself jumping from not only program to program while developing your projects, but from file to file containing a completely different language of code. To simplify this process and speed up the development of elements within your documents, Brackets allows you to select elements within your HTML files, and view their relative CSS styles. To accomplish this, select an element within the HTML example file, and press *Ctrl +E* or *Cmd + E* (depending on your operating system) to display the styles for that element directly within the same HTML file.

No longer do you have to waste time sifting through line after line of CSS in dedicated CSS files to find your element styles. Now Brackets can do all the hard work searching while you continue to write code:

When the inline editor is displayed (as seen in the preceding screenshot under the <body> HTML element tag), not only can you easily edit the styles related to the selected element, but some important data is also displayed. In the top-left corner of the inline style window is the filename of the document containing the relative styles and beside the filename is the line number where the styles can be located.

As simple as the concept of inline editing is, we can take it even further by inspecting the styles of elements that contain multiple styles definitions. For example, looking at the following link element in brackets displays a number of different styles which are all applied to the same element in one way or another. By selecting the different definitions in the inline editor, you can easily switch between each of the style settings, edit them, and continue on your way. Of course this inline editing concept is not only for HTML and CSS, it reaches in your JavaScript development cycle as well. The team behind Brackets is still building more of this inline editing functionality into the application by extending features such as color and gradient selections.

Live Preview

Another great feature already built into Brackets is **Live Preview**. Instead of the traditional method of editing code, saving it, and then moving over to the browser to test it, the Live Preview system simplifies this into an automated test build as you type. When the **Live Preview** button is activated in the top-right corner of the application window, the default system web browser will open containing the current working HTML page. As mentioned, with this feature selected, you can continue to modify the current document and view the reflected changes as you type:

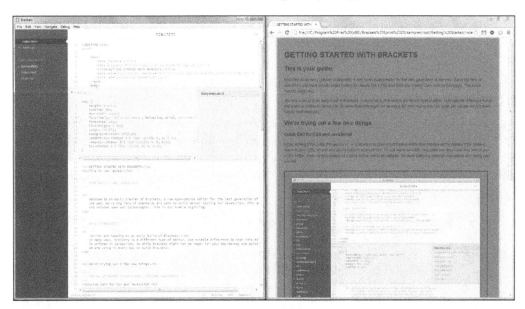

The preceding screenshot illustrates a change to the body element background-color style property, changing it from white to red. This simple automated save and reload functionality is just another piece of Brackets that allows web developers to spend less time doing recurring time consuming tasks.

Plugins

Thanks to the fact that Brackets is open source and created with the same platforms it is intended to be used for, many developers have begun creating their own customized extensions and plugins for Brackets. From adding the ability to do custom code highlighting with the mouse, to added support for code completion, the spectrum of public input has been pretty amazing. Of course you don't have to rely on the public to get new features into Brackets. As stated before, the entire project has been built with the technology you are learning about in this book. So if you are willing to take the jump, attempting to add some new unique feature into Brackets could be a great learning project.

Contributing

The best part of Brackets is not only the fact that it is completely open source, freely available, and actively developed, but the entire application is built on the HTML5 stack. As your web development skill set grows, the Brackets project can be a fantastic place to expand and share your development skills with the rest of the world. The development team consistently appends updates and modifications submitted by the public and is always asking for further input from its users. Since Brackets is still cooking in the development oven, now is a great time to jump aboard and help create what could be the next big HTML5 code editor. All of the project information can be found within the project website pages, as well as the project GitHub page. If you wish to dive even deeper, hop onto IRC and checkout the `#brackets` channel on `freenode.net`.

Sublime Text

If a light-weight code editor such as Brackets is more up your alley, then Sublime Text is another editor worth checking out (`http://www.sublimetext.com`). Sublime is simple and light weight and supports massive amount of programming languages right out of the box, so it can be used for much more than just HTML5 development:

```
File  Edit  Selection  Find  View  Goto  Tools  Project  Preferences  Help

JetPackMan.js          x

1    var JetPackMan = function() {
2        var _jetPackSound = document.getElementById("jetpack");
3        _jetPackSound.addEventListener("ended", handleSoundComplete, false);
4
5        var _explosionSound = document.getElementById("explosion");
6        var _soundPlaying = false;
7
8        var _animationData = Array();
9        var _imageSource = 'imgs/JetPackMan.png';
10       var _currentFrame = 0;
11       var _canvas = document.getElementById("player");
12       var _context = _canvas.getContext("2d");
13
14       var _imageObj = new Image();
15       _imageObj.src = _imageSource;
16
17       var _currentY = 0;
18       var _jetPackOn = false;
19       var _explode = false;
20       var _interval;
21
22       var _xVal = 0;
23       var _yVal = 0;
24       var _widthVal = 0;
25       var _heightVal = 0;
26
27       // Append the Sprite Sheet JSON to a local Array.
28       $.each(JetPackManData['frames'], function(key, val) {
29           _animationData.push(val);
30       });
31
32       _widthVal = _animationData[_currentFrame]['frame']['w'];

Line 27, Column 34                                    Tab Size: 4        JavaScript
```

Sublime's multiple text selection feature is one worth noting. When working on larger documents of code, the need to make the same edit to a large amount of text, such as spacing, seems to come up quite a bit. To alleviate this issue, Sublime uses a multiple text selection and edit feature to allow you to easy modify many parts of the same document with a single change:

As you can see in the preceding screenshot, Sublime also includes a minimized layout of your code to easily allow you to locate specific sections of your code based on how they look. As weird as this may sound, surprisingly it is really effective. Sublime has a ton of other great features making it one of my personal favorite code editors out there.

Available on Window, OS X, and Linux, Sublime can be downloaded and installed for free and used indefinitely. However to remove purchase alerts, a license can be purchased for $70 USD from the Sublime Text website (https://www.sublimetext.com/buy).

Execution and testing

Many of the software titles shown so far have contained their own methods to aid you in the process of testing and debugging your websites and applications. However, the amount of technology out there to test for and test with is growing at a rate which makes it very hard for a specific piece of software to stay on top. Having a library of different applications and services at your disposal will not only allow you to test many different aspects of your project, but possibly save you a ton of time in the process.

Web browser developer consoles

Although we have already spent some time in this book looking into some of the functionality contained within many of the popular browser developer consoles, there are a couple other aspects of the console that are worth looking into when considering frontend execution benchmarks and tests. As your projects grow in size and complexity, the requirement that you spend time optimizing the flow and execution of your application grows with it. If you have ever had the chance to use the Adobe Flash Profiler or Adobe Scout to dig into how and what your application is doing during runtime, you may already understand the benefit of this type of precaution:

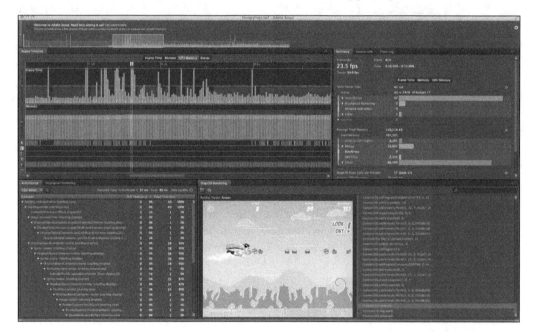

The preceding screenshot is from the new Adobe Scout (`http://gaming.adobe.com/technologies/scout/`) profiling tools used by game developers to look at what is going on inside their game as it is actually being played. Moving out of the realm of Flash development unfortunately means dropping the use of great new applications and profilers such as Scout, however, there are many alternatives available to you as a HTML5 developer, we will just need to go hunting for them.

> During the 2013 Adobe Max Conference, details of a new version of Adobe Scout specifically built for HTML5 development in the works were discussed. Keep an eye out for this fantastic tool's release date on the Adobe website. You can also watch the video demonstration from the conference at `http://tv.adobe.com/watch/max-2013/adobe-scout-profiling-taken-to-the-next-level/`.

We have already spent some time looking at the JavaScript or web developer consoles in many of the popular web browsers today, but there are many more features these panels contain that can aid in running tests and benchmarks on your project prior to releasing it to the public.

Network analysis

Many developer consoles within web browsers contain network consoles which allow you to visualize how the data within your webpages are loading from the perspective of your users. Open the console up prior to loading the page and when the page is loaded, the real-time data is passed into an easy-to-read table that can display exactly what files are being loaded, if they succeeded or failed loading, what the filesize of the asset was, as well as exactly how long it took to load:

Name	Method	Status	Type	Initiator	Size	Time	Timeline
load.php?debug=false&lang=...	GET	200	text/jav...	load.php:153	(from c...	87 ms	
load.php?debug=false&lang=...	GET	200	text/jav...	load.php:153	(from c...	86 ms	
load.php?debug=false&lang=...	GET	200	text/jav...	load.php:153	(from c...	86 ms	
120px-HTML5-logo.svg.png	GET	304	image/png	HTML5:65	553 B	79 ms	
Special:BannerRandom?userl...	GET	200	text/jav...	load.php:127	532 B	48 ms	
420px-HTML5-APIs-and-relate...	GET	304	image/png	HTML5:315	590 B	69 ms	
search-ltr.png?303-4	GET	304	image/png	HTML5:901	425 B	63 ms	
poweredby_mediawiki_88x31...	GET	304	image/png	HTML5:1055	431 B	64 ms	
wikimedia-button.png	GET	304	image/png	HTML5:1052	319 B	63 ms	
28px-Crystal_Clear_app_bro...	GET	304	image/png	HTML5:395	445 B	63 ms	
28px-Internet_map_1024.jpg	GET	304	image/jpeg	HTML5:391	566 B	63 ms	
30px-Commons-logo.svg.png	GET	304	image/png	HTML5:471	572 B	64 ms	
Wiki.png	GET	304	image/png	HTML5:913	500 B	63 ms	
magnify-clip.png	GET	304	image/png	HTML5:317	429 B	60 ms	
data:image/png;base...	GET	Success	image/png	load.php:148	0 B	Pending	
Special:RecordImpression?r...	GET	200	image/png	load.php:2	488 B	36 ms	
data:image/png;base...	GET	Success	image/png	load.php:148	0 B	Pending	
data:image/png;base...	GET	Success	image/png	load.php:148	0 B	Pending	
data:image/png;base...	GET	Success	image/png	load.php:148	0 B	1 ms	

29 requests | 37.9 KB transferred | 423 ms (onload: 424 ms, DOMContentLoaded: 282 ms)

Documents   Stylesheets   Images   Scripts   XHR   Fonts   WebSockets   Other

Combining all of this data can easily allow you to find issues within your webpages that you may have missed during the development phase. One easy thing to look out for is what the total page load size is once the page has completely loaded. Keeping in mind the various methods and speeds at which users connect to the Internet, it is always wise to think of the end user first when attempting to optimize the filesize of the assets used in your projects.

Timeline profiling

With many of the common built-in timeline profiling tools, you can literally hit the record button and capture exactly what is going on under the hood of your application during runtime. When events are captured, they are displayed in real time and displayed with the total memory usage. This data can be extremely helpful when attempting to locate where any potential memory leaks in your application may be taking place:

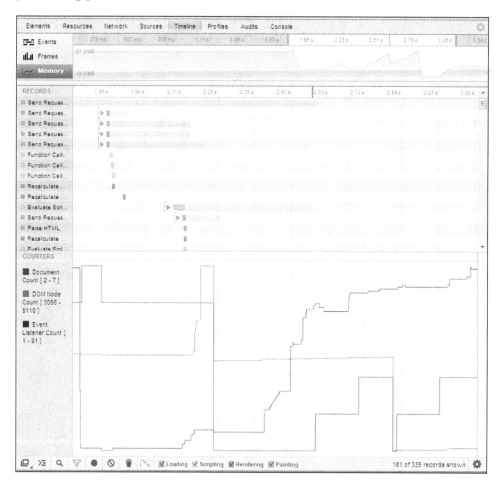

If some of these forms of application analysis methods are foreign to you, don't worry, we will be covering more on this topic in the chapters to come. Spending the time to check out how well your websites and applications actually run on different platforms can save you a ton of headaches post launch.

Stats.js

Dealing with the concept of **Frames per Second** or **FPS** in Flash is regular occurrence. Since the entire platform is built on the concept of a timeline, having your application run at a specific FPS or at its maximum FPS is usually the end goal of every Flash project. During your Flash development career, there may have been a chance you ran into, or even used, a version of Mr. Doob's Hi-ReS Stats script (`https://github.com/mrdoob/Hi-ReS-Stats`). This great little piece of code allows you to easily append an overlay on your applications displaying the FPS over time as well as the current amount of memory your application is using:

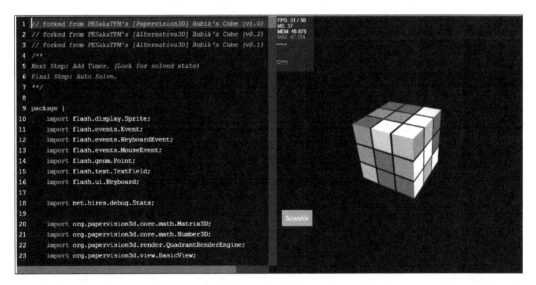

As you can see in the previous example from a prototype found on the great Flash resource site WonderFl (`http://wonderfl.net/c/6fCf`) the stats script is being used to display how well this Rubik's cube application is running as it is used. This is extremely handy when attempting to find locations in the execution of your projects that may be causing issues.

Although the idea of FPS within HTML5 development is not exactly the same, as static HTML pages don't have an active FPS during or after they are loaded. However, when dealing with animation and timer intervals within JavaScript, the FPS concept can be used as we have become used to in Flash development. Thanks to the work of Mr. Doob, the `Stats` script that once only existed for Flash project is now available to be used within your HTML5 projects as well.

Visit `https://github.com/mrdoob/stats.js/` to download the latest version of the project. Implementing the `Stats` display in JavaScript is a little more involved than with ActionScript 3, however, it is still relatively straightforward. Take a look at this example implementation of the `Stats` display from the project documentation:

```
var stats = new Stats();
stats.setMode(1); // 0: fps, 1: ms

// Align top-left
stats.domElement.style.position = 'absolute';
stats.domElement.style.left = '0px';
stats.domElement.style.top = '0px';

document.body.appendChild(stats.domElement);

setInterval( function () {
    stats.begin();

    // your code goes here

    stats.end();
}, 1000 / 60 );
```

The major difference here is the fact that you are required to create the interval from which the `Stats` window will draw its calculations on your own. Since, as mentioned, JavaScript isn't based on a frame-based development paradigm, applying your own method for application intervals is the only way for data such as frames per second to be calculated. This is easily accomplished by using the built-in `setInterval()` method in JavaScript and setting the intended frame rate manually. Since the time a frame will be rendered in will be effectively emulated, we can do some simple math to get things in line to what we are already used to. In the previous example, we have set the interval duration to *1000/60*, where *60* is the intended frames per second value. This calculation is equal to *16.66666666666667* which is the millisecond value to sum 60 intervals in a single second. So after the `Stats` object is created and the display mode is set with the `setMode()` method, you will also need to manually set up the display location on the display.

We will continue to dig deeper into some of these applications as well as overview more platforms that can aid in project testing and benchmarking in the upcoming chapters. As I mentioned a couple chapters ago, the importance of going over your finished project in great detail to test execution time, memory usage, and browser performance is extremely important in making sure you can trust that everyone can view your content as you have intended in design. Web development lacks the benefit of the Flash compiler to automatically optimize our applications prior to runtime. The job is up to you to make sure your programs run smooth.

Summary

The one thing I probably can't stress enough is how important it is for you to go out and explore as many of the different applications and other services that you can. The better understanding you have about what is available to you, as the web developer, the better you can judge what the right tool for the job at hand is. If it hasn't sunk in yet, though similar in many aspects, HTML5 development is far more of an open style of development. Without the need to use a specific application set, you are free to do and use whatever your heart desires. This chapter barely scratches the surface of some of the popular applications developers are using today. However, it is my hope that with this general overview of the software that was explained, you can start developing your own HTML5 applications with the best tool for the job.

In the next chapter, will take a look at some of the popular options for pushing JavaScript even further by compiling not only JavaScript to other programming languages, but other programming languages to JavaScript.

8
Exporting to HTML5

In *Chapter 5, Code Once, Release Everywhere,* we spent some time learning about the CreateJS JavaScript framework as well as the CreateJS Toolkit plugin for Flash Professional CS6 (`http://www.adobe.com/ca/products/flash/flash-to-html5.html`) and how they can easily integrate your pre-existing knowledge of Flash development directly into HTML5 projects. Over the last year, Adobe has adopted this framework to be the official way to work with Flash-based assets in your HTML5 projects. That being said, there are actually a number of other ways that you can achieve somewhat of the same effect when attempting to directly move your Flash-based applications and games into pure HTML5. In this chapter, we will continue to look at some of the third-party tools and applications that may aid you in your asset and code development flow.

In this chapter, we will cover the following:

- Automatically generating HTML5 projects from a Flash SWF with Google's Swiffy
- Manually converting animated assets to HTML5-ready sprite sheets
- Writing your JavaScript libraries and frameworks in ActionScript 3 with Jangaroo
- Targeting all of your platform development needs in a single language source with Haxe
- Building robust web applications using Google's Dart programming language

Google Swiffy

The Swiffy project created by Google (`https://www.google.com/doubleclick/studio/swiffy`) is one of the easiest ways to port your pre-existing Flash applications into HTML5 projects. The aim of the project is to take in the already compiled Flash SWF files, and convert the data within into a JSON object with SVG vector animation data. The resulting Swiffy compiled JavaScript, can then be run directly within a modern web browser with the aid of the Google Swiffy Runtime.

Although this project is still in Beta and has many limitations, Swiffy supports Flash projects written in both ActionScript 2 and ActionScript 3 allowing you to possibly avoid having to ever think about manually converting your AS2 to AS3 projects manually. The support for more complex Flash assets within your projects is growing at a steady rate, however, it will be worth your time to check out the current browser and feature-support lists on the project website prior to usage as it may not fully cover the application you intend to convert (`https://www.google.com/doubleclick/studio/swiffy/gettingstarted.html`). ActionScript 3 support within Swiffy is limited to using specific methods within specific classes to be sure the conversion can properly take place. At the time of writing this book, the ActionScript 3 support within Swiffy contains the following limitations:

- Exception handling is not supported
- Optional arguments are not supported
- XML handling is not supported
- The order of object initialization and construction is not constant

You can find the full, up-to-date documentation for current ActionScript 3 support on the Swiffy ActionScript 3 Support page on the project website (https://www.google.com/doubleclick/studio/swiffy/actionscript3.html). If you head over to the ActionScript Support page, you can get a better sense of what classes and methods can be used within your Flash applications. If your application exceeds the supported properties listed in the project support page, there is a very high likelihood of your application not converting properly.

How does Swiffy work?

To get an idea of how Swiffy works and to see the output and limitations first hand, let's create a simple Flash application and convert it to HTML5 and view what happens. We will start with what is possibly the best case scenario for Swiffy conversions. Our Flash project will contain assets and animations completely created from within the Flash Professional IDE and avoid the use of any ActionScript for the time being. To make this example a little closer to a real-world example, we can pretend this Flash application is a pre-existing banner ad or other simple Flash movie which we would like to display on mobile devices or any other devices that don't have access to the Adobe Flash Player:

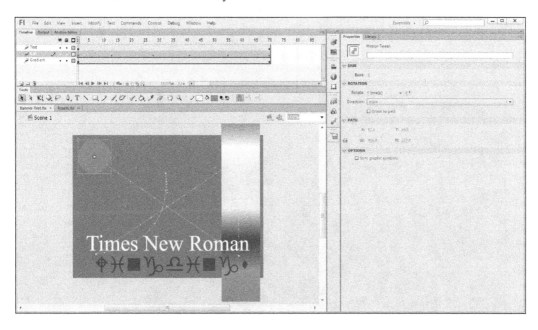

As ugly as the preceding example is, it actually represents some important factors to test. First off, we have a circle which has been motion tweened around the stage. Second, we have a rectangle filled with a gradient background color, again in the vector format. Finally, we have two lines of text: one is a simple use of the **Times New Roman** font and the other is a test of a more complex font such as **Wingdings**. Just like the two shapes, the text will be animated across the stage upon playback. The idea with this test is to see how well Swiffy deals with the extremely common SWF setup of just timeline modified elements. To make this test less complicated, we will also leave out any ActionScript and assume the timeline will loop infinitely.

With the timeline created, we can go ahead and output a SWF of this movie into our project directory. All Swiffy requires to generate its Web-ready output is the single SWF created from your Flash project, so open up a web browser and head over to the Swiffy project website (`https://www.google.com/doubleclick/studio/swiffy`).

 At the time of writing this book, Swiffy will allow you to upload any SWF file that equals or is less than 1 MB in size.

When you are all ready to convert your SWF, use the form on the front page of the project website to upload your SWF to the Swiffy servers. It should only take a moment or two for the results to appear, as shown in the following screenshot:

The results should display something like the preceding screenshot. A preview of the converted SWF will appear in Web-ready display as well as all of the output messages and links to download the output. The supplied QR code on every SWF conversion page will allow you to easily test the generated source on a mobile device to verify it is working properly. As displayed on the output page, you can easily download the HTML document along with all the other data by right-clicking on the link to the external output example (in this case, `Banner-Test.html`) and save the referenced page that way.

Examining Swiffy-generated code

With the content saved onto your local machine, let's take a quick moment to review exactly what has been done, and how we could transplant this asset into a pre-existing website. After opening up the HTML file, the first thing to take note of is the use of external libraries:

```
<script src="https://www.gstatic.com/swiffy/v5.0/runtime.js"></script>
```

This JavaScript call is importing the Google Swiffy runtime from the Google file server and is required to properly display the data following it. Just like CreateJS, the code that has been created is a hybrid of JavaScript and needs a final interpreter in order to properly function. This is a critically important thing to note about Swiffy. Including the `runtime.js` file is an absolute requirement to your project provided any assets generated from Swiffy were added.

Directly after the Swiffy runtime inclusion, you will notice a huge blob of text contained in more HTML `<script>` tags. The following is a snippet of what it looks like:

```
swiffyobject = {"tags":[{"frames":[],"scenes":[{"name":"Scene 1","offs
et":0}],"type":23},{"bounds":[{"ymin":0,"ymax":2240,"xmin":0,"xmax":10
399}],"id":1,"fillstyles":[{"transform":["4738D::1056F199e20k"],"type
":2,"gradient":{"stops":[{"color":[-65536],"offset":[0]},{"color":[-
256],"offset":[42]},{"color":[-16711936],"offset":[93]},{"color":[-
16711681],"offset":[127]}….
```

This data is the JavaScript object which represents all of the data from your assets and animations included in the original SWF. Since our example contained no Bitmap images, and everything within it was vector based, the entire application has been compiled down to 100 percent code and can be displayed with a couple lines of further JavaScript:

```
var swiffyElement = document.getElementById('swiffycontainer');
var stage = new swiffy.Stage(swiffyElement), swiffyobject);
stage.start();
```

Finding Swiffy's limits

All of this is fine and dandy until we start to make things a little more complicated. In the next example, I have created a very simple game in ActionScript 3. The idea of the game is to control the position of the box on the stage by moving your mouse around the visible stage. As time passes, your box will begin to grow and take up more space on the stage. The goal of the game is to go as long as possible without letting your box touch any of the randomly moving black dots. For simplicity, I have not included any user interface in this game. All of the results and output will just be sent to the web browser developer console for the time being. As always, you can check out the example in the working form as it is contained in the downloadable chapter example files:

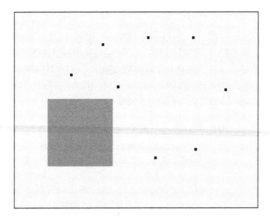

Yes, it is extremely crude, but it covers many common aspects of Flash applications in a manageable number of lines of code, which is perfect for our purposes of demonstration. As mentioned, there is no user interface in the game as any of the game output will just be sent to the Flash output debug window. Let's take a look at the code before going any further so you can take note of the specific features, classes, and variable types that have been utilized:

```
package {

    import flash.display.MovieClip;
    import flash.events.Event;
    import flash.events.MouseEvent;

    // Setting the frame rate is important here as we calculate
    // the users score from how many frames have passed.
    // It's worth noting that the TimerEvent class can be used
    // without any issue by applications converted with
    // Google Swiffy.
```

```
[SWF(backgroundColor="0xEFEFEF", width="1024", height="768",
frameRate="30")]

public class PlayerMoveTest extends MovieClip {
  // Setting a static const variable, defines
  // how many bad guy dots to add to the stage.
  private static const BAD_GUY_COUNT:int = 10;

  // The 'Player' class is a red box created and defined
  // within an SWC included into this project.
  private var _player:Player;

  // An array to hold all of the bad guys created
  // when the game is created.
  private var _badGuys:Array;

  private var _lifeTimer:int;
  private var _playerTarget:Object = new Object();

  /**
   * PlayerMoveTest Constructor
   */
  public function PlayerMoveTest() {
    // Start by creating and adding all of the bad
    // guys to the game stage.
    _badGuys = new Array();
    for(var i:int = 0; i < BAD_GUY_COUNT; i++) {
      // Using MovieClips instead of Sprites
      // as Sprites are not supported by the
      // Google Swiffy compiler.
      var badGuy:MovieClip = new MovieClip();
      badGuy.graphics.beginFill(0x000000, 1);
      badGuy.graphics.drawRect(-5, -5, 10, 10);
      badGuy.graphics.endFill();
      badGuy.x = Math.floor(Math.random() * (1000 + 1));
      badGuy.y = Math.floor(Math.random() * (700 + 1));
      _badGuys.push(badGuy);
      addChild(badGuy);
    }

// Create the users Player object
// Again, this is created within a included SWC.
    _player = new Player();
    _player.x = 100;
```

```
        _player.y = 100;
        _playerTarget.x = _player.x;
        _playerTarget.y = _player.y;
        addChild(_player);

        // Add a on enter frame to update the game stage.
        this.addEventListener(Event.ENTER_FRAME, updateEnviroment,
        false, 0, true);
    }

/**
 * Called on every frame when the game is in a playable
 * state.
 */
    private function updateEnviroment(event:Event):void {
        // Update the life timer, used for player score.
        _lifeTimer++;

        // Set the new player position target.
        // this position is based of the current X and Y
        // position of the user's mouse.
        _playerTarget.x = this.mouseX - 50;
        _playerTarget.y = this.mouseY - 50;

// Calculate the distance to the current
// player target.
        var xDistance:int = _playerTarget.x - _player.x;
        var yDistance:int = _playerTarget.y - _player.y;

        // Update the position of the player object. Use
        // a simple method to ease the position into the
        // target.
        _player.x = _playerTarget.x - (xDistance * 0.9);
        _player.y = _playerTarget.y - (yDistance * 0.9);
        _player.width += 0.5;
        _player.height += 0.5;

// Randomly move the position of each bad guy on
// every frame.
        for(var i:int = 0; i < BAD_GUY_COUNT; i++) {
            _badGuys[i].x += Math.round(Math.random() * (15 - (-15)) +
            (-15));
            _badGuys[i].y += Math.round(Math.random() * (15 - (-15)) +
            (-15));
```

```
// Using the common hitTestObject method
// to check and see if any of these bad guys
// are currently touching the player object.
        if(_player.hitTestObject(_badGuys[i])) {
            // The player is touching a bad guy
            // so stop the on enter frame event
            // and alert the users score.
            this.removeEventListener(Event.ENTER_FRAME,
            updateEnviroment);

            trace('GAME OVER!!!');
            trace('You lasted ' + Math.round(_lifeTimer / 30) + '
seconds.');
            }
        }
      }
    }
  }
```

If you are interested in actually compiling the source of this application, you can find all of the files to open it within Flash Builder as an ActionScript project. Compile the application to a SWF and test the application locally to confirm it is working. If all is well, let's attempt to send this file to Swiffy and see what happens:

> The ActionScript function Array() is not supported.
>
> The ActionScript method flash.display.DisplayObject.hitTestObject() is not supported.
>
> The ActionScript property flash.display.Sprite.graphics is not supported. (3 occurrences)

Provided you followed the steps properly, Swiffy will fail when attempting to convert this SWF and generate the error list in the previous screenshot. Let take a quick look at what went wrong, the limitations, and workarounds that could be put into place to correct the issue. To begin, the first error listed the notice that arrays are not supported by the Swiffy compiler. In our application's case, we used an array to contain all of the bad-guy instances in a single global variable. Without the use of arrays in this or any application, the requirement to manage data in a more primitive manner is required. This issue alone can be the deciding factor when deciding to use Swiffy to do your conversion. Although there are many ways to get around this issue, the fact of the matter is, if you have an application that is littered with arrays, chances are the current version of Swiffy will not be able to help you. Regardless of all that bad news, let's move on to the second issue. Not surprisingly, the hitTestObject method, which is common in ActionScript 3 development, is not supported by the compiler either.

This easy-to-use method can be a life saver when simple collision detection is required in Flash development, but since there is no direct JavaScript equivalent to convert it to. Again, this can be compensated for but the resulting code would be far larger then calling a single method as one is used to in typical ActionScript 3 development. So this can be considered an issue, but not a dead end provided your collision detection is only using the supported methods and properties. The final error listed in our conversion attempt was the use of the `Sprite.graphics` class. If you recall, the code example specifically used MovieClips rather than Sprites, as Sprites are not supported by the Swiffy compiler. However, unlike the `Player` object, which was originally created within the Flash Professional IDE and saved into a SWC, the bad guy objects were created within the code with the use of the internal ActionScript 3 Graphics API:

```
badGuy.graphics.beginFill(0x000000, 1);
badGuy.graphics.drawRect(-5, -5, 10, 10);
badGuy.graphics.endFill();
```

These three lines are the reason for the final error. Since the `MovieClip` object in Flash is built on top of the `Sprite` class, the resulting error follows suit. Since the SWC deals with the creation of the `Player` object, no errors are passed for that object. However, it is worth noting that even with these errors fixed by removing all of the bad guys and only having a box moving around, the successfully converted result still displays nothing on the HTML version of the game. At the moment, it seems Swiffy doesn't support the use of SWC's in the ActionScript 3 project, it is more comfortable using the old school pure Flash IDE development style of application development.

All of this being said, the reality is that the majority of the work Swiffy can reliably do for you is simple Flash applications and movie conversions, not your typical Flash game or application. Despite the lack for many features that have commonly been used in Flash development for years, Swiffy can still be a very handy tool for assets such as integrated website animations or advertisement banners.

Generating sprite sheets in Flash Professional CS6

If you ever intend to port or copy some of your pre-existing Flash-based timeline animations to a HTML5 project, you are going to have to do some conversion of your own. As you have seen in the examples in this book, timeline animations just don't exist in the HTML5 stack. Therefore, you will need to convert the animation sequence into a new format that can be displayed properly on the Web. One of the easiest options is converting the animation into a video file and using the `<video>` tag element to play it back. Unfortunately, converting bitmap or vector assets into a video file that can properly be played back on the Web will result in a ton of quality loss. To top that off, the video playback will be very heavy resulting in slower application load times. Finally, videos in HTML5 lack many important features such as support of alpha transparency, resulting in all of your assets contained in a fully visible rectangular container. To get around all of these issues, many web developers are turning to the tried and true method of sprite sheets. The concept behind sprite sheets is pretty simple. Take all of the frames in your animation sequence, place them all side by side on the same image (with a transparent background), and save the image as an uncompressed PNG file. This way, when loaded by a client over the Web, downloading a single file is all that is needed to have the entire animation sequence in memory ready for playback. Converting your Flash-based timeline animations into sprite sheets manually, by copy and pasting each frame into a PNG document, is a long a tedious undertaking. Thankfully, it is one undertaking you will not need to deal with as Flash Professional CS6 has incorporated a sprite sheet generator right in the IDE.

Using the sprite sheet generator in Flash CS6 is painfully simple. The good folks at Adobe have managed to create a tool that will easily have you using your Flash animations in your HTML5 projects in minutes. Though simple to use, the feature can be a little hidden, so let's quickly take a look at the sprite sheet generator in action and place some of the results in a working HTML5 document to test.

For example purposes, I have created a very simple example of a Flash animation on the timeline which includes only three different shapes. Each shape is displayed for only 5 frames for a total of 15 frames of animation:

 As always, you can find all the example files in the downloadable chapter examples.

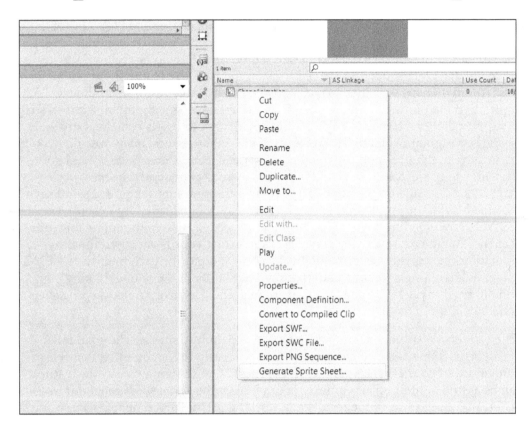

Locate the MovieClip within the library of the Flash project and right-click on it. Reviewing the context menu displayed when right-clicking on any MovieClip, you will find a **Generate Sprite Sheet** option. Select this option and you will be presented with the new, feature rich, **Generate Sprite Sheet** window:

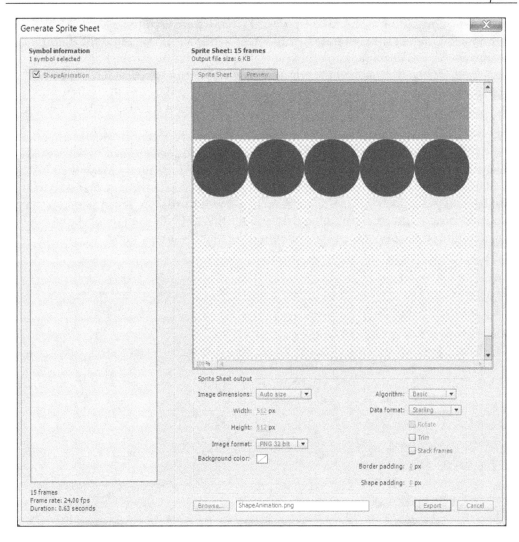

Upon initial inspection, you can see every frame in your animation has automatically been appended to the same document and lined up in a grid format. As mentioned, this animation contains 15 frames, therefore, every frame has been appended to the sprite sheet **Preview** window and is displayed with the default configuration. Before saving this output, let's check out some of the options available to see if we can optimize this sprite sheet any further.

We can start by getting a general overview of what we are about to export. At the bottom-left corner of the **Generate Sprite Sheet** window, you will find the details of the current MovieClip containing the frame count and duration based on a specific frame rate. On the right side of the window, you can see an easy-to-view preview of what the sprite sheet will look like when generated under the current configuration. Selecting the second **Preview** tab will display the animation running in its native form.

Below the preview window is all of the configuration properties available to you when exporting the animation assets and dataset. The dimensions of the exported image can be automatically sized by Flash or configured manually to set the available area where your animation frame can be placed. The image format can also be configured as PNG or JPG formats to allow for further compression on the exported image. It is recommended that you set this as PNG with no background unless required to allow for proper image background transparency:

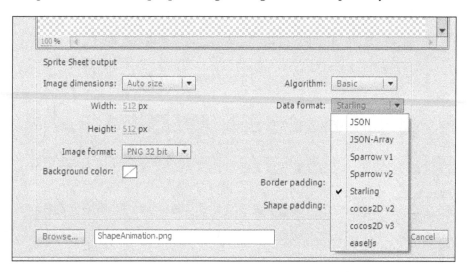

The right size of the configuration properties contains the settings for the dataset export. Since the image exported for the sprite sheet will only contain the frame assets and no animation data, the sprite sheet will require some form of data in order to properly playback. You will usually have no issue when using the basic algorithm from the available slicing algorithms. With the basic setting, sprites are arranged in nice uniform rows in an easy-to-use grid layout. This is the optimal output setting when dealing with any simple animation. The other current option for algorithms is the **MaxRects** option. This option is used to attempt to pack the frames as tightly together as possible. The reason one would do this is to minimize the exported image filesize to allow for faster download times over an Internet connection. Once an algorithm has been selected, we can move on to probably the most important setting in this export window. The **Data format** selection allows you to set the data export format to specifically work with how ever you are developing your HTML5 application. Support for **The Sparrow Framework** for iOS development (`http://gamua.com/sparrow`), **The Starling Framework** for ActionScript 3 (`http://gamua.com/starling/`), as well as **Cocos2D** (`http://cocos2d.org/`) have been included. As a HTML5 developer, the three main export settings you will probably be most interested in are the **JSON**, **JSON-Array**, and **easeljs** options. Exporting the dataset as a simple JSON export will allow you to use the data universally as JSON in the open standard for human-readable data storage. The **JSON-Array** setting is extremely similar with the difference of storing the data in JSON arrays rather than direct objects. The difference between the two will really only affect how you interpret the data within your code. Finally, the **easeljs** export setting allows you to automatically prepare the exported animation for inclusion in your CreateJS, or EaselJS project. This export setting is handy when you are attempting to include an external asset within another Flash project into a pre-existing CreateJS toolkit-based project:

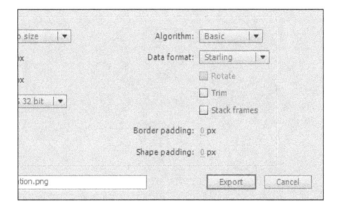

The final settings in the configuration are the **Trim** and **Stack frames** options. Trimming the frames in the sprite sheet will remove any unused empty space between each of the elements within. This will again optimize your end result by minimizing the exported image filesize. Finally, the **Stack frames** option allows you to further optimize your animation by removing or stacking any frames that are identical in your animation.

Since there will be no need to store the same image twice since the exported dataset will contain the timeline information, these assets can be removed without issue:

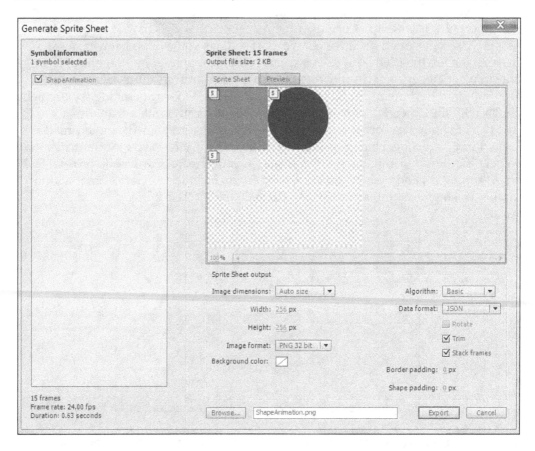

With all of these settings covered, let's export this animation with the settings in the previous screenshot to see what we get for an output. When the **Export** button is clicked, the window will close when completed, and you will be able to find the exported material in the root of your project directory. With the **JSON** setting appended to the **Data format** option, two files are exported. The first file is the sprite sheet image in the PNG format:

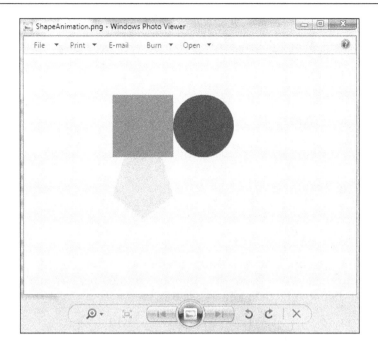

The second file is our JSON output containing all of the frame positions and sizes of the animation. The following is a snippet from the exported JSON containing the animation data for the first three frame of animation:

```
{"frames": {

"ShapeAnimation0000":
{
   "frame": {"x":0,"y":0,"w":100,"h":100},
   "rotated": false,
   "trimmed": false,
   "spriteSourceSize": {"x":0,"y":0,"w":100,"h":100},
   "sourceSize": {"w":100,"h":100}
},
"ShapeAnimation0001":
{
   "frame": {"x":0,"y":0,"w":100,"h":100},
   "rotated": false,
   "trimmed": false,
   "spriteSourceSize": {"x":0,"y":0,"w":100,"h":100},
   "sourceSize": {"w":100,"h":100}
},
"ShapeAnimation0002":
{
```

```
      "frame": {"x":0,"y":0,"w":100,"h":100},
      "rotated": false,
      "trimmed": false,
      "spriteSourceSize": {"x":0,"y":0,"w":100,"h":100},
      "sourceSize": {"w":100,"h":100}
    },
    "ShapeAnimation0003":
    {
      "frame": {"x":0,"y":0,"w":100,"h":100},
      "rotated": false,
      "trimmed": false,
      "spriteSourceSize": {"x":0,"y":0,"w":100,"h":100},
      "sourceSize": {"w":100,"h":100}
    },
```

The data is extremely simple to read and understand which is good, as from this point out without the use of a game development framework or CreateJS, we have to interpret and display this data and assets ourselves:

```html
<!DOCTYPE html>
<html lang="en">
  <head>
    <meta charset="utf-8" />
    <title>ShapeAnimation Sprite Sheet Example</title>

    <style>
      #animation {
        width:100px;
        height:100px;
        overflow:hidden;
      }
    </style>

    <script type="text/javascript" src="js/jquery-1.9.1.min.js">
    </script>
    <script>
    var animationData = Array();
    var currentFrame = 0;

    $(document).ready(function() {
      // Get the Sprite Sheet JSON
      $.getJSON('ShapeAnimation.json', function(data) {
        // Save each of the objects into an array.
        $.each(data['frames'], function(key, val) {
          animationData.push(val);
```

```
        });

          // Start the animation.
          runAnimation();
        });
      });

      function runAnimation() {
        // Update the CSS properties of the Sprite Sheet image.
        $('#animation img').css('margin-left',
        animationData[currentFrame]['frame']['x'] * -1);
        $('#animation img').css('margin-top',
        animationData[currentFrame]['frame']['y'] * -1);

        // Update the frame counter and reset if needed.
        currentFrame++;
        if(currentFrame == animationData.length) currentFrame = 0;

        // Keep calling this method every 200ms.
        setTimeout(runAnimation, 200);
      }
    </script>
  </head>

  <body>
    <div id="animation">
      <img src="ShapeAnimation.png">
    </div>
  </body>
</html>
```

Due to the tremendous support for CreateJS in Flash Professional CS6, the export and usage of the EaselJS setting for sprite sheets is definitely the easiest way to go. However, as demonstrated in the previous code snippet, with the standardized JSON export methods, you can implement any Flash animation as a sprite sheet into your HTML5 projects with relative ease.

 If you are interested in learning more about sprite sheets but you don't want to spend time creating all of the assets, head over to Google images and search for sprite sheets. You will find an endless resource of great sprite sheets to test your applications with. Of course, you should always be sure to have permission or ownership of any asset when used on a public facing website.

Jangaroo

The story behind the development of Jangaroo (`http://www.jangaroo.net`) is actually pretty interesting. Created by the development team at CoreMedia (`http://www.coremedia.com`), Jangaroo was built out of the frustrations the internal development team had with the current JavaScript development capabilities. Rather than dealing with many of the common syntax issues that JavaScript possess, the development team at CoreMedia set about to create a ActionScript 3 to JavaScript compiler written in Java. As absurd as that may sound, the actuality is that Flash developers can easily continue writing in a familiar syntax while specifically targeting HTML5-based web development. Jangaroo aims to allow developers to write high quality JavaScript frameworks and applications with the power of ActionScript 3. In a nutshell, it will take in ActionScript 3 files, and with the use of its compiler written in Java, convert them into ready to use JavaScript:

So why would anyone want to avoid writing native JavaScript and begin writing ActionScript 3 for the next HTML5 project? Well, as a developer with previous experience writing ActionScript 3, you can probably already answer this question from all of the examples and overviews so far in this book. When it comes to writing large robust applications in HTML5, the lack of packages, classes, and proper inheritance in JavaScript can begin to create a minefield of code which can be tricky to manage. By allowing yourself to continue developing your applications in a language that you are not only used to, but allows for easier management of the classes in your project, you can surpass many common hurdles that would have arisen during a pure JavaScript development cycle.

The heart of the Jangaroo project is the Jangaroo ActionScript 3 to JavaScript compiler called `jooc`. The compiler will take in your ActionScript `.as` files and export them as compiled JavaScript `.js` files. To install and run Jangaroo, you will need to begin by making sure you have installed an up-to-date version of the Java Runtime Environment (http://www.oracle.com/technetwork/java/javase/downloads/index.html) as well as Maven (http://maven.apache.org). The installation and setup of these two pieces of software may seem intimidating, but be sure the process is extremely straightforward and well-documented, so I will leave that process up to you.

 One note worth making when dealing with installing the Java Runtime Environment on your computer is to be sure the JAVA_HOME environment variable is properly set. If you encounter any issue during the installation of testing process of Jangaroo, this will be a good place to start debugging.

To give you an example of a simplified development cycle of a JavaScript-driven application created with ActionScript 3 and compiled with Jangaroo, let's use the HelloWorld example that can be found on the project website (http://www.jangaroo.net/tutorial):

```
package {
/**
 * The most simple Jangaroo class on earth.
 */
public class HelloWorld {
  /**
   * Let the browser display a welcome message.
   */
  public static function main():void {
    window.document.body.innerHTML =
    "<strong>Hello World from Jangaroo!</strong>";
```

```
        }
    }
}
```

As you can see in the code example, the syntax available to your ActionScript classes is a hybrid of common ActionScript 3 as well as some special window and document object references to allow you to integrate your application into the browser properly. If you are interested in learning more about the language and code syntax options when preparing ActionScript 3 for the Jangaroo compiler, head over to the **Writing Code** page in the official Jangaroo documentation (`http://www.jangaroo. net/tutorial/writing_code`).

The bulk of Jangaroo is open source and the project code and assets can be found on the CoreMedia Github page (`https://github.com/CoreMedia`).

Haxe

Keeping on the topic of compiling applications and other programming languages directly to JavaScript, I should take a moment and cover some of the exciting features in the world of Haxe development:

Haxe (http://haxe.org) is its own standalone open source programming language. Where most programming languages are built for a specific application type in mind, JavaScript for the Web, ActionScript for Flash, Haxe can be compiled and run on a variety of platforms and devices all from the same source code. Haxe source can selectively be compiled into JavaScript, Flash, PHP, C++, C#, and Java and with your prior experience with ActionScript 3 and new skills you have learned in JavaScript, learning the Haxe language syntax is a breeze.

Although cross-platform development may not be of interest to you right now, having at least a basic understanding of what languages such as Haxe offer may allow you to fill some more gaps in your development skill set. Just for some final clarity before we move on, let's take a quick peek at an example snippet of Haxe code which can be found on the **Code Snippets** page on the Haxe project website (http://haxe.org/doc/snip). The following code is an example of implementing the popular sorting method, Quicksort (http://en.wikipedia.org/wiki/Quicksort). Since we already have an idea of what this sorting algorithm is attempting to accomplish, let's review this code to mainly get an idea of class, method, and variable syntax in the Haxe programming language:

```
class Quicksort {

    static var arr = [4,8,0,3,9,1,5,2,6,7];

    static function quicksort( lo : Int, hi : Int ) : Void {
        var i = lo;
        var j = hi;
        var buf = arr;
        var p = buf[(lo+hi)>>1];
        while( i <= j ) {
            while( arr[i] > p ) i++;
            while( arr[j] < p ) j--;
            if( i <= j ) {
                var t = buf[i];
                buf[i++] = buf[j];
                buf[j--] = t;
            }
        }
        if( lo < j ) quicksort( lo, j );
        if( i < hi ) quicksort( i, hi );
    }

    static function main() {
        quicksort( 0, arr.length-1 );
        trace(arr);
    }
}
```

As you can see directly in the first line, Haxe has full class support unlike JavaScript. This concept alone may be a selling point as ActionScript developers moving over into Haxe will find many more similarities which are unavailable in JavaScript. Other features such as static functions, strict variable typing, and common debug methods such as `trace()` are just a couple more of the great features within Haxe that specifically let a developer with previous ActionScript 3 development experience shine.

> If you are interested in learning more about the exciting world of Haxe development, checkout the book *Haxe 2 Beginners Guide, Packt Publishing* (`http://www.packtpub.com/haxe-2-beginners-guide/book`).

Haxe itself is a beast of a project. The ability to cross compile your application source code directly to almost every modern platform available is an extremely valuable asset when you are developing a project with very specific platform requirements. Even if you intend to target only HTML5 web projects with your Haxe source code, having the ability to move your application to another platform with only a couple clicks of the mouse is pretty amazing. Also, as with many of the other platforms and compilers we have reviewed in this chapter, Haxe can alleviate many of the common complaints web developers have with JavaScript syntax. The project is still relatively new although many developers have already jumped on the bandwagon. If developing your next application in Haxe sounds like an interesting challenge, I highly recommend looking into it some more.

Google Dart

With the goal of helping developers from all platforms build complex, high-performance client apps for the modern Web, Google's Dart (`https://code.google.com/p/dart/`) is another great example of pushing web development, more specifically JavaScript development, to the limit. Just like Haxe, Dart is an open-source project that uses its own specific programming language to compile into Web-ready JavaScript documents and just like Jangaroo, Dart was built out of the frustrations with the limits of the current web development platforms. In an attempt to bring a new structured, single language workflow Google has released a *Technology Preview* of the Dart project for early testing and feedback from the web development community:

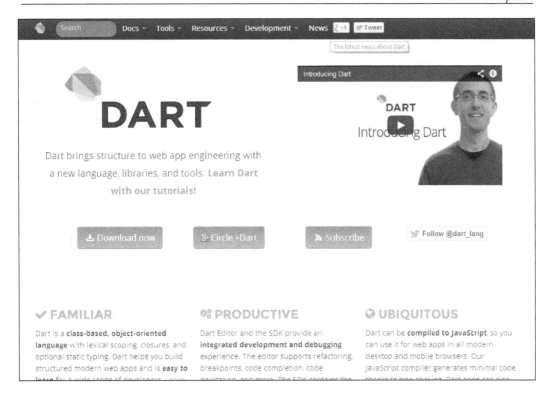

Of course, since Dart is built on its own language syntax, there will be a learning curve involved when first starting out. To aid in the strain of learning a new language, I highly recommend checking out the official Dart Editor. The Dart Editor (http://www.dartlang.org/docs/editor/) is probably the easiest way to get up and running with Dart development.

It supports features such as real-time error and syntax checking to alert you of any issues before you compile, as well as code completion to help you understand what can be done with each method and property:

The Dart Editor, like many others, is built on the popular Eclipse IDE. As simplified as the code editor is, this can be considered another win for anyone with Flash Builder experience as the interface will be extremely familiar. I say this editor is simplified because the editor does not come as a plugin for Eclipse, instead it comes packaged as its own standalone Eclipse-based editor with all of the unnecessary elements removed from it.

Like the overview of Haxe, I will keep this brief as Dart is still a very new project and I have yet to personally meet anyone who has developed a popular web application with it. That being said, there is absolutely no reason to discredit a language such as Dart. As the JavaScript specification evolves and browser support follow suit, the need for these projects may become less. However, as any Flash developer knows, the ability to compile projects with a proper debug and output flow can allow them to find and fix issues faster than many traditional methods of writing client-side scripts.

Summary

During the course of this chapter, we spent some time looking at some projects that are pushing the limits of web application development from websites and libraries such as Google's Swiffy project that easily allow you to convert simple Flash SWF files directly to a Web-friendly HTML and JavaScript configuration, to familiar methods of exporting Flash vector and bitmap animations into Web-ready sprite sheets right from within the Flash Professional IDE. Projects such as Haxe, Dart, and Jangaroo give developers new options when attempting to create their HTML5 projects. The native JavaScript that will drive their application can actually be written in a completely different language altogether. Extending the capabilities of JavaScript into other languages may seem backwards at first, but the reasons for creating these projects generally all come down to the lack of common language syntax and development flow issues developers have when writing JavaScript. As mentioned earlier, none of the projects or features within specific applications mentioned in this chapter are required when developing you next HTML5 project. Arming yourself with the knowledge of what projects and platforms web developers have available to them right now will allow you to come to better conclusions as to the best way for you to tackle your next HTML5 project.

I have to stress, the list of applications, features, and compilers mentioned in this chapter is only a small fraction of what is available to you when working with JavaScript. If you are interested in seeing more projects that can compile to and or extend JavaScript, head over to `http://altjs.org` to get a start. There you will find a listing of projects that target beginner to advanced developer styles, so I am sure there will be something there to interest you. Many of these projects are based off of CoffeeScript (`http://coffeescript.org`), yet another dedicated language that compiles directly to JavaScript, which is yet another great project I recommend checking out. The number of projects related to extending JavaScript's development flow and abilities seems endless, and growing every day. No one can ever expect you to know all of them, but having a general understanding of what is out there and what many of these platforms can do will allow you to make faster and better decisions when setting out to develop your next project.

In the next two chapters, we will begin taking everything we have covered up to this point into an actual HTML5 application development flow. We will cover many of the important aspects every developer should be aware of when developing for the Web as well as a way to properly test your application as you develop. Finally to wrap everything up, we will take that application to the Internet and cover some ways to publish and maintain your project once it is live.

9
Avoiding the Roadblocks

Up to this point in the book, we have covered many of the new and exciting aspects of web development with HTML5. However, during this time we have only ever looked at each feature as an individual aspect rather than a piece of a larger project. When it comes to building applications for the real world, you will inevitably have to begin merging these new features together to build the appropriate feature set within your app. In this chapter, we will build a playable game using some of the new and old features available to you as a web developer. Beginning with a version built-in Flash, we will then build a direct port of the application into HTML5 and discuss the differences and issues you may encounter while dealing with assets and functionality that you have become used to in the ActionScript and Flash world of development.

The Jet Pack game

The application we will build is a simple 2D, side scrolling game with simplistic controls that can easily be converted to touch event for mobile devices. To keep things easy to explain and understand, I have modeled this game after the popular Helicopter Game (http://www.helicopter-game.org/) that has been played all over the Internet for many years.

The following screenshot shows the Helicopter Game:

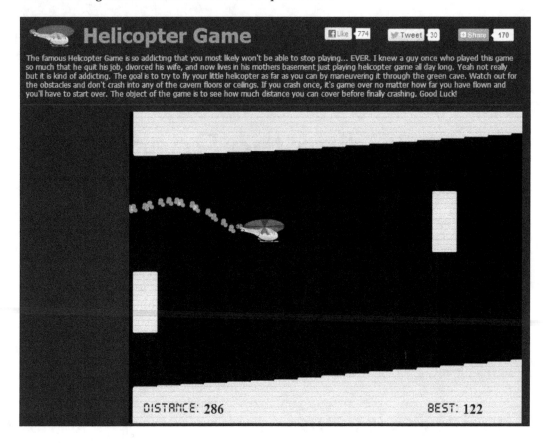

Although there are already many versions of this game on the Internet, the most popular ones are written in Flash, cutting out many users on mobile and desktop browsers from playing it. The gameplay and controls are extremely simplistic and only require the player to use a single key on their keyboard or use their mouse to click instead.

Rather than attempt to directly copy this popular game, we will use it as a starting point for gameplay design. To add our own personal touch to the game, we will switch the helicopter character to a little man with a jet pack. Before we get started, take a look at the following screenshot of the game in action to get a better idea of what our end result will look like. Of course you can always play the game yourself by checking out the Flash and HTML versions of this application located with the example files for this chapter:

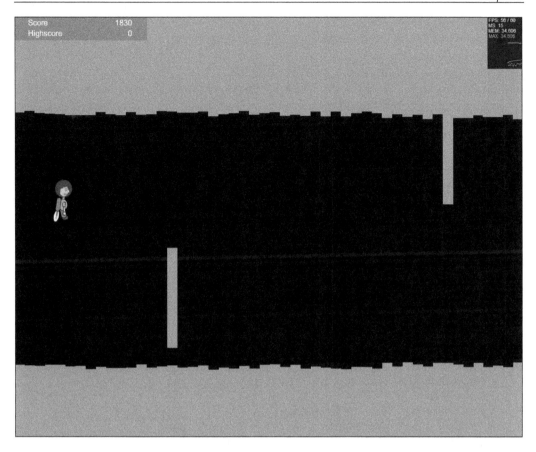

You play this game as the character, the Jet Pack man, displayed on the left of the previous screenshot. Your goal is to control the character's altitude by activating his jetpack. As your character travels deeper into the cave system, not only will the cave become increasingly tighter, but there will be randomly placed obstacles which you will need to pilot yourself around. Gravity plays an important role as well since when your jetpack is not activated, your player will begin falling back down to the ground. The level objects are dynamically generated in real time as the player travels deeper into the cave and constrained to tighter positions as the difficulty increases. During every interval of the game source code, each section of the level is checked for collision with the player to determine if the game is over or not. Each interval of the game also increases the player's current score, so the deeper into the cave you travel, the higher your score will be. High scores are tracked within the game instance and displayed within the UI to allow the player to easily see what the next attempt's goal will be.

As I mentioned before, we will initially look at this game's source code written in ActionScript 3 to get an understanding of how I have written it. Of course this comes with the disclaimer that although some aspects of this games code may work for you in other projects, the source code for this game has been set up to aid in our learning and understanding of ActionScript 3 to HTML5 conversions. This game has not been optimized to the point it should be for public release and I will do my best during this chapter to point out what some of these short comings are. With all of this in mind, let's jump right into the source structure of the Flash version of this Jet Pack game.

Building the game in Flash

To keep things easy to understand we will keep the line and file count to a minimum for this game. We will begin with the base class for our ActionScript project named `Game`. Check out the following condensed base class example to get an idea of the game's code structure. You can always look at the full version in the downloadable chapter example files:

```
package {
  import flash.display.Sprite;
  import flash.events.Event;
  import flash.events.KeyboardEvent;

  [SWF(width='1000', height='800', backgroundColor='#000000',
  frameRate='60')]
  public class Game extends Sprite {
    private var _levelBlocks:Array = new Array();
    private var _interval:int;
    private var _blockInterval:int;
    private var _player:JetPackMan;
    private var _difficulty:int = 10;
    private var _speed:int = 10;
    private var _keyDown:Boolean;
    private var _score:int;
    private var _highScore:int;
    private var _scoreBoard:ScoreBoard;
    private var _gameOver:Boolean;

    public function Game() {
      generateLevel();
      createPlayer();
      displayScore();

      this.addEventListener(Event.ENTER_FRAME, updateI terval,
      false, 0, true);
      stage.addEventListener(KeyboardEvent.KEY_DOWN, onKeyDown,
      false, 0, true);
```

```
    stage.addEventListener(KeyboardEvent.KEY_UP, onKeyUp, false,
    0, true);
}

// Starts a new game.
private function startNewGame():void {
    // Reset the game switches and counters.
    _gameOver = false;
    _score = 0;
    _speed = 10;
    _difficulty = 10;

    for each(var block:LevelBlock in _levelBlocks) {
        block.destroy();
        removeChild(block);
    }
    _levelBlocks = new Array();

    removeChild(_player);
    _player.destroy();
    _player = null;

    generateLevel();
    createPlayer();

    this.addEventListener(Event.ENTER_FRAME, updateInterval,
    false, 0, true);
}

// Adds the score board to the stage.
private function displayScore():void {
    _scoreBoard = new ScoreBoard();
    _scoreBoard.x = -40;
    _scoreBoard.y = -20;
    addChild(_scoreBoard);
}

// Generates the beginnings of a new level.
private function generateLevel():void {
    for(var i:int = 0; i < 20; i++) {
        var randomHeight:int = (Math.floor(Math.random() *
            (_difficulty - (_difficulty - 10) + 1)) + (_difficulty -
            10));
        var levelBlock:LevelBlock = new LevelBlock(_speed, 800 +
            (20 * i), randomHeight - 10, 20, 100);
        _levelBlocks.push(levelBlock);
        addChildAt(levelBlock, 0);
```

```
        randomHeight = (Math.floor(Math.random() * (_difficulty -
          (_difficulty - 10) + 1)) + (_difficulty - 10));
        var bottomLevelBlock:LevelBlock = new LevelBlock(_speed, 800 +
          (20 * i), (randomHeight * -1) + 750, 20, 100);
        _levelBlocks.push(bottomLevelBlock);
        addChildAt(bottomLevelBlock, 0);
    }
}

// Creates and adds a player object to the stage.
private function createPlayer():void {
  _player = new JetPackMan();
  _player.x = 80;
  _player.y = 400;
  addChild(_player);
}

// Called on keyboard key down.
private function onKeyDown(e:KeyboardEvent):void {
  if(_gameOver) startNewGame();
  _keyDown = true;
}

// Called on keyboard key up.
private function onKeyUp(e:KeyboardEvent):void {
  _keyDown = false;
}

// Game interval. Called on each frame.
private function updateInterval(e:Event):void {
  _score = _score + 1;
  _scoreBoard.score.text = String(_score);

  if(_keyDown) {
    _player.jetPackOn();
    _player.y = _player.y - 5;
  } else {
    _player.jetPackOff();
    _player.y = _player.y + 5;
  }

  _interval++;
  var increaseSpeed:Boolean = false;
  if(_interval >= 100) {
    increaseSpeed = true;
    _difficulty = _difficulty + 5;
```

```
  //_speed++;
  _interval = 0;
}

// Update every block
for each(var block:LevelBlock in _levelBlocks) {
  block.update();

  if(block.hitTestObject(_player)) {
    _player.explode();
    _gameOver = true;

    if(_score > _highScore) {
      _highScore = _score;
      _scoreBoard.highscore.text = String(_highScore);
    }

    this.removeEventListener(Event.ENTER_FRAME,
    updateInterval);
  }

  if(increaseSpeed) block.setSpeed(_speed);
}

// Check if new blocks need to be added
if(_levelBlocks[_levelBlocks.length - 1].currentX() < 2000)
{
  var randomHeight:int = (Math.floor(Math.random() *
  (_difficulty - (_difficulty - 10) + 1)) + (_difficulty -
  10));
  var levelBlock:LevelBlock = new LevelBlock(_speed, _
  levelBlocks[_levelBlocks.length - 1].currentX() + 20,
  randomHeight - _difficulty, 20, 100 + _difficulty);
  _levelBlocks.push(levelBlock);
  addChildAt(levelBlock, 0);

  randomHeight = (Math.floor(Math.random() * (_difficulty -
  (_difficulty - 10) + 1)) + (_difficulty - 10));
  var bottomLevelBlock:LevelBlock = new LevelBlock(_speed,
  _levelBlocks[_levelBlocks.length - 1].currentX(),
  (randomHeight * -1) + 750, 20, 100 + _difficulty);
  _levelBlocks.push(bottomLevelBlock);
  addChildAt(bottomLevelBlock, 0);
}

// Add a random block every now and then to make things
interesting.
```

```
     // We will base the frequency of random blocks on the
     // current difficulty in the game.
     _blockInterval++;
     if(_blockInterval > 5000 / _difficulty) {
       _blockInterval = 0;

       randomHeight = (Math.floor(Math.random() * (750 - 5 + 1))
       + 5);
       var randomY:int = (Math.floor(Math.random() * (750 - 5 +
       1)) + 5);
       var randomBlock:LevelBlock = new LevelBlock(_speed,
       _levelBlocks[_levelBlocks.length - 1].currentX(), randomY,
       20, 100 + _difficulty);
       _levelBlocks.push(randomBlock);
       addChildAt(randomBlock, 0);
     }
   }

  }
}
```

This single class manages to take care of the majority of the gameplay and user interactions. The game is constantly updated based on the current difficulty factor set within the game. As the game progresses, the difficulty is translated into scrolling speed as each asset within the level is updated and set to change its x position value in larger amounts. Although there are two more classes to support the creation of the Player as well as all of the LevelBlock, I will leave that to you to dig into.

Converting game assets

To start preparing this game to be ported to HTML5, we will begin with the assets used within the game, converting and preparing each of them for the web. To create the user interface and player object within this game, I have created and published a Flash SWC which is included into this ActionScript project in Flash Builder. The assets within the SWC contain not only the objects and animations used in the game, but the sounds as well as shown in the following screenshot:

As you can see in the previous screenshot, my crudely hand drawn Jet Pack man has a timeline based key frame animation sequence attached to him to allow him to visually turn on and off his jetpack as well as explode when he impacts any wall. This timeline animation has some simple ActionScript appended to some of the frames which allow for easy stopping and looping for the animation sequence.

To convert the Player MovieClip into an HTML5 ready asset, we will use the Sprite Sheet Generator tool we discussed in previous chapters as shown in the following screenshot:

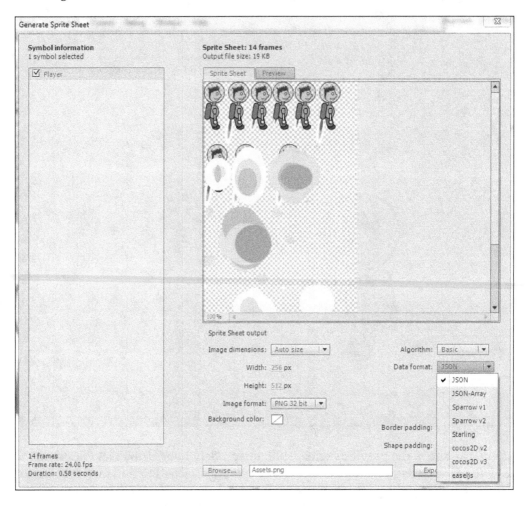

After condensing the image into the smallest layout possible and optimizing the output properties in the **Generate Sprite Sheet** window, set the **Data format** property to **JSON** and export the data. The compiled Sprite Sheet as well as the **JSON** file will be used to replicate the Player's animation from our HTML5 conversion. Once we have prepped the Player Sprite Sheet, we can put it aside for the time being while we convert the remainder of the assets.

Now let's move on to preparing the audio used within the game. The audio assets within the Flash SWF can easily be prepared for HTML5 by simply locating the source MP3 files and placing them within the HTML5 game project directory. Since the MP3 files are supported for use within HTML5 under the `<audio>` element, no further preparation will be needed in order to get the audio ready for our conversion. The tricky part with HTML5 audio only comes when you need to deal with it in the code, which we will get into shortly.

Without the use of the Flash Timeline or any other HTML5 sprite sheet library, we will have to import and manipulate the Sprite Sheet data of our Player completely on our own. Handy calls like `gotoAndPlay();` and `stop();` do not exist in JavaScript, so we will need to recreate that functionality on our own. This may sound like a monumental task, but rest assured, Sprite Sheets images and datasets contain all of the necessary information required for you to display them properly. All you need is to understand the data format and the properties that need referencing. Since Sprite Sheets are broken up into frames, the concept of playback control via numerical frame referencing should be extremely familiar to you. The frames that have been exported within the Sprite Sheet dataset will directly correspond to the numerical value of the frames within the source MovieClip in Flash. However, since the frame data in the **JSON** file is in an array, we will encounter an `off by one` error if we don't compensate for the fact numerical array keys start at 0 and not 1. Again, it's worth mentioning that this method of displaying the Sprite Sheet is just one of thousands of implementations of Sprite Sheets in HTML5. Many developers have created their own open source projects to alleviate much of the stress of having to do this yourself within every one of your projects.

> There are a ton of great open source resources on the web that can aid in Sprite Sheet integration into your HTML5 project. One library worth checking out is `http://www.spritely.net`, a fully HTML5 and jQuery based Sprite Sheet library.

Take a look at the condensed version of the converted `JetPackMan` class which is shown in the following JavaScript. This will give you a much clearer idea of frame control for this Sprite Sheet:

```
var JetPackMan = function() {
  var _jetPackSound = document.getElementById("jetpack");
  _jetPackSound.addEventListener("ended", onSoundDone, false);

  var _explosionSound = document.getElementById("explosion");
  var _soundPlaying = false;

  var _animationData = Array();
  var _imageSource = 'imgs/JetPackMan.png';
```

```javascript
var _currentFrame = 0;
var _canvas = document.getElementById("player");
var _context = _canvas.getContext("2d");

var _imageObj = new Image();
_imageObj.src = _imageSource;

var _currentY = 0;
var _jetPackOn = false;
var _explode = false;
var _interval;

var _xVal = 0;
var _yVal = 0;
var _widthVal = 0;
var _heightVal = 0;

// Append the Sprite Sheet JSON to a local Array.
$.each(JetPackManData['frames'], function(key, val) {
  _animationData.push(val);
});

_widthVal = _animationData[_currentFrame]['frame']['w'];
_heightVal = _animationData[_currentFrame]['frame']['h'];


// Starts the animation sequence.
this.startAnimation = function() {
  runAnimation();
}


// Turns the Jet Pack on.
this.jetPackOn = function() {
  _jetPackOn = true;

  if(!_soundPlaying) {
    _jetPackSound.play();
    _soundPlaying = true;
  }
}


// Runs the character's animation sequence.
function runAnimation() {
  // Clear the entire canvas as the player sits in its own.
  _context.clearRect(0, 0, 1000, 800);
```

```
  if(_jetPackOn) {
    if(_currentFrame == 0) _currentFrame = 1;

    if(_currentFrame == 5) {
      _currentFrame = 0;
    } else {
      _currentFrame++;
    }
  }

  if(_explode) {
    if(_currentFrame < 7) {
      _currentFrame = 7;
    } else {
      if(_currentFrame < 13)
        _currentFrame++;
      else
        return; // The explosion has finished, stop the
        interval.
    }
  }

  _currentY = _yVal;

  _context.drawImage(
    _imageObj,
    _animationData[_currentFrame]['frame']['x'],
    _animationData[_currentFrame]['frame']['y'],
    _animationData[_currentFrame]['frame']['w'],
    _animationData[_currentFrame]['frame']['h'],
    _xVal,
    _yVal,
    _animationData[_currentFrame]['frame']['w'],
    _animationData[_currentFrame]['frame']['h']
  );

  _widthVal = _animationData[_currentFrame]['frame']['w'];
  _heightVal = _animationData[_currentFrame]['frame']['h'];

  // Call the animation interval again.
  setTimeout(runAnimation, 1000/60);
}


// Called on jetpack sound effect complete.
function onSoundDone(e) {
```

```
      _soundPlaying = false;
  }


  // Turns the Jet Pack off.
  this.jetPackOff = function() {
    _jetPackOn = false;
    _currentFrame = 0;
  }


  // Explodes the JetPackMan.
  // To be called on level collision.
  this.explode = function() {
    _explode = true;
    _jetPackOn = false;
    _explosionSound.play();
  }

  this.setX = function(x) { _xVal = x; }
  this.setY = function(y) { _yVal = y; }
  this.currentX = function() { return _xVal; }
  this.currentY = function() { return _yVal; }
  this.currentWidth = function() { return _widthVal; }
  this.currentHeight = function() { return _heightVal; }

  // Destroys the JetPackMan.
  this.destroy = function() {
    _explosionSound = null;
    _jetPackSound = null;
  }
}
```

This method of graphic manipulation, though similar to the concepts used in the Flash Timeline, differ in that we are using 100 percent bitmap data which requires us to manually redraw the visible area of the Sprite Sheet on each frame interval. During each update interval to the animation sequence, we utilize the built in drawImage(); method to append the updated frame location to the HTML <canvas> element. This means that if the pre-existing visible data that had been drawn to the canvas in the previous frame is not manually removed from the canvas, the next drawImage(); call will just append the new frames graphics over top of the old. To avoid this issue we call another built in method, clearRect();, with the position values of where the pre-existing graphic was located. This may understandably sound confusing, however there is a very easy way to visualize this Sprite Sheet manipulation in action. If you open the HTML5 version of the Jet Pack game included within this chapter's example files and comment out the `clearRect();` within the `runAnimation` function, you can now play the game and see what the Player element will look like during runtime. As time passes and more frames are displayed on top of each other, it can quickly become a mess of layered images that will never get updated. As annoying as this is, it does serve a great purpose as it could be utilized for some very interesting visualizations. However, since we only want one character in our game at a time we must be sure to clean up the canvas display on each interval.

Although it is avoided in this example, another important note worth making about integrating this Sprite Sheet is the issues you may encounter while attempting to import the **JSON** dataset containing the Sprite Sheet frame properties as follows:

```
$.getJSON('json/JetPackMan.json', function(data) {
  // Your code here…
});
```

If used for external data loading, the popular jQuery `getJSON` method (`http://api.jquery.com/jQuery.getJSON/`) will attempt an AJAX request to the external data source in order to read the data and pass it back into the return method. However if you are executing the JavaScript from your local machine without the use of a web server, your browser will not accept the request and display a warning that looks something like the following console screenshot:

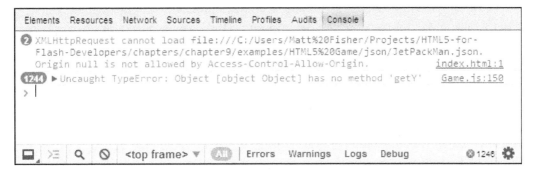

One way of fixing this issue is by simply publishing your HTML5 project to a working web server. From there you can open up the reference to the data from the website URL in a browser. You could also setup your own web server on your computer to have the ability to connect to `http://localhost` in order to view your content. Projects like WAMP (`http://www.wampserver.com/en/`) and MAMP (`http://www.mamp.info/en/index.html`) are all-in-one packages including the Apache web server, MySQL Server and PHP. These server setups, traditionally run on Linux servers, allow you to easily emulate the environment that your website will eventually reside on and give you all the benefits from the software stack described above.

Of course the content you run on your local web server will not be public on the Internet, so you won't be able to share it with your friends unless you start performing some network configuration (you can search for "port forwarding" on Google if you're interested). The final and probably the more logical way to fix this issue when attempting to run this code locally without a web server is to strip the data from inside the JSON Sprite Sheet output and append it into the JavaScript source which is included in the HTML document of the game as follows:

```
var JetPackManData = {
  "frames": {
    "Player0000": {
      "frame": {"x":0...
```

By simply appending the JSON object as it is exported from Flash to a standard JavaScript variable, we can now call the JetPackManData variable rather than a jQuery getJSON() call allowing us to run this game locally with no further Access Control issues.

> The Mozilla Developer Network has a great resource for more detailed information as to why Access Control issues may occur (https://developer.mozilla.org/en-US/docs/HTTP/Access_control_CORS).

Another issue you may encounter, depending on the browser size you use to play this game on, is browser page scrolling or other unwanted actions when the user is attempting to control the player within the game.

Converting ActionScript classes

Since you have already got a glimpse of the converted game source by checking out the Player class which has been modified to deal with Sprite Sheets rather than the Flash Timeline, let's continue down that road by looking at how we can set up the base class of the application in HTML5. To aid in a couple of event listeners and element selection, I have included the jQuery library within this project. I have already made note of this controversial decision in the previous chapters of this book, but it is worth noting again that many developers dislike the usage of jQuery simply for use with element selection. Since the game we are currently converting to HTML5 is extremely simplistic, there really is no need for jQuery within this example. However, if you were to take this simple game source and extend it into a more developed game with rich UI and better game play, the use of a library like jQuery will easily become extremely valid.

The following source is a simplified copy of the Game.js file which is included within the HTML5 version of this game. I have simplified the code and further added commented documentation to aid in understanding how the flow of this game source operates:

```javascript
// Wait for the page load to finish before starting the game.
$( document ).ready( function() {
  // Create a new instance of our Game object.
  // This is effectively like declaring our base class
  // in our Flash Builder ActionScript project.
  var game = new Game();
});

// Declaring the Game Object
var Game = function() {
  // Setup all of the private object variables.
  var _levelBlocks = Array();
  var _interval = 0;
  var _blockInterval = 0;

  // Calls the (JetPackMan) object source we just reviewed above
  var _player = new JetPackMan();

  var _difficulty = 10;
  var _speed = 10;
  var _keyDown = false;
  var _score = 0;
  var _highScore = 0;
  var _gameOver = false;
  var _gameInterval;

  // Use the 'game' canvas for level assets.
  var _canvas = document.getElementById("game");

  // Append the stats display to the stage for benchmarking.
  var _stats = new Stats();
  _stats.setMode(0);
  document.body.appendChild(_stats.domElement);
  _stats.domElement.style.position = 'absolute';
  _stats.domElement.style.left = '960px';
  _stats.domElement.style.top = '41px';
  _stats.domElement.style.zIndex = '2';

  // Prepare the initial aspecs of the level.
```

```
        generateLevel();

        // Create a player object for the user to control.
        createPlayer();

        // Set up Enter Frame and keyboard even listeners.
        // To emulate the 60 frames per second runtime in the Flash
        // version of this game, we divide 1000 by the specific frame
        // rate.
        _gameInterval = setInterval(
          function() {
            // On every frame interval
            updateInterval();
          }
        , 1000 / 60);

        // Set up the keyboard event listeners as they were set up
        // in the Flash version.
        $(document).keydown(function() { onKeyDown(); });
        $(document).keyup(function() { onKeyUp(); });

        // Do the same for the mouse click events.
        window.addEventListener('mousedown', onKeyDown, false);
        window.addEventListener('mouseup', onKeyUp, false);

        // Finally add support for touch events.
        window.addEventListener('touchstart', onKeyDown, false);
        window.addEventListener('touchend', onKeyUp, false);


        /**
        * Starts a new game.
        * Note: The structure of this function declares it as a
        * private function within the Game object scope.
        */
        function startNewGame() {
          // Reset the game switches and counters.
          _gameOver = false;
          _score = 0;
          _speed = 10;
          _difficulty = 10;

          // Clear all level blocks by calling the destroy method
          // on each of the active blocks.
```

```
// NOTE: By appending the _levelBlocks.length to a
// variable prior to looping over the Array, we avoid
// having to duplicate the same lookup multiple times.
var l = _levelBlocks.length;
for(var i = 0; i < l; i++) {
  _levelBlocks[i].destroy();
}
_levelBlocks = new Array();

// Remove player.
_player.destroy();
_player = null;

generateLevel();
createPlayer();

// Start the game interval event again.
_gameInterval = setInterval(function() { updateInterval(); }, 1000
/ 60);
}

/**
 * Generates the beginnings of a new level.
 * By running this prior to starting the game, we can
 * assure that there is some level already created for the
 * Player to initially fly into.
 */
function generateLevel() {
  // Run a loop to generate LevelBlocks on both the top
  // and bottom of the level.
  for(var i = 0; i < 20; i++) {
    // Top LevelBlocks
    // Base the height of the LevelBlock on the
    // current game difficulty.
    var randomHeight = (Math.floor(Math.random() * (_difficulty - (_
    difficulty - 10) + 1)) + (_difficulty - 10));
    var levelBlock = new LevelBlock(_speed, 800 + (20 * i),
    randomHeight - 10, 20, 100);
    // Once created, add the LevelBlock reference to
    // the _LevelBlocks Array.
    _levelBlocks.push(levelBlock);

    // Bottom LevelBlocks
    // We will perform the same operation as above
```

```
        // with some some changes to place this block on
        // the bottom of the level.
        randomHeight = (Math.floor(Math.random() * (_difficulty -
        (_difficulty - 10) + 1)) + (_difficulty - 10));
        var bottomLevelBlock = new LevelBlock(_speed, 800 + (20 *
        i), (randomHeight * -1) + 750, 20, 100);
        _levelBlocks.push(bottomLevelBlock);
    }
}

/**
 * Creates and adds a player object to the stage.
 */
function createPlayer() {
  _player = new JetPackMan();
  _player.setX(80);
  _player.setY(400);
  _player.startAnimation();
}

/**
 * Called on keyboard key down.
 */
function onKeyDown(e) {
  // Start a new game if the current one has ended.
  if(_gameOver) startNewGame();

  _keyDown = true;
}

/**
 * Called on keyboard key up.
 */
function onKeyUp(e) {
  _keyDown = false;
}

/**
 * Game interval. Called on each frame.
 */
function updateInterval(e) {
  _stats.begin();

  // Update the player's score.
```

```
_score = _score + 1;
$('#scoreboard .score').html(String(_score));

// Move player
if(_keyDown) {
  _player.jetPackOn();
  _player.setY(_player.currentY() - 5);
} else {
  _player.jetPackOff();
  _player.setY(_player.currentY() + 5);
}

// Speed game up as it plays
_interval++;

// Check if the interval is far enough to increase
// the difficulty factor.
var increaseSpeed = false;
if(_interval >= 100) {
  increaseSpeed = true;
  _difficulty = _difficulty + 5;
  //_speed++;
  _interval = 0;
}

// Update every block
var l = _levelBlocks.length;
for(var i = 0; i < l; i++) {
  _levelBlocks[i].update();

  // This is where things get really interesting.
  // Since we do not have access to the
  // hitTestObject() method like in ActionScript 3
  // we will need to do our own collision detec-tion.
  // This process is further explained after this
  // code example.
  if(
    _levelBlocks[i].currentX() < _player.currentX() +
    _player.currentWidth()  &&
    _levelBlocks[i].currentX() +
    _levelBlocks[i].currentWidth()  > _player.currentX() &&
    _levelBlocks[i].currentY() < _player.currentY() +
    _player.currentHeight() &&
    _levelBlocks[i].currentY() +
    _levelBlocks[i].currentHeight() > _player.currentY()
```

```
) {
  _player.explode();
  _gameOver = true;

  // Check for highscore.
  if(_score > _highScore) {
    _highScore = _score;
    $('#scoreboard .highscore').html(String(_highScore));
  }

  // Like the Flash version, we need to stop
  // the game interval once the user has hit
  // a part of the level. To do this, we can
  // utilize the clearInterval() method and
  // pass in the _gameInterval reference.
  window.clearInterval(_gameInterval);
}

// If the condition for the game speed to increase
// was met and the increaseSpeed Boolean is set to
// true, call the setSpeed method on each of the
// LevelBlocks.
if(increaseSpeed) _levelBlocks[i].setSpeed(_speed);
}

// As time passes and the LevelBlocks scroll across
// the screen we need to check if new blocks need to be
// added in order to keep the level filled with blocks.
// To do this, we just monitor the X position value of
// last block in the _levelBlocks Array.
if(_levelBlocks[_levelBlocks.length - 1].currentX() < 2000) {
  // Just as in the generateLevel() method, we
  // create a block on both the top and bottom
  // and set its height based on the _ difficulty.
  var randomHeight = (Math.floor(Math.random() * (_difficulty
  - (_difficulty - 10) + 1)) + (_difficulty - 10));
  var levelBlock = new LevelBlock(_speed,
  _levelBlocks[_levelBlocks.length - 1].currentX() + 20,
  randomHeight - _difficulty, 20, 100 + _difficulty);
  _levelBlocks.push(levelBlock);

  // Bottom
  randomHeight = (Math.floor(Math.random() * (_difficulty -
  (_difficulty - 10) + 1)) + (_difficulty - 10));
  var bottomLevelBlock = new LevelBlock(_speed,
```

```
      _levelBlocks[_levelBlocks.length - 1].currentX(),
      (randomHeight * -1) + 750, 20, 100 + _difficulty);
      _levelBlocks.push(bottomLevelBlock);
  }


  // To make the game interesting, we add a random block
  // every now and then to make things interesting.
  // We will base the frequency of random blocks on the
  // current difficulty in the game.
  _blockInterval++;
  if(_blockInterval > 5000 / _difficulty) {
    // When the condition is met, reset the counter.
    _blockInterval = 0;

    // Create random height and Y position values
    // to keep things interesting. This method of
    // generating a random number within a range
    // is one of the most common.
    // Math.floor(Math.random()*(max-min+1))+min;
    randomHeight = (Math.floor(Math.random() * (750 - 5 + 1)) +
    5);
    var randomY = (Math.floor(Math.random() * (750 - 5 + 1)) +
    5);
    var randomBlock = new LevelBlock(_speed,
    _levelBlocks[_levelBlocks.length - 1].currentX(), randomY,
    20, 100 + _difficulty);
    _levelBlocks.push(randomBlock);
  }

  _stats.end();
  }
};
```

In print, this may seem like a ton of code but in reality this is a very simplistic example of a 2D game built in JavaScript. Be sure to read over the comments included in the code which highlight what each part of the code accomplishes and how it is laid out. When all is said and done and the main `index.html` file is opened up in a HTML5 compliant web browser, you will hopefully see the resulting Jet Pack game in 100 percent HTML5 as shown in the following screenshot:

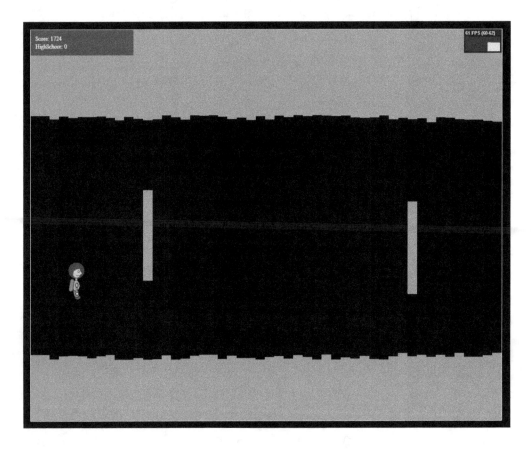

Notice that we have even managed to get a statistics readout at the top right corner of the game area just like in our Flash version. Just like how we reviewed in *Chapter 7, Choosing How You Develop*, we utilize the stats display made possible by the same developer (Ricardo Cabello Miguel also known as Mr. Doob) who provided us with the stats display we used in Flash. Checkout the GitHub page for `Stats.js` (`https://github.com/mrdoob/stats.js/`) to learn more about the project.

Dealing with audio and playback

Using the knowledge we have gained during the overview of HTML5 audio file type and codec support in this book, we can set up the audio for this game pretty easily. Rather than using the SWC importing method that was used in our Flash project, when importing audio into an HTML5 project, we can just append the reference to the source directly into the body of the HTML document inside of a `<audio>` element as follows:

```html
<!DOCTYPE html>
<html lang="en">
  <head>
    <meta charset="utf-8" />
    <title>Jet Pack</title>

    <link rel="stylesheet" type="text/css" href="css/Game.css">

    <script src="js/jquery.min.js"></script>
    <script src="js/Stats.js"></script>
    <script src="js/LevelBlock.js"></script>
    <script src="js/JetPackMan.js"></script>
    <script src="js/JetPackManData.js"></script>
    <script src="js/Game.js"></script>
  </head>

  <body>
    <canvas id="game" width="1000" height="800"></canvas>
    <canvas id="player" width="1000" height="800"></canvas>

    <div id="scoreboard">
      <p>Score: <span class="score">0</span></p>
      <p>HighSchore: <span class="highscore">0</span></p>
    </div>

    <audio id="explosion" src="audio/explosion.mp3"></audio>
    <audio id="jetpack" src="audio/jetpack.mp3"></audio>
  </body>
</html>
```

By default the audio will not play and because we excluded the option to create playback controls, there will be no visible element created within the HTML document during page render. Therefore to begin utilizing the audio in JavaScript, which will allow us to play it on-demand, we begin by referencing the element that was appended into the HTML document as follows:

```
var _jetPackSound = document.getElementById("jetpack");
```

With the audio file referenced, we can easily begin to control the playback by calling the `play()` method on the `_jetPackSound` variable. However, to avoid overlapping the same audio track multiple times during the game play, we can also append an event listener to the element to be called when the sound playback has completed as follows:

```
_jetPackSound.addEventListener("ended", onSoundComplete, false);
```

By creating the event handler for this listener, we can also update the `_soundPlaying` Boolean variable located in the `JetPackMan` class. From this point forward, we can now easily determine if the sound effect is playing or not from anywhere within the `JetPackMan` object.

 You can find some more detailed information on HTML5 audio and video playback control in JavaScript on the Mozilla Developer Network website `https://developer.mozilla.org/en-US/docs/HTML/Using_HTML5_audio_and_video`.

Rewriting AS3 code that can't be directly converted

As I mentioned in one of the previous code examples earlier, the lack of the commonly used `hitTestObject()` method from ActionScript 3 in any HTML5 project means that many of these common yet complex pieces of functionality need to be written yourself. In the example Jet Pack game in HTML5, we use one of the more simplistic methods of collision detection by checking over the Players bounding box or the area that the Player takes up and compare it with each one of the LevelBlocks that has been generated. This condition, when simplified, looks something like the following code:

```
if(
  a.x < b.x + b.width && a.x + a.width > b.x && a.y < b.y +
  b.height && a.y + a.height > b.y
) {
  // 'a' is touching 'b'
}
```

One of the tricky aspects of implementing a functionality like collision detection is that with the advent of the Canvas element in HTML5, there are multiple ways to create and manipulate elements within your HTML document. Flash applications have the advantage of utilizing some great built-in functionality because the development structure is far more structured. When developing HTML5 applications that are heavily dependent on JavaScript, the development flow becomes a little more of a wild west setting.

When digging around to see how other developers may have implemented a feature like collision detection, a great resource as always is Github. The Github project search allows you to narrow your searches down to a specific programming language making it that much easier to find an open source project that may help you out (`https://github.com/search?l=JavaScript&q=Collision +Detection&ref=cmdform&type=Repositories`).

Mobile platform support

Since we now have an HTML5 ready version of our game, one of the initial benefits that we can consider is the fact that most mobile device browsers will support the playback of this application. However, because we have set up the game specifically to be controlled via the user's keyboard, we have not created a control method for users that don't have access to one. Correcting this issue in the case of our Jet Pack game is actually pretty easy since our control system only uses one input. In reality, we have two options as to how we implement this feature as almost every mobile browser that supports touch events registers them as click events as well. This means that we can either implement the same keyboard event listener as a specific touch event or as a common mouse click event. The upside of setting the mouse event over the touch event is that the mouse event will also register for any user who happens to play the game on a device with a mouse as well. Using only default JavaScript syntax we can accomplish this with the following code:

```
window.addEventListener('mousedown', onKeyDown, false);
window.addEventListener('mouseup', onKeyUp, false);
```

As you can see, since we don't condition the key press in the `onKeyDown` or `onKeyUp` methods, we can simply tie the mouse event to the same event handler and call it a day. Depending on whether you have rather used touch events instead of mouse events, we would only have to modify the event parameter within the `addEventListener` call as follows:

```
window.addEventListener('touchstart', onKeyDown, false);
window.addEventListener('touchend', onKeyUp, false);
```

The Mozilla Developer Network also contains a detailed outline of what Touch Events and the properties within are available to you when developing the touch-enabled HTML5 applications (`https://developer.mozilla.org/en-US/docs/DOM/Touch_events`). Although this is a Mozilla site, most of the documentation is cross browser compliant.

Probably one of the most troubling aspects of testing this game on a mobile device is the fact that the canvas element utilized to display the game elements has a static width and height. The width and height I chose to originally create the game are 1000px by 600px. These dimensions may render properly on some mobile devices, but the chances are if you were to play this on a phone, some area of the canvas will either be cut off from display, or presented in a manner that scales the canvas to fit the screen as shown in the following screenshot:

The previous screenshot is taken directly from a Samsung Galaxy S2 and clearly shows how the game is cut off from the default view in the landscape display. Zooming in and out of the page is still available as an interactive browser feature, but even when zoomed out when the game is in landscape display, I am unable to view the entire viewable game area. Now check out the next screenshot taken on the same phone of the game in portrait display:

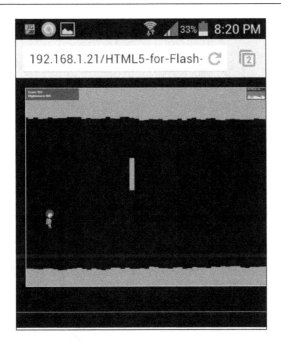

Now with the page view completely zoomed out, we can see the entire game area but the bottom half of the viewable area is wasted as the game is set up to display in a 1000px x 600px display. This issue, though painful to deal with, is actually very common to many Flash developers. If you have developed any web applications in Flash that require a scalable display, you would have had to write event listeners in your application to watch for window resizing and move the position of the elements within your application accordingly. You can update the canvas size from JavaScript easily with calls to your elements width and height properties with the following code:

```
myCanvas.width = 1920;
myCanvas.height = 1080;
myCanvas.style.width = "1920px";
myCanvas.style.height = "1080px";
```

This setup covers all of your bases by updating the CSS style of the element as well as the base element width and height values. Of course, with this update you will also have to manually update the position values for all of the playable elements that are being displayed in this game. If you wish to continue digging more into the source of this game, I advise either attempting to extend the gameplay or working with the Canvas element resizing for dynamic window display sizes.

Summary

By using an application originally built in Flash, in this chapter we have covered some more interesting aspects of HTML5 development. By developing the HTML5 Version of our game without the use of any third party JavaScript libraries, we can easily compare the two development paradigms. In reality, Flash and HTML5 development are extremely similar. Asset preparation and manipulation stands out as one of the most complicated aspects of transitioning your ActionScript and Flash development experience over to HTML5 development. Understanding your limitations, regardless of whether they are browser or device specific is a key factor in making sure you're ready to display your content to as many users as possible.

In the next and final chapter of the book, we will continue putting together working HTML5 applications with more emphasis on preparation for public release. We will attempt to push the limits of what HTML5 can do with peripherals like the webcams and microphones, and discuss what your next steps in HTML5 development could be once you have finished this book.

10
Preparing for Release

Throughout the chapters of this book we have covered many different applications and tools for developing your HTML5 content. As with the Flash development cycle you have become accustomed to, you will usually need to spend some time optimizing your application for use on the web in the final stages of your HTML5 application development flow. Thankfully, just like the asset management and coding stages of our HTML5 development, there are a ton of great resources to aid in the preparation of moving your application onto a public-facing web server. When testing your HTML5 applications locally on the computer you are developing them on, your local network, unless specially configured, will not allow the content to be viewed on any other computer, either on your local network or on the Internet. If you were to install a web server on your computer and configure your networking to allow incoming connections, only then could you share your work with others on the Internet. To avoid any domain name or security issues, the common way to host your work on the Internet is to purchase a web hosting plan from a vendor online. This way your content is external from your working version and is placed on a server specifically dedicated to host your web content. This process isn't new for HTML5 by any means and is typical of what you would have done with your Flash **SWF** files, provided you had the same intentions. However, since HTML5 projects are not compiled into a single binary file such as Flash, we will need to take great care in making sure our project assets and code are properly set up to deliver a fast and secure experience to our end users. In this chapter, we will conclude the book by looking over many of the most optimal ways to prepare your project for the web.

Targeting supported web browsers

Many developers fail to constantly test their work in multiple web browsers during HTML5 development, either because they are too lazy to spend the time to do it, or they just all together forget. Easily one of the biggest issues you will encounter when testing and publishing your final application for public usage will be browser support. If you didn't manage to test your project in various browsers on different platforms, you may be surprised when a user complains that your application doesn't work for them. As HTML5 still is the new kid on the block, many browsers are still running to catch up with the feature support needed to display your HTML5 content properly.

Keeping up-to-date with what current web browsers support in the realm of HTML5 feature support can be an extremely important asset to gain as a developer. Keeping yourself and your project out of impending doom, because you were able to spot a lack of support on a specific device or platform early, cannot only save you tons of time, but money as well. A great "One Stop Shop" for web browser HTML5 feature support checks is http://caniuse.com. After opening the site in a web browser you can easily select any of the specified HTML5 features and look into what browsers, and more importantly what browser versions support that specific feature:

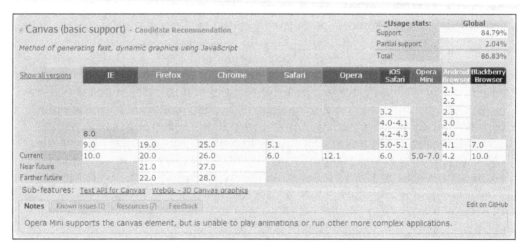

Taking a look at the preceding screenshot of the **Canvas** tag element support statistics (at the time of writing this book), we can see that the **Canvas** element is now supported by around 85 percent of browsers. This site is almost a must have when sitting down to create your initial technical outline for your project. With even a slight idea of some of the features in HTML5 you may use in your project, you can simply jump over to `http://caniuse.com` and determine what your end users will be required to use to properly view your content.

`http://html5readiness.com` is a great example of a great HTML5 project in action as the site uses the data from `http://caniuse.com` to display the HTML5 **Readiness** in an easy to view, single page, interactive graphic.

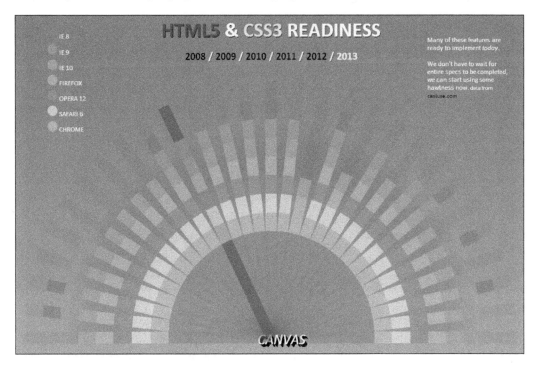

This can be a great resource just like `http://caniuse.com`, however your clients or designers may like it even more for its ease of use and feature support timeline visualizations.

Having the overview of global browser support is a great resource, but if you are interested in digging into the specifications and statistics of the browser you use on your computer, head over to `http://html5test.com` and let the site score your browser.

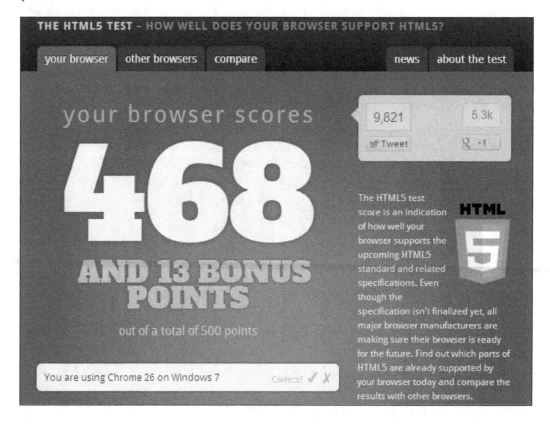

The score generated by the site can be taken as a general overview of all of the HTML5 features that this site tests your browser for. Scrolling down the results page, you will find the complete outline of each of the tested features and if it passed the test or not.

Microdata	0/15
Microdata	No ✗

Web applications	18/20
Application Cache	Yes ✓
Custom scheme handlers	Yes ✓
Custom content handlers	No ✗
Custom search providers	Yes ✓

Security	20
Sandboxed iframe	Yes ✓
Seamless iframe	Yes ✓
iframe with inline contents	Yes ✓

With these easy to use tools that are all accessible online for free, you have all of the data at your fingertips to allow for proper planning and outlining of your HTML5 applications. Keep in mind that as new browsers are released and current versions are updated, this data will continue to evolve. You may even find that some of the data you referenced at the beginning of your project development has changed by the time you finish. Therefore, testing your project for browser compatibility during development is always worth the extra effort.

Be sure to also checkout the HTML5 tests for mobile browsers as well at `http://html5test.com/results/mobile.html`. There you can easily find out which current mobile devices best support not only the features your HTML5 application utilizes, but also the HTML5 specification as a whole. This resource can be of great help when also looking to purchase your next mobile phone or tablet.

Client-side tests

With the amount of mobile and desktop devices that have an HTML5-compliant browser, growing at an exponential rate, the requirement for developers to test applications or web content on a variety of different setups has become a requirement. Unfortunately, the amount of time required to set yourself up with testing environments on all of these devices can add up very quickly. To save yourself copious amounts of time during the testing phase, you may be interested in checking out http://www.browserstack.com.

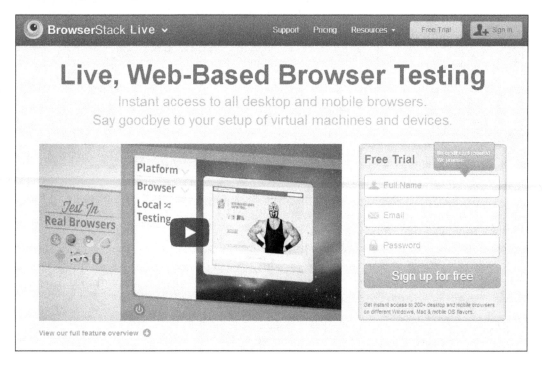

After signing up with BrowserStack, you can easily access all of the modern desktop and mobile browsers right from the service. Rather than having to configure each machine and browser independently, BrowserStack has done all of the hard work for you by only delivering access to the specific browser of your choice already preconfigured with development tools. BrowserStack is a paid service, but free trials are available if you are interested. Personally I still suggest doing this type of testing manually at least once, to see how much you can justify the cost of a service like this. If you are the type of person with 10 computers sitting in your basement, by all means set up your own testing environment. You can also always set up a number of virtual machines on your development computer to enable you to turn on and off your testing machines from a single computer. Regardless of how you do it, it will only usually be a matter of time before you are sick and tired of spending countless hours just maintaining your testing environment and a service such as BrowserStack may be the ultimate solution.

Browser Nightly builds

If you are really pushing the limits of what HTML5 can do, it may be a wise decision to test your content on the absolute latest version of all of the intended browsers that will be viewing your site. With privately developed browsers such as Internet Explorer, you will have to wait for Microsoft to release or prerelease the next version, but with open source browsers such as Google Chrome (`https://www.google.com/intl/en/chrome/browser/`) or Mozilla's Firefox (`http://www.mozilla.org/en-US/firefox/new/`), you can download the Nightly or actively developed version of the software to see what direction the next version is heading in.

Google Chrome browser's nightly build is referred to as the Canary build and can be found at `https://www.google.ca/intl/en/chrome/browser/canary.html`. As you can see from the tagline in the preceding project website screenshot, this build of Chrome is absolute latest and comes with the warning of its possible instability right out front. It's worth keeping in mind that you can safely install the standard version of Google Chrome on your computer to continue to utilize for normal web usage. The Canary build can be opened at any time and is preset to continually update itself from the Google distribution server when a new version is posted for public usage.

Of course, as mentioned, Mozilla has their own nightly build of Firefox available for download as well at `http://nightly.mozilla.org`.

The nightly builds of Firefox currently come in both the desktop and mobile versions of the web browser and again can easily be installed side-by-side with your preexisting version of Firefox stable on your computer. Using these development versions of popular web browsers not only allows you to test your code on software that will soon be available, but it also give you an inside look at some of the new and exciting features that the general public may not be able to use until the next stable release.

So is it really worth the time to test on these browsers, that, in effect, no one is really using yet? Well, being preemptive with your development can really pay off for applications that may go untouched from updates or patches on the Internet. If you don't manage to catch the fact that your HTML5 web application isn't working in the browser that was released a couple months after you published your application, that could be a really bad thing. On top of that, spending time with these new web browsers will only make you more aware and savvy to what features you can utilize when developing your applications. You will begin to learn more about the inner workings of a specific browser's development and release cycles as well.

WebRTC

The move to utilize media inputs, such as camera and microphones, within your HTML5 applications at an all-time high, WebRTC has come to provide a solution to this issue. The WebRTC project is currently supported by Google, Mozilla, and Opera, and the project website can be found at `http://www.webrtc.org`. From a Flash developers perspective, the concept of using web cameras and microphones without the need for third party plugins should get you even more excited about HTML5 development. The features that WebRTC has started to bring to the hands of HTML5 developers pushes the limits of what HTML5 can do even closer to that of Flash.

> If you have a friend online and you want to test a simple WebRTC web cam chat application, head over to `http://apprtc.appspot.com` and connect to the server which will return an ID for your user. Send that ID to a friend along with the URL to the site and connect to each other online in a pure HTML5 audio and video chat.

Since WebRTC is still a very new specification, only some of the modern browsers available right now support it and unfortunately for developers, the support methods are a little bit different for each browser. This initial step that any developer working with WebRTC should make is to check if the current browser even supports this feature. This can be done with some JavaScript function such as the following code snippet:

```
function hasGetUserMedia() {
  return !!(navigator.getUserMedia ||
            navigator.webkitGetUserMedia ||
            navigator.mozGetUserMedia ||
            navigator.msGetUserMedia
         );
}
```

As you can see, the methods for interacting with the User Media object element within JavaScript differ from `getUserMedia` all the way to `msGetUserMedia`, depending on the type of web browser attempting to load it. By conditioning all of the ways to lookup the user media object into a single return statement, this function will either return the user media object, if the browser supports it, or return a value of false if nothing was found. With this `hasGetUserMedia` function applied into an HTML5 project, we can easily incorporate the function call into further code, that applies the user's web cam feed onto the web page if available.

```
var video = document.getElementById('camera');
if(hasGetUserMedia()) {
```

```
    navigator.webkitGetUserMedia(
{
audio: true,
video: true
}, function(stream) {
video.src = window.URL.createObjectURL(stream);
        }, onConnectionFail);
    } else {
        alert('WebRTC is not supported!');
    }
```

The initial line of this code example applies the element with the ID of camera to the variable video. This element in the HTML document is actually a video tag element and looks like the following:

```
<video id="camera" autoplay></video>
```

You may also recall that the video element can be styled by CSS3 properties, giving you a ton of design options for displaying the web camera video feed. So let's extend these WebRTC related code snippets into a working example with some CSS3 styles. We will start by creating our initial HTML page to be displayed in the web browser.

```
<!DOCTYPE html>
<html lang="en">
  <head>
    <meta charset="utf-8" />
    <title>Web RTC Demo</title>
    <style>
      .grayscale {
        -webkit-filter:grayscale(1);
      }
      .sepia {
        -webkit-filter:sepia(1);
      }
      .blur {
        -webkit-filter:blur(10px)
      }
    </style>
  </head>

  <body>
    <video id="camera" autoplay></video>
    <p>
      <button id="button0">Clear Styles</button>
      <button id="button1">Grayscale</button>
```

```
            <button id="button2">Sepia</button>
            <button id="button3">Blur</button>
        </p>
        <script src="js/webrtc.js"></script>
    </body>
</html>
```

Within this HTML page we have also added some simple CSS3 filters with unique class names for each. Each of the different CSS styles appended into the HTML document also have an HTML button element to correspond with it, located within the body of the document. Finally we reference the external JavaScript file that will deal with the WebRTC functionality which we will create next.

With the HTML file saved and a new file open to write our JavaScript into, we can append the code snippets we have already looked at, as well as some code to append the CSS styles, to the video element, when the user clicks the buttons on the HTML page.

```
var video = document.getElementById('camera');
var clearBtn = document.getElementById('button0');
var grayscaleBtn = document.getElementById('button1');
var speiaBtn = document.getElementById('button2');
var blurBtn = document.getElementById('button3');

if(hasGetUserMedia()) {
  navigator.webkitGetUserMedia({audio: true, video: true},
  function(stream) {
    video.src = window.URL.createObjectURL(stream);
  }, onConnectionFail);
} else {
  alert('getUserMedia() is not supported in your browser');
}

// Checks if the users browser has Web RTC support.
function hasGetUserMedia() {
  return !!(navigator.getUserMedia ||
          navigator.webkitGetUserMedia ||
          navigator.mozGetUserMedia ||
          navigator.msGetUserMedia
        );
}

// Called if the connection to the video stream fails.
var onConnectionFail = function(e) {
  console.log('ERROR: User Media connection failure!', e);
};

// Clear Styles
```

```
clearBtn.addEventListener('click', function() {
  video.className = '';
});

// Grayscale
grayscaleBtn.addEventListener('click', function() {
  video.classList.add('grayscale');
});

// Sepia
speiaBtn.addEventListener('click', function() {
  video.classList.add('sepia');
});

// Blur
blurBtn.addEventListener('click', function() {
  video.classList.add('blur');
});
```

As you can see, the bulk of this JavaScript is dealing with the CSS manipulation of the video element and not the setup of the web camera stream. Setting up a WebRTC connection to the end user, provided their browser supports it, is easily accomplished with a few lines of a JavaScript.

Thankfully, I was smart enough to add in the blur effect to hide myself using this example in the preceding screenshot. Keep in mind that just like camera and microphone connections in Flash, the stream is completely local to the user and not sent to any other server unless you have manually added that feature into the application. For applications such as multi-user chat and public streaming, you will require a server to send your audio or video stream to. Node.js would be a perfect place to begin if this type of HTML5 development sounds exciting to you. There is even a Node.js package dedicated to dealing with WebRTC (`https://npmjs.org/package/webrtc.io`) to help get you started in the right direction.

Privacy can be a huge issue when it comes to gaining the ability to stream audio and video over the Internet without the use of third party plugins such as Flash Player. Therefore, web browsers will always prompt the end user for approval, when an attempt is made to connect to their media channels via WebRTC. If you are developing HTML5 applications that plan on utilizing features in WebRTC, this is an important fact to remember. If a user decides to opt out of enabling their microphone or web camera, the user experience of your application may break all together. Another step that some browsers such as Google Chrome are taking to keep you safe online is by applying a unique icon to any browser tab that has an active media stream attached to it. Regardless of whether the stream is delivering the content to a third party server or just using it locally, the icon will always be visible.

As you can see in the preceding screenshot, when WebRTC has been activated in Google Chrome and the user is streaming audio or video to the website, the browser tab gains a glowing red recording icon to alert you that the feed is active.

If you are interested in learning more about not only the origins of the WebRTC project and its support on modern browsers, but also about how to properly utilize it in your projects, check out the great article on *Capturing Audio & Video in HTML* on `http://www.html5rocks.com/en/tutorials/getusermedia/intro/`.

What's even more exciting about WebRTC is the possible future for the technology. As you have seen in the overview of this technology so far, the aim is really to get audio and video working without dependencies on the web. However, there is also a goal to get a dedicated data channel working in WebRTC, which could enable a slew of amazing new web-based technology, as your computer could really act as its own server while using specific web applications.

WebGL support

WebGL, like WebRTC, is one of the new and exciting features to start seeing high quality support on many modern web browsers on desktop and on mobile. Taking advantage of hardware-accelerated graphics on a client's computer or device can enable you to bring many of the fully-featured 2D and 3D animations and interactions you may have used while developing Flash projects in the past. When attempting to verify if the browser you are using supports WebGL, the easiest tool for verification can be found at http://get.webgl.org.

If your browser passed the WebGL verification tests, the site will be displayed as shown in the previous screenshot, rendering a 3D wireframe rotating cube, and the text alerting you of the results. You can of course utilize http://caniuse.com to check what browsers currently support WebGL as well as dig into the official WebGL public wiki found at http://www.khronos.org/webgl/wiki/Main_Page.

> If you are interested in learning more about the exciting world of WebGL in HTML5, check out the *WebGL Beginner's Guide* found on the Packt Publishing website (http://www.packtpub.com/webgl-javascript-beginners-guide/book).

WebGL on mobile browsers

Depending on the intensity of the WebGL application you are viewing, you may notice extremely slow frame rates, as well as, applications that may become unresponsive. As WebGL has gained support on a small number of devices and browsers, the development community is slowly creating optimizations for mobile experiences utilizing this technology. Unfortunately, the processing power between most desktop and a mobile devices are still pretty far apart, therefore the requirement for developers to optimize their experiences if intending for mobile browsers to view them is critical.

A great resource for checking out WebGL content on your mobile device is the Three.js project page found at `http://threejs.org`. From the index of projects and examples on the main page, you can easily get a sense of how some of the coolest WebGL examples run on any device.

 If you are interested in getting a more in depth look at any web browsers' WebGL capabilities, check out `http://webgl-bench.appspot.com` for an online benchmarking tool to help examine and display your WebGL rendering statistics.

Allowing users to find your work

Although search engine indexing is not directly related to HTML5, since you are coming from a Flash developer's perspective, it is definitely worth noting. Many search engines have become increasingly better at parsing Flash content for search engine results, but at the end of the day, creating a full Flash site will require you to perform some work around to have your content displayed properly, when someone attempts to search for it. Search engine bots will have a much easier time reading your HTML5 projects as they have a more direct approach to reading the important data about the pages on your website.

With the growth in what HTML element tags may now contain, the ability to tag specific elements on your site, specifically for search engines, is a new and exciting way to optimize your website's search engine optimization. One of the key aspects of web content the Google search engine is looking for in recent years is content related to authorship. For instance, if you have an article or piece written by a specific author on your site, you can easily integrate the author's information as meta data within the HTML page.

When tagged properly, this will not only allow the search engines, but also social websites, to easily parse those specific pages' content with ease. For instance, consider some of these methods for defining specific elements in your HTML source:

```
<!--
    Link to a Spanish version of your site, defined by the
    'hreflang' parameter.
-->
<link hreflang="es" href="index_es.html" rel="alternate">

<!-- The link to the authors website (external) -->
<link rel="author" href="https://www.johnsmith.com⬛>
```

In these examples, we append the `rel` and `hreflang` tag elements to aid in describing a link's content preemptively.

```
<a rel="license" href="licensing.html">License information</a>
<a rel="next" href="index3.html">Next</a>
<a rel="prev" href="index1.html">Previous</a>

<link rel="search" href="http://www.johnsmith.com/search.xml">

<figure id="myfigure>
  <img src="cat.jpg" alt="Kitty Cat">
  <figcaption>A Photo of my Cat</figcaption>
</figure>
```

Although none of these tags are technically required when developing your HTML documents, the effort to put meta data into your content, especially if it will be dynamically supplied, will more likely than not result in better traffic and search engine result ranking once your web site has been published online.

As mentioned, many social websites such as Google+ or Facebook will attempt to parse your web pages content to create a detailed link structure back to your site. The more viable content and meta data that you can supply to the websites and systems that attempt to read it, will result in better link structure and information output when users link back to your site.

The HTML5 History API

If you happen to have built a website completely in Flash before, you may have had experience with using JavaScript libraries such as SWFAddress (http://www.asual.com/swfaddress) to emulate the URL update functionality typical to normal web page display. If you are unaware of this project, or the idea of URL updating, the concept is simply that when you load a new page on the Internet, the URL in the address bar changes according to the location of the page you are viewing. With typical HTML web content, each page is displayed in a new HTML document, therefore the URL could easily be defined for each section of the website. With a website built in Flash, all of the content will be compiled into a single SWF that will be embedded on a single HTML page. So when the content changes in the Flash, there will be no change in the address bar of the web browser as no new page was requested. By including SWFAddress into your Flash project for the web, you can easily send a command via the SWFAddress JavaScript API to append customized updates to the address bar of the web browsers. Most importantly, if a user was to hit one of the custom URLs that your application has utilized, you can easily skip the user experience directly to a section of your application that they originally intended to visit. With the rise in popularity of features such as the Canvas element and AJAX requests in HTML5, the need for many websites to physically reload the web page on every request is dropping. Therefore, a system similar to SWFAddress is needed to properly integrate your sites on the web.

The HTML5 History API (`http://www.whatwg.org/specs/web-apps/current-work/multipage/history.html`) is your key to not only controlling the address bar of the clients web browser, but also to control many elements of their browsers history records to enable the browsers' back-and-forward functionality to continue to work. Although some of the older versions of popular modern browsers lack support for the HTML5 History API, the overwhelming majority of the latest versions of all browsers available now seem to support this feature (`http://caniuse.com/#feat=history`). However, when attempting to use any feature where you are not 100 percent positive every use will have support, some initial checks are usually worth the effort. To check for history API support, we can attempt to lookup the type of the `history.pushState` object which is responsible for writing changes to the browsers page history.

```
if (typeof history.pushState === 'undefined') {
  // The HTML5 History API is Unavailable...
} else {
  // The HTML5 History API is Available!
}
```

Provided everything passes, you are good to read and write data to the clients browser history. Mozilla has written a fantastic outline of the History API and its usage which can be found at `https://developer.mozilla.org/en/docs/DOM/Manipulating_the_browser_history`.

 For a down to earth example of the HTML5 History API in action, check out the online demo and source code from HTML5 Demos (`http://html5demos.com/history`).

The important factor to note in regards to the History API and search engine optimization is the freedom that your applications have when it comes to referencing application state in the URL displayed in the browser address bar. Setting unique URLs to specific locations and elements in your content will allow for easier debugging and generation of user statistics and analytics.

Premade testing and benchmark solutions

In previous chapters, we have covered and utilized features of many modern web browser developer tool sets, mainly utilizing the JavaScript console for easy output and code debugging during development. Many of these pre-installed developer tool sets within popular web browsers also include many tools that allow you to not only dig into your own websites structure to locate issues, but debug other websites on the Internet to get an idea of their inner workings as well.

Google's web development toolset

When it comes to tools for debugging and analyzing HTML5 content in the browser, Google has really stepped up to the plate by creating not only the Chrome Developer Tools (`https://developers.google.com/chrome-developer-tools/`) but the Google Web Toolkit (`https://developers.google.com/web-toolkit/overview`) as well. All of these tools combined can be utilized to do a majority of the deep down application debugging that your application may require prior to public deployment. For instance, if you have managed to develop your own HTML5 game and need to dig into the game structure and flow to determine where optimizations are required, you can go through the process of writing tests for each and every element of the game, or you can use a tool like Google's Speed Tracer (`https://developers.google.com/web-toolkit/speedtracer/index`).

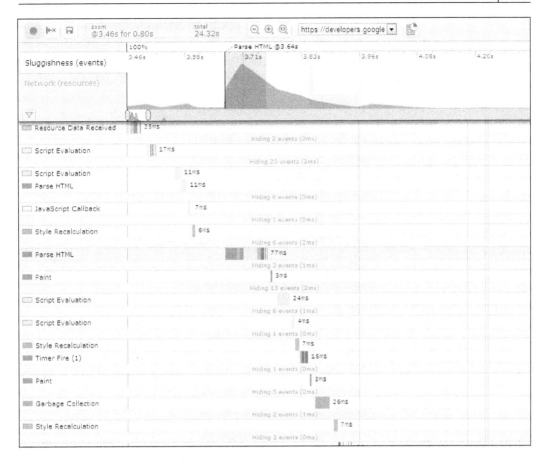

As you can see in the screenshot of Speed Tracer in action, the application manages to dig deep into the application runtime to display statistics on many aspects of how the active application is actually running on a given machine. Within the statistical output is the time to load, time to execute, time to display, and so much more. Simple websites that display content and video in a traditional manner may not find any benefit in using a tool that digs this deep. However, for anyone interested in building robust interactive Canvas, WebGL or any other heavy computation, or calculation applications that may require debugging of the runtime, this tool is defiantly worth looking into.

For the vast majority of HTML5 development, the Chrome Developer Tools is a browser feature that many web developers can't live without. With the entire toolset included in every installation of Chrome, you can easily open and start debugging any website with the tool in seconds. From inspecting the page elements and their associated styles with the Elements Inspector, displayed in the following screenshot, to displaying the load time of every internal and external request made by your page on load and during runtime with the Network Inspector, almost everything you need to debug your content is in one handy built in window.

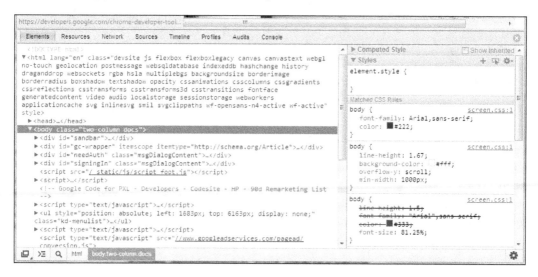

Since Google has been promoting this piece of software extremely well in the last couple years, I really don't need to go into great detail of its usage here. There are more than a couple of amazing video tutorials that can easily be found on the project website along with great documentation of every feature within the application feature set.

The Chrome Developer Tools project website contains a bunch of great resources both video and in text to aid in understanding everything the extension is capable of doing. Be sure to head over to `https://developers.google.com/chrome-developer-tools/docs/videos` and check it out.

As time passes, you will probably find yourself quickly opening and closing this extension as you browse the web. As a developer, one the great aspects of HTML5 development is that when the content is public, so is the code that run it. Digging into how someone managed to create web content that amazed you is a very easy way to get extremely knowledgeable about the HTML5 stack.

YSlow website grading

Although many of us hated getting our grades in school, having someone grade your website can be an incredibly useful resource. The YSlow (`http://yslow.org`) browser extension is an open source project that can be added to Chrome, Firefox, Opera, Safari, and many other forms of web-based content. Upon opening and activating the extension, you can run the system on the website you currently have opened in your web browser. Consider the YSlow extension window after we run the tests on `http://www.packtpub.com`.

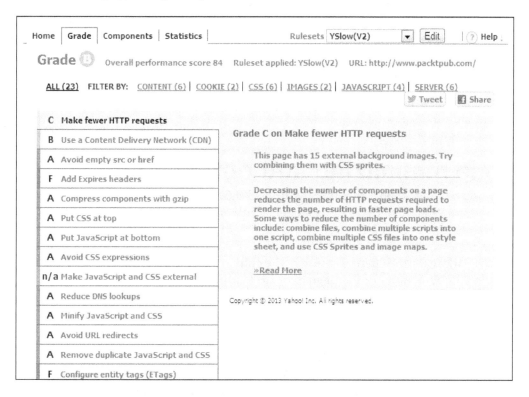

In the top left corner of the extension window, you can see that the website was given a B grade. Now without any detail on what makes up the grade, that data is effectively useless. So to confirm the graded result, let's dig into why this site received the grade it did. Below the grade in a color coded list you will find the individual tests results from all of the areas that are examined by YSlow. For the vast majority of the tests, the Packt Publishing website scored very well. However, the test concluded that for one, the site can make fewer HTTP requests, meaning that too much of the code and assets that make up the page are referenced from a variety of external resources. Secondly, the test results also display bad results for the inclusion of expire headers.

This means that there are many assets on the page with caching expire times very far in the future. Configurations like this could very well cause some users to see page content during page load that has actually been updated on the server. Because the cache time for some assets is set so far in the future, if the user has been to your site before, their web browser may not re-request the same asset, thinking that since the cache time is so far away, there is no possibility that the data could have changed.

 If you are interested into how YSlow manages to do what it does, be sure to head over to the project GitHub page to learn more (`https://github.com/marcelduran/yslow`).

YSlow covers a lot more than just the short list of results you can see in the previous screenshot. Since the test literally only takes a couple seconds and the browser extension setup of the application allows you to install it in seconds, I highly recommend downloading this extension and testing it out; not only on your web content but others as well.

Code minimizing and obfuscation

After you have finished developing your HTML5 application, you may notice that the amount of referencing to external JavaScript and CSS files may have gotten a little out of hand. One of the easiest ways to begin the battle for faster page loads is to minimize your JavaScript and CSS source code into the smallest file size possible. This will allow for the client to retrieve the content over the Internet in a shorter time allowing the remainder of the page to finish loading.

Some CSS compilers such as LESS (`http://lesscss.org`) and SAS (`http://sass-lang.com`) contain the ability to minimize your CSS automatically, saving you the hassle of remembering to do it yourself after every update to your site. However, if you are not using a CSS compiler, there are still many great ways to accomplish the same task. One of my personal favorite online resources for CSS compression is `http://www.csscompressor.com`. This easy to use CSS compressor gives you the ability to not only configure the actions performed to optimize your CSS, but also control the level of compression as well. To get a better idea of what this compression looks like, consider the following example CSS syntax:

```
#example {
  width:800px;
  height:600px;
  overflow:hidden;
  margin-right:10px;
  top:20px;
}
#example a {
```

```
    color:#FFFFFF;
    text-decoration:none;
}
#example li {
  line-height:20px;
  color:#EFEFEF;
  padding-left:20px;
}
#example .alert {
  display:none;
}
```

There is nothing really special about these CSS styles other than the fact that we are styling only the #example tag element and its inner content. This CSS example really will just serve as an example as to what you would probably be used to seeing all over your projects. Of course your final application will probably contain far more than four CSS properties, but the end result will be the same regardless of CSS source code size. To keep things simple and conserve space within the book, we will just use these styles.

After opening up a web browser and heading over to http://www.csscompressor.com, we can copy these styles into the large text area on the site.

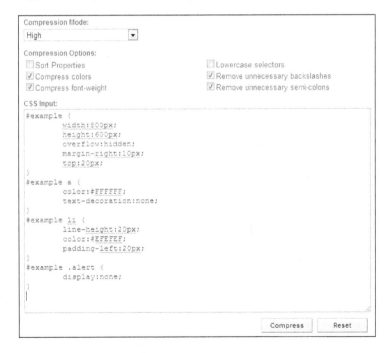

Before we begin our CSS compressor, take note of the options above the text input area. Although this specific CSS minimizing website is only one of many freely available on the Internet, the general configuration properties are the same. As you can see by the previous screenshot, you also have the option of selecting **Sort Properties** which will output your CSS styles sorted into minimalistic configurations effectively optimizing your code. Most important is the dropdown selector which allows you to choose the Compression Mode for the compressed output. For instance, selecting **High** and compressing our example CSS would output the following:

```
#example{width:800px;height:600px;overflow:hidden;margin-
right:10px;top:20px}
#example a{color:#FFF;text-decoration:none}
#example li{line-height:20px;color:#EFEFEF;padding-left:20px}
#example .alert{display:none}
```

Since our example CSS is simple to begin with, the amount of work done to compress our code in the configuration is pretty minimal. Effectively all the compressor needed to do was remove all extra whitespace from the supplied CSS and place all of the element properties on single lines. This may seem like a minimal amount of work and output, but the fact of the matter is that the compressed CSS source is now 14.8 percent smaller in file size than the originally supplied source. For only a couple minutes of work, that is a huge amount of optimization. We can take it even one step further by selecting the **Highest** option for the Compression Mode. With this option selected, the compressor will now put the entire compressed CSS source on a single line. With this setup, our file size drops another 2.2 percent totaling 16 percent file size reduction.

```
#example{width:800px;height:600px;overflow:hidden;ma
rgin-right:10px;top:20px}#example a{color:#FFF;text-
decoration:none}#example li{line-height:20px;color:#EFEFEF;padding-
left:20px}#example .alert{display:none}
```

As mentioned, file compression like this is not only for your CSS source code. This technique is actually even more useful for JavaScript. As your JavaScript source is usually responsible for all of the client side actions, the size of your source code can grow extremely large. Not only can this external source code be large in file size, but it may also contain some semi-sensitive code that you would prefer the end user not to be aware of. Of course JavaScript is no place for hard coding user names and passwords, but if you were to write a game in JavaScript, you probably wouldn't want users to locate the method to progress to the next level. You can use JavaScript compression to aid in your fight for code privacy, but of course always remember that JavaScript is a client-side language. No matter how hard you try, the end user will always have access to your source code, so always keep that in mind while developing your applications.

JavaScript compression is common amongst many popular JavaScript libraries and frameworks, many of which we have already looked at in this book. The jQuery (http://jquery.com) library comes in two different packages, Development and Production. The difference between the two being that the Production version is compressed, ready for use online, whereas the development version is the user friendly JavaScript source ready for further manipulation. Websites such as http://www.minifyjavascript.com are a great online resource for accomplishing this task with your own custom JavaScript that is included within your HTML5 projects.

External dependencies

As your HTML5 projects become more and more feature rich, the requirement to include external dependencies such as jQuery or various jQuery plugins will probably increase just the same. By the end of your application development cycle you could possibly have over a dozen external JavaScript files referenced from a single HTML file. Although from a human standpoint, the segregation of all of your application's functionality in separate files may be optimal for ease of development, when it comes to publishing all of these files on the web you are effectively making your end users connection do more work when attempting to load your content. Since each piece of the JavaScript (or CSS) functionality may be broken in different files, the browser will need to individually request and receive each and every file referenced in the document before the document can finish loading. One solution to this issue is to combine all of the external third party JavaScript or CSS files into a single file for your HTML documents to request. This way only a single request will be made to the server, cutting down on page load times and bandwidth consumption. However, in most cases you will probably only want to combine JavaScript and CSS content that you do not plan on editing in the future. When all of your files are combined into one, the difficulty factor when the time comes to debug issues can be increased. Keeping your custom JavaScript and CSS in their own files can allow for far easier editing and republishing.

After your published site is live on the Internet for a while, regardless of whether you update it or not, there is a high likelihood of the dependencies that your application utilizes may fall out of date. Developers behind the projects your application uses may release small bug fixes to entire version updates to their libraries or frameworks without your knowledge. Although your application should live on without issue, provided it did before, you may be so inclined to update a specific plugin to gain the newest feature set or security fixes. If the updated version of, for example, a jQuery Plugin was published to a site where the utilized version of jQuery was either out of date or incompatible, you will probably encounter various issues when attempting to run your application.

The issue may be easily resolved by updating your site's utilized version of jQuery to the required version; however if the other plugins you are using are not compatible with the newest version of jQuery you appended, those may break as well.

It is because of this downward spiral that I stress two specific things all HTML5 developers should be aware of. Firstly, attempt to stay on top of the development progression of the external dependencies you utilize in your projects. Even if you are not interested in an expanded feature set, the developers of these projects often release security updates and code optimizations. Finally, attempt to spend the time to properly research and test if updating any of the dependencies your projects uses will directly affect any of the other dependencies that work alongside it.

Making deployment easy

If you are working on a HTML5 site or application that will require constant updates, you may be interested in finding ways to ease the pain of manual file updating when it comes to publishing updates to your web server. Manually updating specific files over a FTP or SFTP connection to your web server that may be in different directories can easily become a pain. Finding ways to automate any time wasting process is usually a point of interest for any developer. So for the sake of your sanity in future projects, let's cover a few of the interesting options available to web developer for automating many processes from compressing code to deploying a website.

Creating tasks with Grunt

Grunt (`http://gruntjs.com`) is a relatively new kid on the web development block but has seen extremely active development since its inception in 2011. The concept behind the software is pretty simple—automation. The key to Grunt's success in the HTML5 web developer community is the fact that the scripts you write to perform your customized tasks automatically are entirely written in JavaScript. This allows anyone, with experience writing JavaScript, to create tasks that would normally be created with BASH scripts or some other command line deployed programming language.

GRUNT
The JavaScript Task Runner

→ Getting Started   ≫ Plugins   📄 Documentation   ⚙ API

Latest Version
- Stable: v0.4.1
- Development: N/A

Ads by Boooup

Latest News

Why use a task runner?

In one word: automation. The less work you have to do when performing repetitive tasks like minification, compilation, unit testing, linting, etc. the easier your job becomes. After you've configured it, a task runner can do most of that mundane work for you—and your team—with basically zero effort

Why use Grunt?

The Grunt ecosystem is huge and it's growing every day. With literally hundreds of plugins to choose from, you can use Grunt to automate just about anything with a minimum of effort. If someone hasn't already built what you need, authoring and publishing your own Grunt plugin to npm is a breeze.

Grunt is built on the Node.js (`http://nodejs.org/`) framework and requires Node.js to be installed on the machine utilizing it. Because of Grunt's relationship with Node.js, you can locate plugins to begin the foundation of your Grunt tasks and install them the same way you install the Node.js packages. In terms of automated deployment of your website source to a web server, you would probably need to start by figuring out how to establish a connection from your Grunt scripts code to a web server via FTP or SFTP. Fortunately, as mentioned, the Node.js Package Manager or NPM system can set you off on the right foot with a quick search for Grunt SFTP on `https://npmjs.org`. In the results you will locate the grunt-sftp-deploy (`https://npmjs.org/package/grunt-sftp-deploy`) plugin which will give your Grunt tasks the ability to easily connect and deploy your local website source to an external web server over a SFTP connection.

> If you are interested in learning more about Grunt or want to install it on your computer, head over to the official Grunt documentation at `http://gruntjs.com/getting-started` and follow the *Getting Started* tutorial.

In reality, when it comes to creating customized tasks with Grunt, your imagination is really the limit. If you ever find yourself doing the same task over and over and want to automate the repetition, regardless if the issue is a personal or global one, writing some code to perform the automation for you can be a really great learning experience and time saver. Head over to the Grunt Plugins page on the office project site (`http://gruntjs.com/plugins`) to find more inspiration for great tasks that you can create or utilize.

Deploying content with Git

Another piece of software you will probably find yourself using if you haven't already is Git (`http://git-scm.com/`). Git is a free and open source version control system utilized by both large and small projects around the world. Most developers can't fathom a world where they didn't use version control software of some kind and most web developers who use it, use Git. The majority of Git's success in the world of web development is not only because it is such a great and reliable piece of software, but because websites such as Github (`https://github.com`) and BitBucket (`https://bitbucket.org`) have been created to allow developer to store their code privately or share it publically. Rather than freely distributing code as an archived ZIP file, developers can download the entire repository of code which include all of the previous edit history made by other developers who have contributed. This also means that if you were to make a change to someone else's code, they can still retain the right to choose to integrate your edits into their release. The benefits of version control could fill an entire book, so if you are not using Git or some other form of version control yet, be sure to dig deeper into it.

Using Git to automatically deploy your web content can be a little tricky to set up at first, but once configured, the setup can not only allow you to publish content to your web server easily, but any other developer that may be working on the same application as well. Git utilizes the idea of branches to allow developers to work in their own environment of the applications code without stepping on other developer's toes. When both developers have completed the updates to the application in each of their branches, Git can be utilized to merge the edits in the two branches back into a single file automatically. By utilizing the concepts of branches, developers can agree to make a specific branch (usually the Master branch) the working branch that is deployed on the applications web server. If you were to append the Git repository on the web server itself and call the Git pull command from a web based script, anyone from your development team could easily push the latest version of the website from the Git repository to the active web server without ever having to connect via FTP or SFTP and manually copy files over.

If you are interested in learning more or curious as to how to go about setting this type of solution up for one of your web based HTML5 project, check out the git-deploy project on Github (`https://github.com/git-deploy/git-deploy`).

Summary

In this chapter, we spent some time going over some of the common aspects for preparing your HTML5 application or website for deployment on a public web server. Although there is no common practice for project preparation for the web, there are many aspects like optimization of code and file structure that, when given the proper amount of time, will keep your content stable and keep delivery times from server requests to a minimum. Sometimes anticipating issues is not a reality until you have had valid user testing completed on your project. This form of user testing, unless you have a team at your disposal, usually comes in the initial launch of your application to the public. Making sure that your application is set up in a way to report errors or generate statistics will decrease the time it takes for you to locate and correct any issues that may arise. Even additions as simple as appending Google Analytics (`http://www.google.ca/analytics/`) into your site will enable you to view where users may have hit a dead end or bad request.

The road to learning HTML5 and what it has to offer the web development community is an endless commitment that will extremely benefit your career as a developer. Though still in its early stages, this latest version of the HTML specification has proved to be one of the most important aspects of moving the web into a more application-like infrastructure. The world of HTML5 development has opened its doors to developers coming from many development skillsets in other languages. As a developer with experience in Flash and ActionScript 3, not only do you already have a leg up in terms of the learning curve JavaScript has to offer, but the understanding every Flash developer has of multimedia and its integration in code will be an invaluable skill to constantly fall back on as you continue to learn.

Finally, I would like to give you my full appreciation for taking the time to read through the pages of this book. It is my hope that your venture into HTML5 development was as pleasant as my own. The amazing projects that have sprung up in the last couple years are a testament to the excitement surrounding HTML5 and the new features that have been added to the specification. Some new and exciting framework or library is put into the community spotlight every week it seems. As great as the variety of projects can be, the vast sea of great 3rd party content available to utilize in your project means to make valid decisions of what to use, you need to keep up to date with as much as you can. Hop on your favorite social network, find some other developers with similar interest to your own, and start a new project to push the limits of what you can accomplish with HTML5. Who knows, maybe I will end up using a library you wrote in my next project!

Index

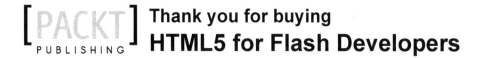

Thank you for buying
HTML5 for Flash Developers

About Packt Publishing

Packt, pronounced 'packed', published its first book "*Mastering phpMyAdmin for Effective MySQL Management*" in April 2004 and subsequently continued to specialize in publishing highly focused books on specific technologies and solutions.

Our books and publications share the experiences of your fellow IT professionals in adapting and customizing today's systems, applications, and frameworks. Our solution based books give you the knowledge and power to customize the software and technologies you're using to get the job done. Packt books are more specific and less general than the IT books you have seen in the past. Our unique business model allows us to bring you more focused information, giving you more of what you need to know, and less of what you don't.

Packt is a modern, yet unique publishing company, which focuses on producing quality, cutting-edge books for communities of developers, administrators, and newbies alike. For more information, please visit our website: www.packtpub.com.

Writing for Packt

We welcome all inquiries from people who are interested in authoring. Book proposals should be sent to author@packtpub.com. If your book idea is still at an early stage and you would like to discuss it first before writing a formal book proposal, contact us; one of our commissioning editors will get in touch with you.

We're not just looking for published authors; if you have strong technical skills but no writing experience, our experienced editors can help you develop a writing career, or simply get some additional reward for your expertise.

Designing Next Generation Web Projects with CSS3

ISBN: 978-1-84969-326-4   Paperback: 288 pages

A practical guide to the usage of CSS3 - a journey through properties, tools, and techniques to better understand CSS3

1. CSS3 properties and techniques have been applied to complete web projects

2. Explains tools to deal with CSS increasing in complexity, such as experimental vendor prefixes

3. Fast and concise style focused primarily on practical aspects like implementation techniques and fallback strategies

HTML5 iPhone Web Application Development

ISBN: 978-1-84969-102-4   Paperback: 338 pages

An introduction to web application development for mobile within the iOS Safari browser

1. Simple and complex problems will be covered with examples and resources that backup the approach and technique.

2. Real world solutions that are broken down for multiple target audiences; from beginner developers to technical architects.

3. Learn to build true web applications using the latest industry standards for iOS Safari.

Please check **www.packtpub.com** for information on our titles

HTML5 and CSS3 Responsive Web Design Cookbook

ISBN: 978-1-84969-544-2   Paperback: 204 pages

Learn the secrets of developing responsive websites capable of interfacing with today's mobile Internet devices

1. Learn the fundamental elements of writing responsive website code for all stages of the development lifecycle

2. Create the ultimate code writer's resource using logical workflow layers

3. Full of usable code for immediate use in your website projects

HTML5 Data and Services Cookbook

ISBN: 978-1-78355-928-2   Paperback: 486 pages

Over hundred website building recipes utilizing all the modern HTML5 features ands techniques!

1. Learn to effectively display lists and tables, draw charts, animate elements and use modern techniques such as templates and data-binding frameworks through simple and short examples.

2. Examples utilizing modern HTML5 features such as rich text editing, file manipulation, graphics drawing capabilities, real time communication.

3. Explore the full power of HTML5 - from number rounding to advanced graphics to real-time data binding - we have it covered.

Please check **www.packtpub.com** for information on our titles